ACTION! 3

Key Stage 3 Science

PARKSTONE GIRLS' GRAMMAR SCHOOL

This Book is lent to:—

Georgina Smyth MDP	9T 2006

This book is the property of the School and must be returned on request. If lost or unfairly used the pupil will be expected to replace it. It must not be marked in any way.

Louise Petheram

Phil Routledge

Lawrie Ryan

Text © Louise Petheram, Phil Routledge and Lawrie Ryan 2003
Original illustrations © Nelson Thornes Ltd 2003

The right of Louise Petheram, Phil Routledge and Lawrie Ryan to be identified as authors of this work has been asserted by them in accordance with the Copyright, Designs and Patents Act 1988.

All rights reserved. No part of this publication may be reproduced or transmitted in any form or by any means, electronic or mechanical, including photocopy, recording or any information storage and retrieval system, without permission in writing from the publisher or under licence from the Copyright Licensing Agency Limited, of 90 Tottenham Court Road, London W1T 4LP.

Any person who commits any unauthorised act in relation to this publication may be liable to criminal prosecution and civil claims for damages.

Published in 2003 by:
Nelson Thornes Ltd
Delta Place
27 Bath Road
CHELTENHAM
GL53 7TH
United Kingdom

03 04 05 06 07 / 10 9 8 7 6 5 4 3 2 1

A catalogue record for this book is available from the British Library

ISBN 0 7487 6796 7

Illustrations by Lisa Berkshire, Ian West and IFA Design Ltd
Page make-up by Tech Set Ltd

Printed and bound in Italy by Canale

Contents

Biology

9A Inheritance and selection   5

Why are offspring similar but not identical?   6
Looking at variation   9
Producing new breeds   11
Breeding farm animals   13
How do we get new varieties of plant?   14
Comparing different varieties   15
Clones   16
Summary   19
End of unit Questions   20

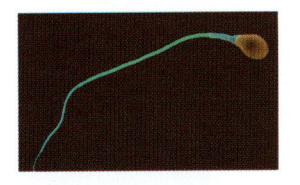

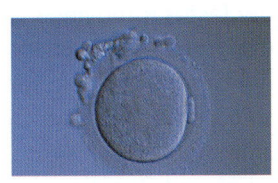

9B Fit and healthy   21

What do we mean by fit?   22
Breathing   25
Smoking   28
A healthy diet   30
Alcohol   33
Exercise and fitness   34
Drugs   36
Summary   39
End of unit Questions   40

9C Plants and photosynthesis   41

Building our knowledge of photosynthesis   42
How do plants make food?   43
Measuring photosynthesis   47
The leaf   48
What happens to the glucose produced in leaves?   49
Plant plumbing   50
Green plants in the environment   52
Reviewing your work   54
Summary   55
End of unit Questions   56

9D Plants for food   57

Where does our food come from?   58
Plants and fertilisers   62
Competing plants   66
Plants and pests   68
What is the perfect place for growing plants?   70
Summary   71
End of unit Questions   72

Chemistry

9E Reactions of metals and their compounds   73

Properties of metals and non-metals   74
Metals reacting with acids   78
Metal carbonates reacting with acids   82
Metal oxides reacting with acids   84
Neutralisation and salts   86
Preparing salts   88
Summary   89
End of unit Questions   90

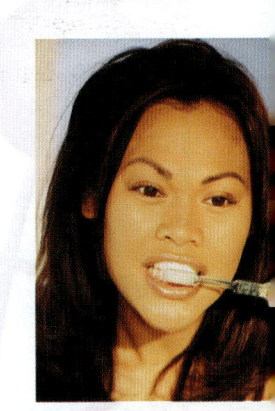

9F Patterns of reactivity   91

Tarnished metals   92
Metals reacting with water   95
The reactivity of metals with dilute acids   98
Metals reacting with oxygen   100
Displacement reactions   101
Reactivity linked to the sources and uses of metals   104
Summary   105
End of unit Questions   106

9G Environmental chemistry   107

Different types of soil   108
Weathering of rocks and
   building materials   112
What causes acid rain?   113
The effects of acid rain   115
Monitoring pollution   118
The issue of global
   warming   121
Summary   123
End of unit Questions   124

9H Using chemistry   125

Energy from burning fuels   126
Energy from other chemical reactions   129
More useful exothermic reactions   131
Making new materials   132
A closer look at chemical reactions   134
Making magnesium oxide   137
A closer look at combustion   139
Summary   141
End of unit Questions   142

Physics

9I Energy and electricity   143

How is energy involved in
   doing useful things?   144
How does electricity
   transfer energy?   147
What are we paying for
   when we use
   electricity?   151
Where do we get
   electricity from?   154
How can we reduce the
   waste of energy?   157
Summary   159
End of unit Questions   160

9J Gravity and space   161

What is gravity?   162
How does gravity change?   164
How have our ideas about
   the solar system
   changed?   167
What keeps the planets
   and satellites in orbit?   168
Artificial satellites   170
Summary   173
End of unit Questions   174

9K Speeding up   175

How fast is it moving?   176
How do forces affect speed?   179
How can we increase speed?   182
Using graphs to show changes in speed   186
Summary   189
End of unit Questions   190

9L Pressure and moments   191

What is pressure?   192
Pressure in gases and liquids   195
How do levers work?   199
How do things balance?   201
Summary   205
End of unit Questions   206

How to revise   **207**

Biology Revision
(Units 7A–7D, 8A–8D)   **210**

Chemistry Revision
(Units 7E–7H, 8E–8H)   **218**

Physics Revision
(Units 7I–7L, 8I–8L)   **226**

Glossary   **234**

Index   **236**

Acknowledgements   **240**

4

9A Inheritance and selection

Introduction

In this unit we will build on some of the ideas covered in Units 7A, 7B and 7D. We will revise some of the things you learned about then and look in greater detail at how characteristics are inherited by individual organisms. We will also look at ways in which humans can use our knowledge of inheritance and selection to produce new varieties of animals and plants.

You already know

- that individual members of a species show variation
- that variation can be inherited or caused by environmental factors
- that sexual reproduction involves the fusion of a male and female sex cell

In this topic you will learn

- about characteristics that are inherited and how these can be used in selective breeding
- why selective breeding is important
- about variations that are caused by environmental differences

1 What can you remember?

Look at the drawing.
a Make a list of variations you can see between members of the same species.
b Is each of these variations **inherited** or **environmental**?
c What other variations might there be that you cannot identify just by looking at the organisms?

BIOLOGY   Inheritance and selection

A1 Why are offspring similar but not identical?

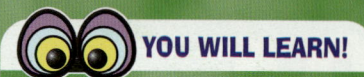

YOU WILL LEARN!
- that cells have a nucleus that contains information that passes from one generation to the next
- that when fertilisation happens, genetic information from the male and female combines
- that fertilisation produces a new individual that has a unique set of genes
- how eggs and sperms are specialised cells
- that fertilisation is similar in animals and plants

In topic 7B 'Reproduction' you learnt that the nucleus of every cell contains a set of genes. These genes contain all of the **genetic information** needed to make an individual organism. Each gene has information needed to control the development of one characteristic e.g. eye colour or hair colour. A group of genes is called a **chromosome**. Human cell nuclei have 46 chromosomes in 23 pairs.

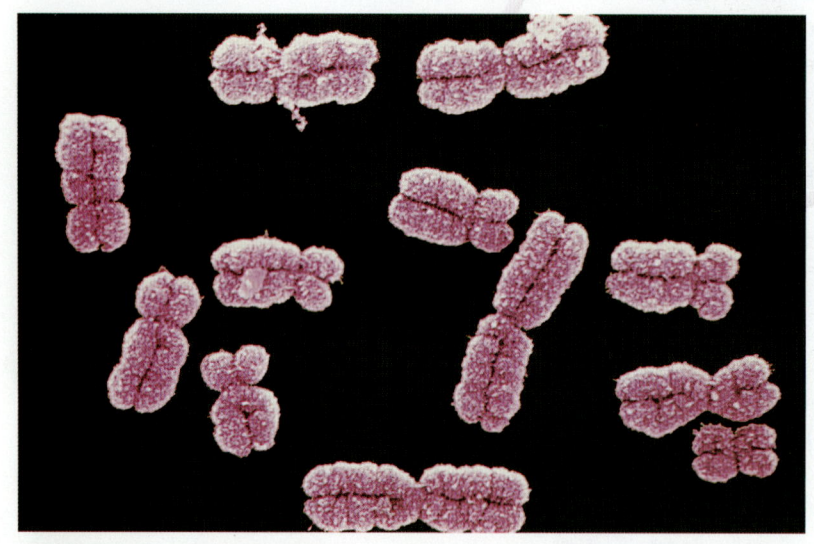

Chromosomes

Sperm and eggs are different from all other cells in the body. They are made in a special type of cell division called **meiosis**. Egg and sperm cells only have half the number of chromosomes found in all the other cells in the body. Plants also have genes and pass on genetic information to their offspring. Plants have **pollen** instead of sperm and **ovules** instead of eggs.

Eggs, sperm, pollen and ovules are all sex cells and are called **gametes**.

When gametes are formed they have half the genes found in the parents' cells. Each gamete will have a different set of genes, so each gamete is unique. Imagine a very simple organism with ten genes. Each gamete from this organism will have five genes. There are a lot of different ways of combining five genes from a set of ten genes. In a human there are thousands of genes, which means there are millions of millions of ways of combining them in each gamete.

Did you know

Genes are made of a chemical called **deoxyribonucleic acid**. Luckily we normally just call it **DNA**!

BIOLOGY **Inheritance and selection**

PARENT'S GENES

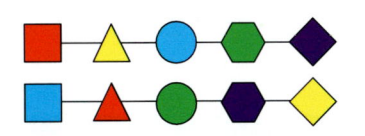

The parent has ten genes arranged in two sets.

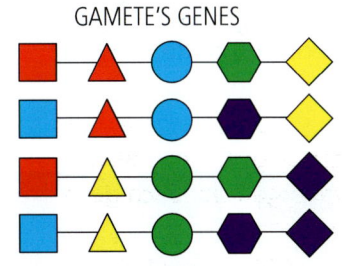

GAMETE'S GENES

Here are four different combinations of five genes in the gamete. How many more are there?

Parent's genes can combine in many different ways

1 Bringing genes together

Review the work you did in 7B about where eggs and sperms are formed and how a sperm fertilises an egg.

Draw a set of diagrams that summarise this whole process. Make sure you show how genetic information is transferred from parents to their offspring.

Make another set of drawings to show how genetic information is passed on in plants.

2 Some FAQs

Some year 7 pupils have some questions that they want answers to.

Try to answer them. Some simple diagrams might help you to explain.

Why do I look like my older brother?

How do identical twins happen?

Why do I look much more like my identical twin sister than my other sister?

Can identical twins be a boy and a girl?

My mum is having twin test tube babies. Two of her eggs were mixed with sperm in a dish then put back in her body. Will they be identical twins?

Is fertilisation in plants the same as in animals?

BUT MY TEACHER SAID ALL MY JEANS COME FROM MY PARENTS!

BIOLOGY   Inheritance and selection

Eggs and sperms

Eggs and sperms are special cells with a special job to do.
They are **adapted** to carry out their job.

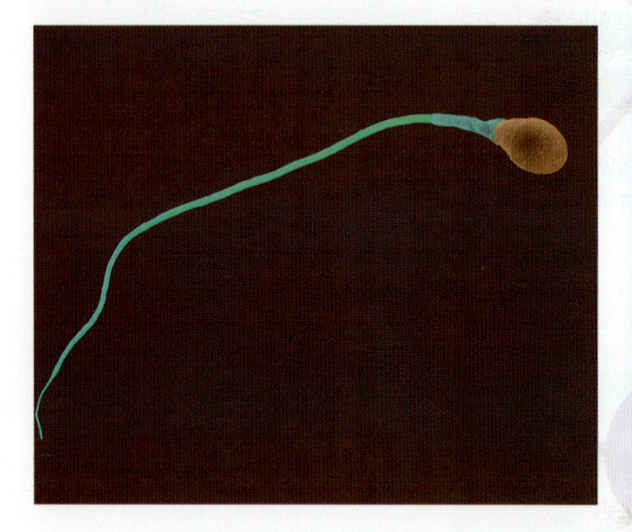

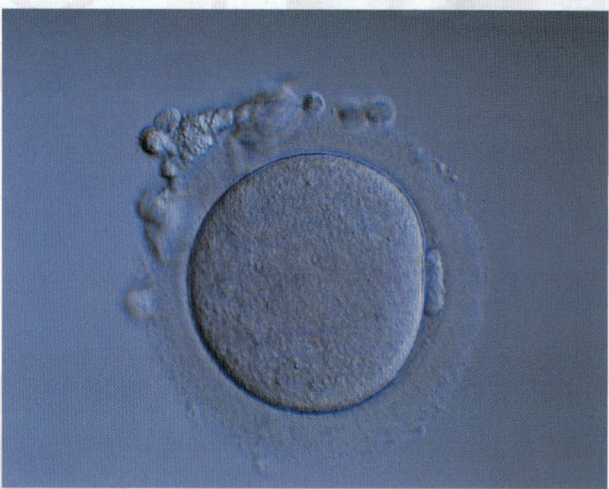

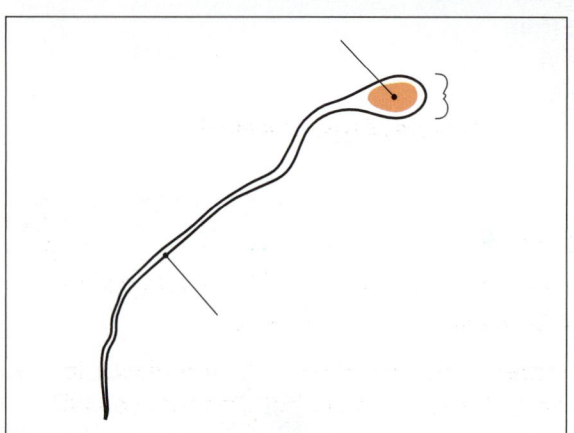

Human sperm   Human egg

3 Specialised cells

Draw and label a diagram of an egg and a sperm to show how they are adapted to carry out their job.

4 The human genome project

This is a major worldwide science project. Use the Internet to find out more about this project.

BIOLOGY   Inheritance and selection

A2 Looking at variation

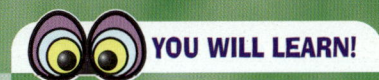

YOU WILL LEARN!
- that variations in a species can be due to environmental factors
- how to decide which measurements and observations to make
- how to design tables to record data
- how to use a spreadsheet to analyse data and draw graphs
- how to draw conclusions about variation

Have you ever looked at the salad section in a supermarket? You want a lettuce but there are so many different ones to choose from! They are all the same species but there are many different **varieties**.

See if you can identify the varieties in the photograph.

Gardeners and farmers can grow many different varieties of the same crop.

These are all types of lettuce!

1 Are there differences in a variety?

Your teacher will give you some specimens from a particular variety of a crop. Broad beans are a good example (although you could try to investigate a different crop).

What differences are there between individual specimens? Try to think of things that you can easily measure such as length. What else could you measure?

If each group of 2 or 3 pupils measures ten specimens each, then by putting the class results together you should have data from a large sample.

A spreadsheet would be a very useful way to handle the large amount of data that you will produce.

Calculate the average for each of the measurements you make. Better still, get your spreadsheet to calculate it for you! Use the spreadsheet to produce frequency charts for each of the measurements you make. Comment on the shape of your frequency chart.

2 Comparing varieties

Try making the same measurements on a different variety of the same crop as you used in Activity 1. Put your data into a new spreadsheet and compare the average and the frequency charts for each measurement.

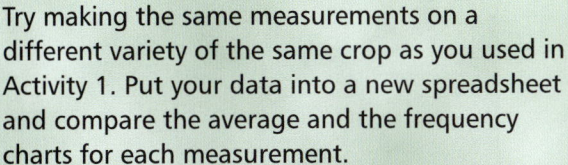

a Do the different varieties show any noticeable differences?

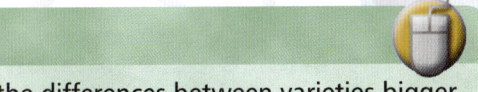

b Are the differences between varieties bigger than the differences within the varieties? How does the data support your answer?

c How reliable is your data?

BIOLOGY   Inheritance and selection

As well as size, there are many other differences between varieties. Most of these are more difficult to measure.

Different varieties of plants often taste quite different. Farmers try to grow varieties that have a long 'shelf life'. A lot of plant varieties are grown because they are resistant to diseases. The time taken for a fruit to ripen can vary from one variety to another. Varieties of the same crop can be quite different in colour. Even things like tomatoes can come in many different shades of red.

3 Which is the best crop to grow?

Read the paragraph above about differences between varieties of the same crop.

a For each of the differences, try to explain why it is important.
b For each one, try to think of a way you could measure that difference.
c Why is it important that supermarkets are able to compare different varieties of the same crop?

In *Ascent! Book 1*, you saw that there are differences between identical twins even though they have identical genes. All of the specimens from one variety of plant have very similar or even identical genetic information yet there are still differences between them. So how do these differences occur?

Genes give an individual the **potential** to develop in a particular way. The **environment** can help decide if it actually reaches its potential.

Points to discuss

A gardener plants two potatoes from the same plant on the same day. Both have identical genes. After five months he digs up each plant, collects the potatoes that have grown and weighs them. One plant produces 1.0 kg of potatoes while the other produces 1.5 kg.

Can you think of some reasons that might explain these differences?

4 Genetic or environmental?

Think about differences between plants of the same species.

Draw up a table to show if they are genetic, environmental or a combination of both.

Draw a similar table to sort out the differences in humans.

BIOLOGY Inheritance and selection

A3 Producing new breeds

YOU WILL LEARN!
- that selective breeding involves mating together individuals with particular inherite...
- that dif... have be... selectiv...
- that se... in new... and pla...

Although there are many breeds of dogs, they all belong to the same species.

Alsatian

Dachshund

St Bernard

Yorkshire terrier

Golden retriever

Border collie

Bulldog

Greyhound

1 Dogs

The pictures show several breeds of dog. They all belong to the same species yet they look very different from each other.

a Make a list of the features they have in common.
b Make another list of the features that are different.
c How did these different breeds come about?

11

BIOLOGY   Inheritance and selection

Humans and dogs have lived together for thousands of years. At first, the dogs were wild. (They may actually have been wolves!) Living close to humans was an easy way of getting food. The humans benefited by being protected by the wolves. When these early humans went hunting the wolves went with them.

Over the years, the humans encouraged the wolves to breed. Perhaps they chose the dogs with longer legs to breed from as they would be the fastest for hunting. This would mean the gene for longer legs was passed on to the next generation. Over many generations this would lead to a dog with much longer legs than the original wolf. At the same time, humans may have also chosen to breed smaller, less fierce dogs to keep as pets. By carefully choosing which individual animals to mate, humans gradually produced many different breeds of dog. This is called **selective breeding**. Most of these breeds originally had a particular job. Today, most dogs are bred to keep as pets although there are still many working dogs.

Did you know

The word 'terrier' comes from the French word *'terre'* which means earth. Terriers were originally used by hunters to crawl into burrows and chase out the animals that lived there.

2 Working dogs

Look at the pictures of dogs on the previous page. Use secondary sources, such as the Internet, to find information about other breeds of dog.

Find out (or try to guess) what they were originally used for.

Decide which characteristics help them to carry out their particular job.

Make a display to show what you find out.

A particular gene, or group of genes, controls each of the characteristics you identified in Activity 2. Dog breeders select animals that show the characteristic they want in their offspring. By choosing an individual with that characteristic they are choosing an individual that carries the right version of the gene.

So far in this section we have looked only at dogs. There are many other examples of domesticated animals and plants that have different varieties due to selective breeding. What examples can you think of? Were they bred for a particular job? The pictures opposite show three varieties of horse. What were they bred for? What features are important in these horses?

Shire horse

Pit pony

Racehorse

BIOLOGY — Inheritance and selection

A4 Breeding farm animals

YOU WILL LEARN!
- that farm animals have been bred to have certain 'desirable' characteristics
- how to make links and connections in your written work to explain a point
- how to 'skim' written information to find out if it is useful

In Britain, the main animals found on farms are cattle, pigs, sheep and poultry (mainly hens and turkeys). What are these animals used for? What features will farmers want in their animals? Some of these features are connected with the product that comes from the animal. Other features can also be important. For example, Hereford bulls are often mated with Friesian cows. This gives good quality meat and animals that have a distinctive white shape on the face that helps farmers to identify each animal. Other features can be connected with where the animal lives. For example, sheep that live on cold hill farms need thicker wool than those on warmer, low-lying farms.

1 Desirable animals

Look at the animals named above. Think about what they are used for and what characteristics will be desirable. Make sure you explain your answer carefully linking your sentences with words like 'because' and 'therefore'. Here is an example:

*'Many cattle are mainly used in the dairy industry, **therefore** farmers want cows that produce a lot of milk. Farmers want dairy cattle to be placid **because** they have to be moved twice a day for milking'.*

1. Write your own descriptions of some desirable characteristics in farm animals, linking them to the reasons why they are desirable.
   Try to find out additional information from books, cd-roms and the Internet. 'Skim' through your sources to find the information needed to answer these questions:
2. Where did farm animals originate?
3. Have desirable characteristics changed through the years?
4. What are 'rare breeds' and why is it important to keep them?

Present your findings in a display or booklet about 'Farm Animals' or do a short presentation to the rest of your class.

Did you know ?

Farmers on some ranches in America who tried to raise cattle found that they could not survive the harsh conditions. So they cross bred domestic cattle with bison (North American buffalo). They produced an animal with good quality meat that could survive the tough winter conditions. They called the new breed the *beefalo*!

Points to discuss

Can different species be crossed to get desirable characteristics? Look at D1 in *Ascent! Book 1*. Can you find out the desirable characteristics of mules?

Did you know ?

Turkeys come from America – not Turkey!

I WANT TO VISIT MY COUSINS BUT I'M NOT SURE WHERE THEY ARE!

WHY NOT TRY AMERICA, BUT NOT AT THANKSGIVING!

13

BIOLOGY — Inheritance and selection

A5 How do we get new varieties of plant?

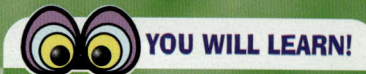

YOU WILL LEARN!
- that plant breeders select healthy plants with particular characteristics to breed from
- that fertilisation of an ovule by a pollen cell produces a new individual
- how plant breeders make sure pollen from one particular flower is used to pollinate another flower

In A2 you saw several varieties of lettuce. The photograph on the right shows different varieties of tomato. Can you name them? Can you name any varieties of other fruits or vegetables?

As well as a different appearance, there are many other less obvious differences between different varieties of the same plant. Some of these were mentioned in A2.

1 Plant varieties

a Make a list of visible differences in the plant specimens opposite and in the picture on page 5.
b What other differences might there be? Explain why each one is important.

Tomatoes come in many varieties

These desirable characteristics are achieved by plant breeders carefully crossing plants. For example, they might cross a plant with good flavour with another that is resistant to cold. But how do they do this? In animals it is easy because farmers can, for example, make sure that a particular bull only mates with a particular cow. But pollen is carried by the wind or by insects. Isn't it? Well, yes, normally it is. Plant breeders, however, do not rely on something as random as the wind or a bee! Can you remember the work you did in *Ascent! Book 1* about pollination?

Pollen is produced on the stamen. It is deposited on the stigma by an insect or by the wind. A plant breeder wants to cross plant A and plant B.

In a flower, the pollen and the ovules are not normally ripe at the same time. The plant breeder takes pollen from a flower on plant A using a small brush. He, or she, then transfers the pollen to a flower on plant B. All of the stamens on the second flower are then removed and the flower is wrapped in polythene to keep any other pollen away.

2 Selective pollination

Write out a set of step-by-step instructions on how to selectively pollinate one plant with pollen from another.

Use diagrams to illustrate your instructions.

Explain the importance of each step.

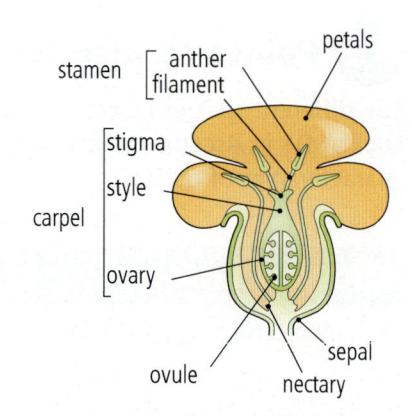

Cross-section through a flower

BIOLOGY   Inheritance and selection

A6 Comparing different varieties

1 Worm's Eye Foods

Worm's Eye Frozen Foods claim that their frozen peas are identical to fresh peas. Your class have the task of testing this claim.

You will be given two samples of peas:

i   fresh peas from the pod
ii frozen peas which have been allowed to thaw.

What differences could there be between the peas? How can you measure them? How can you make it a fair test?

There are some obvious differences that are easy to measure like size and mass. But what about things like taste and colour? What about the time needed to cook the peas? What about the tenderness of the peas?

These are all important differences between varieties of pea, especially for a food manufacturer. They have laboratories set up to find out the answers to these questions. Imagine your science laboratory is part of the Worm's Eye factory and your class are its team of scientists.

Think of ways to answer the questions above. Different members of the class can take responsibility for different investigations. Put the results together and produce a report for Worm's Eye.

Tasting is best done in a Food Technology Room. If you are in a science laboratory special precautions will have been taken to avoid contamination as normally eating and drinking are banned!

YOU WILL LEARN!

- how to decide on a question to be investigated
- how to choose an appropriate sample size
- how to choose the method and apparatus to carry out an investigation
- how to draw conclusions from an investigation
- how to evaluate an investigation

Did you know?

Frozen pea manufacturers need their peas to have exactly the right level of tenderness before freezing them. They use a piece of apparatus called a *pea tenderometer*!

When the peas are ready to be picked, they pick them right away – even in the middle of the night!

They claim their product is 'fresher' than fresh peas because they are frozen within a few hours of being picked whereas real fresh peas can take several days to get to the shops.

A food scientist at work

15

BIOLOGY   Inheritance and selection

A7 Clones

YOU WILL LEARN!
- that, in cloning, all genetic information comes from one parent
- to think about some of the ethical questions about cloning

ATTACK OF THE CLONES — STAR WARS EPISODE II

You have probably heard of **clones**, especially if you are interested in science fiction. Perhaps you have heard of Dolly the sheep. Maybe you have read newspaper stories about **cloning**. So what is cloning?

A clone is an individual whose genetic information all comes from one parent. Dolly the sheep was produced by cloning in 1997 by a team of scientists led by Ian Wilmut in Edinburgh.

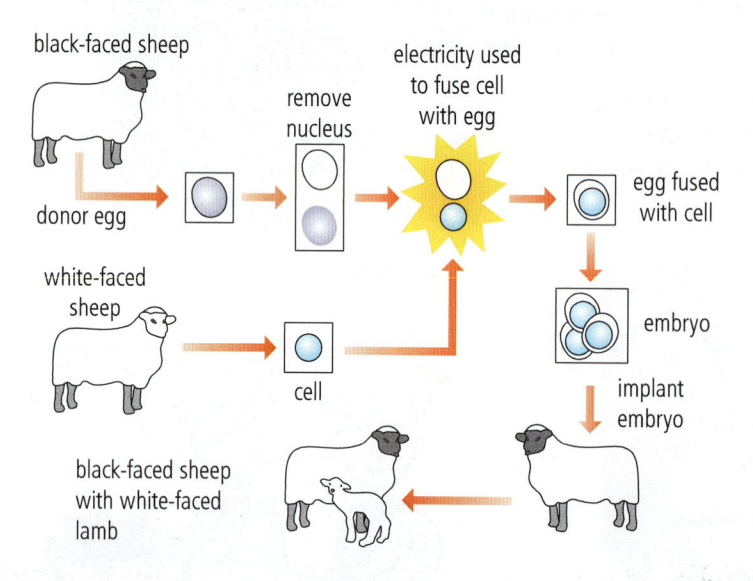

Did you know

Although Dolly has given birth to lambs of her own her health deteriorated as she developed arthritis. She was put to sleep when she was only six years old, which is young for a sheep.

Diagram: black-faced sheep → donor egg → remove nucleus; white-faced sheep → cell; electricity used to fuse cell with egg → egg fused with cell → embryo → implant embryo → black-faced sheep with white-faced lamb.

The nucleus was removed from a cell from the udder of a white-faced sheep. This nucleus was used to replace the nucleus from an egg of a black-faced sheep. The egg started to divide. It was then implanted into the uterus of another black-faced sheep. It grew and produced a lamb with exactly the same genetic information as the white-faced sheep.

Since then, Dolly has given birth to lambs of her own, all produced by normal sexual reproduction. Many other animals have since

Did you know

Woolly mammoths died out about 10 000 years ago. The remains of some mammoths have been found in Siberia, frozen in ice. Because the bodies were frozen, tissue with DNA is still present. Some scientists think it may be possible to take DNA from the remains of a mammoth and implant it into the egg of an elephant. They think they could produce a cloned mammoth.

16

BIOLOGY   Inheritance and selection

been cloned including cows, monkeys, pigs, mice and a gaur (an endangered species of ox from Asia).

1 Cloning animals

a Write a newspaper article about cloning animals. What are the benefits of cloning? Is it safe?

b Many scientists now think it is possible to make a clone of a human. Do you think this should be allowed? Have a class debate about the **ethics** of cloning humans. You will have to find out as much as possible about the subject. You should be able to argue the case for or against cloning.

Although cloning seems totally futuristic, people have actually been producing clones for thousands of years. Remember that a clone is an organism whose genetic information all comes from one parent. We call this **asexual** reproduction. Asexual means 'without sex'.

Many plants reproduce naturally by asexual or **vegetative** reproduction.

The spider plant produces lots of 'plantlets' that hang down from a special stem. When these touch the ground they grow roots. Eventually, the stem breaks away and the plantlet becomes a separate plant, genetically identical to its parent.

Spider plant

2 Taking cuttings

Many plants can be **propagated** by taking **cuttings**.

Get a geranium plant.

Find a stem that is not flowering.

Cut off the stem just below where a leaf joins. Remove the bottom leaf.

Dip the cut end in rooting powder.

Put the cutting in compost. After a couple of weeks the cutting will develop roots. The new plant has identical genetic information to its parent and is a clone.

Taking a cutting

17

BIOLOGY   Inheritance and selection

Another method of making cloned plants is called **grafting**. Rose growers use this method. Rose growers try to develop new flowers by crossing roses with the characteristics they want. When they have a new flower they want to produce many plants with exactly the same genes.

The diagram shows how the graft is made. Only the top part of the new plant has the desired genes but that's all right because that's the bit that makes flowers! Many grafted plants can be made from a single parent plant.

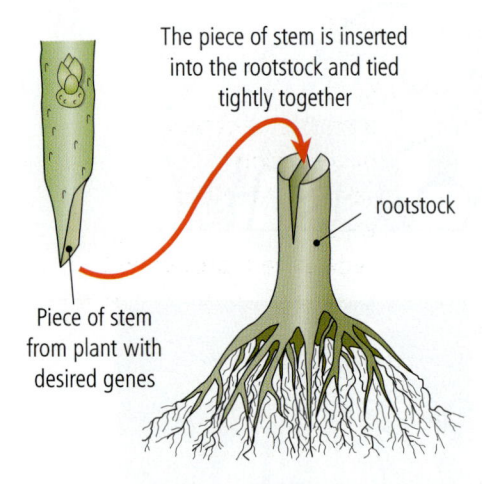

The piece of stem is inserted into the rootstock and tied tightly together

rootstock

Piece of stem from plant with desired genes

The rootstock is planted. Eventually, the stem and rootstock grow together

graft which has grown together

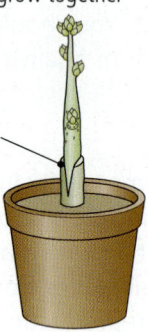

Making a graft

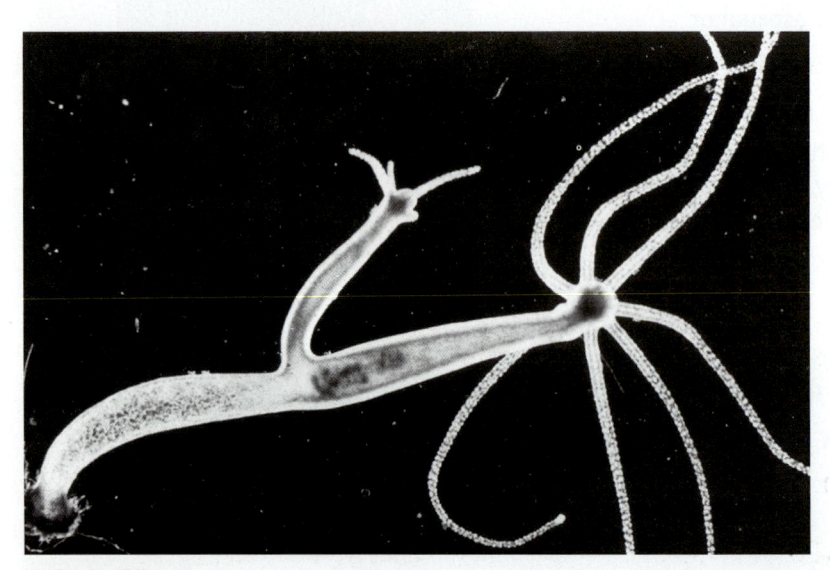

Hydra budding

Did you know

The hydra is a simple animal that lives in ponds. It can reproduce by **budding**. When it is big enough, the bud breaks off and becomes a separate animal, a clone of its parent.

It is named after the Hydra of Greek mythology. Find out about the Hydra and explain why the pond creature is named after it.

BIOLOGY — Inheritance and selection

Summary

All cells have a nucleus containing **genes**. Genes are made of a chemical called **DNA**. A group of genes is called a **chromosome**. Genes carry the **genetic information** needed to make an individual organism. When a male **gamete** fertilises a female gamete, genetic information from both parents combines to make a new individual with a unique set of genes. This happens in both animals and plants.

All individuals show **variation**. **Inherited variation** is due to differences in genes, while **environmental variation** is due to how and where the individual organism lives.

Mating together individuals that have a particular characteristic can produce new breeds of animals. This is called **selective breeding** and has resulted in many new breeds of animals. These include dogs, cats and most farm animals.

Selective breeding has also produced new varieties of plants. These include plants grown for their flowers as well as crops used for food. Plant breeders have to make sure that only pollen from the desired plant is used to fertilise the ovules.

Clones are organisms with genetic information which is identical to their parent's. Plants produce clones naturally by a form of **asexual** reproduction called **vegetative** reproduction. Humans can make use of this to produce new plants by taking **cuttings** and by **grafting**.

In recent years, cloning has produced animals. This has caused a lot of ethical debate, especially about the possibility of cloning humans.

Key words

- asexual
- chromosome
- clone
- cloning
- cutting
- DNA
- environmental variation
- gamete
- gene
- genetic information
- graft
- inherited variation
- propagation
- selective breeding
- variation
- vegetative reproduction

Summary Questions

1. Draw a diagram of a sperm cell and an egg cell and explain how they are adapted to carry out their functions.

2. **a** Explain why the same two parents have children who are different from each other.
   b Explain why identical twins have identical genetic information while non-identical twins do not.

3. Two plants grown from identical cuttings will not look identical. Explain why.

4. Give some examples of inherited characteristics that are desirable in a sheep.

5. Find out about how gardeners and farmers produce strawberries, apples and potatoes that are genetically identical to an original plant with desirable characteristics.

6. You are going to interview a scientist who wants to produce a cloned human. Write down five questions you would ask her.

7. Write a newspaper article about a scientist who wants to clone a mammoth. Make sure you explain the method that he will use but in language that is suitable for an average member of the public.

BIOLOGY — Inheritance and selection

End of unit Questions

1 Herefords and Friesians are two breeds of cattle.
Herefords produce high quality meat. Friesians produce lots of milk.
The drawings below show a Hereford cow and a Friesian cow.

Hereford cow   Friesian cow

a i The two breeds of cattle are different in appearance from each other. What causes the variation between the two breeds? *1 mark*

ii Suggest **three** environmental factors which can affect the amount of meat or milk cattle produce. *3 marks*

b The drawing shows a calf produced by mating a Hereford bull with a Friesian cow. Cattle bred in this way will produce both high quality meat and a high milk yield.

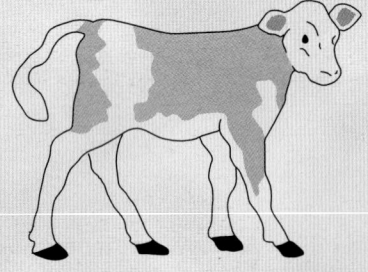

i What term is used to describe this deliberate mating of two different breeds of animals to produce offspring with particular characteristics? *1 mark*

ii Farmers want their cattle to produce high quality meat and a high milk yield. Suggest **three other** characteristics which farmers might want their cattle to have. *3 marks*

2 Gareth was writing to a pen-friend. This is how he described himself:

I am a boy   I weigh 600 N
I am 16 years old   I speak French
I have brown eyes   I have a scar on my chin
I am 1.8 m tall

a From the list choose **two** features that he must have inherited and which will not have been affected by his environment. *2 marks*

b From the list choose **two** features which will have been affected by both inherited **and** environmental factors. *2 marks*

c Gareth measured the heights of the 16-year-old pupils at his school. He recorded the distribution in a bar chart.

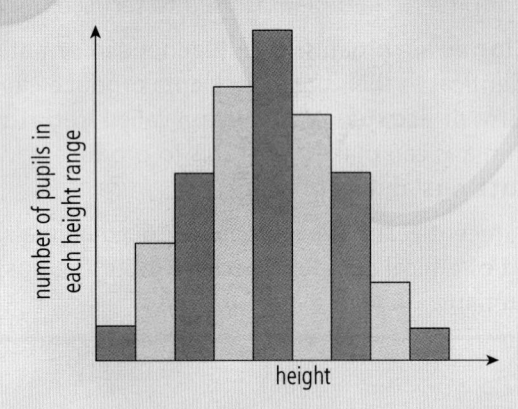

He also collected data about the features in the list below.
Which two features would show a similarly shaped distribution to Gareth's bar chart? Choose the correct letter.

A Ability to roll the tongue
B Presence of ear lobes
C Mass of the pupil
D Circumference of the head
E Sex of the pupil

2 marks

9B Fit and healthy

Introduction

In this unit you will revise some of the work on cells and reproduction from year 7; on nutrition, exercise and respiration from year 8; and on inheritance from year 9. You will look in more detail at the effects of these on our health. Further work will include finding out about the effects of smoking, alcohol and drugs on the human body. The skeleton and muscles are essential parts of the human body and you will find out how to keep these working efficiently.

You already know

- what makes up a balanced diet and why this is needed for healthy growth
- about the exchange of gases in the alveoli
- that the developing fetus obtains materials from the mother's blood through the placenta
- some characteristics that can be inherited

In this topic you will learn

- how the human respiratory, digestive and circulatory systems interact to keep us healthy
- about the functions of the skeleton
- about ways in which diet, exercise, smoking and drugs affect health

1 What can you remember?

Look at the drawing above.
a Make a list of the unhealthy activities of the family in the picture.
b Write out some advice on what they should do to improve their health.
c Make a poster or leaflet called 'Getting your family fit'.

21

BIOLOGY Fit and healthy

B1 What do we mean by fit?

YOU WILL LEARN!
- how fitness is related to the systems of the body
- that fitness is different for different people
- that several systems of the body are needed to obtain energy from food
- the chemical equation for respiration

Are you fit? How do you know? What does it mean to be fit? Look at the photographs. Are all of these people fit?

They are probably all fit but in different ways. There are four ways of looking at fitness:
- Speed – having fast reactions and being able to move quickly
- Stamina – being able to keep on doing exercise for a long time
- Strength – having strong muscles that can exert a lot of force
- Suppleness – being able to bend, stretch and twist easily

These different fitness S-factors depend on different systems of your body working well. For example, to increase your stamina you need to develop your digestive, respiratory and circulatory systems. Developing these requires a combination of exercise and the right food. Smoking damages the respiratory and circulatory systems.

Points to discuss

What systems of the body need to work well for people to develop strength, suppleness and speed?

1 S-factors

Look at the photographs.

a Are the people in each photograph fit? Explain your answer.
b For each of the activities, put the S-factors in order of importance.
c Outline what is required to develop each of the S-factors.

BIOLOGY   Fit and healthy

2 Measuring your fitness

Here are some simple ways to compare fitness:

- **Measuring fat**. Use special callipers to measure the thickness of fat on the back of your upper arm. To do this you should have your arm hanging loosely by your side.
- **Recovery time**. This should give an idea of your stamina. Measure your resting pulse rate. Exercise for a measured period of time then find out how long it takes your pulse rate to return to normal. If possible you can use datalogging equipment to measure this and produce a graph of the results.
- **Strength**. Measure your muscle strength by squeezing a set of bathroom scales.
- **Speed**. Time how long it takes to run a short distance such as 20 m.

Use the ideas above and your imagination to devise a 'fitness index'. This should allow you to measure your own fitness, and compare it with other people, taking into account all four of the S-factors. Does a person's age have anything to do with their fitness? Can you include this in your fitness index?

If you have any health problems discuss these with your teacher before you start.

Energy and fitness

Think back to topic 8B. All forms of exercise need energy. Our energy comes from the food we eat. To release the energy from food we need to convert the food to glucose. Then the glucose has to react with oxygen. This happens in a reaction called **respiration** that takes place in the cells of our body. Carbon dioxide and water are the products of this reaction. We can sum up respiration using this equation:

glucose + oxygen → carbon dioxide + water + energy

When you run, you need lots of energy to be released in your leg muscles.

3 Getting it all together

Look at the equation for respiration.

a Which body systems are required to make it work? Topics 8A and 8B will help you to remember.
b Draw a diagram or flowchart to summarise how these different systems work together to make respiration happen.

The equation above is for **aerobic respiration**.

c What does this mean?
d What do we mean by **anaerobic respiration**? (You learnt about it in 8B)
e What are the differences between aerobic and anaerobic respiration? Draw a table to summarise them.

BIOLOGY   Fit and healthy

The table below shows the effects of some different types of activities:

Exercise	Strength	Stamina	Suppleness	Speed
Badminton	**	**	***	**
Climbing stairs	**	***	*	*
Cycling	***	***	**	*
Disco dancing	*	****	**	*
Football	***	***	***	***
Golf	*	*	**	*
Gymnastics	***	**	****	**
Hill walking	**	***	*	*
Jogging	**	****	**	*
Swimming	****	****	****	**
Tennis	**	***	***	***
Weight-training	****	*	*	*

**** excellent effect   *** very good effect   ** good effect   * no real effect

4 Fitness programme

a Which of the exercises in the table are best for improving
   i   speed
   ii suppleness
   iii stamina
   iv strength?
b Which exercises would be best for
   i   a busy office worker who finds it difficult to find time to exercise
   ii a 25-year-old who has not done any sport since she left school at the age of 18
   iii a 30-year-old who normally plays football once a week and who has decided to enter a marathon in 10 months?
c Look at the man in the cartoon. He's trying to get fit.
   Do you think he is going the right way about it?
d What is he doing wrong?
e Think up a fitness programme that he could follow over a six week period to improve his fitness sensibly.
f What special care should he take?
g Draw a poster aimed at school leavers to advise them of the importance of carrying on with some type of sport. You could include reasons why they should exercise, the sort of things they could do and give them some ideas about the places where they could do it.

BIOLOGY   Fit and healthy
B2 Breathing

YOU WILL LEARN!
- that the lungs, diaphragm, rib cage and its muscles are essential for breathing
- that reducing the chest volume pushes air from the lungs

You should be familiar with the structure of the lungs from *Ascent!* 8 B4.

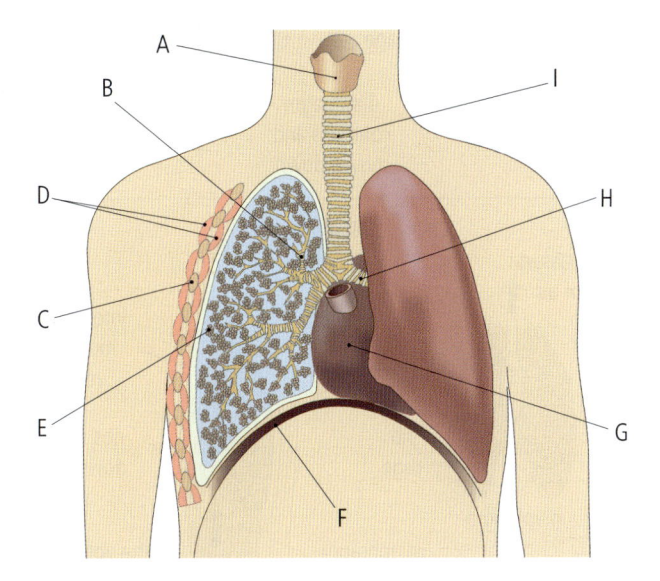

The human respiratory system

1 Review

a Give the names of the parts of the human breathing system indicated by the letters on the diagram.

b Draw a mind map or diagram to show how gases are exchanged in the lungs. You should include the movement of oxygen, carbon dioxide and water vapour and the structure of the alveoli, bronchioles, bronchi and trachea.

How do we breathe?

Put your hand on your rib cage. Breathe in deeply. What happens? Breathe out deeply. What happens? Now, take shallow breaths, like you normally do when you are sitting at rest. How does it compare? We can get a better understanding of breathing by looking at a couple of models.

Look at the diagram of the human breathing system. Between the ribs there are some muscles. These are called **intercostal** muscles. These muscles move the rib cage when they contract. The diaphragm is a large sheet of muscle below the lungs.

When we breathe in, the **external** intercostal muscles contract. This moves the rib cage upwards and outwards. At the same time, the diaphragm contracts and moves down. These movements make the chest cavity or **thorax** bigger. Air is drawn into the lungs. Breathing in is called **inspiration**.

BIOLOGY   Fit and healthy

When we breathe out, the muscles of the diaphragm relax and it returns to its dome shape. The external intercostal muscles relax and the rib cage drops down and inwards. The thorax volume decreases and air is forced out. Breathing out is called **expiration**.

When we are at rest, our breathing is shallow and it is the diaphragm that does most of the work. The external intercostal muscles are more important when we are breathing deeply.

The internal intercostal muscles are not used in normal breathing – only when we breathe out very hard.

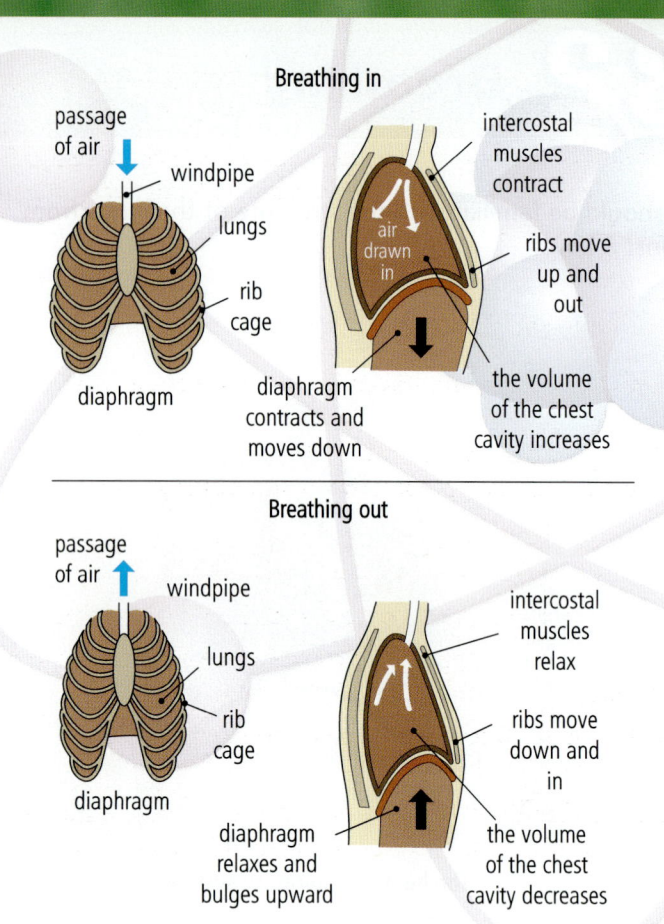

Breathing in

- passage of air
- windpipe
- lungs
- rib cage
- diaphragm
- intercostal muscles contract
- air drawn in
- ribs move up and out
- diaphragm contracts and moves down
- the volume of the chest cavity increases

Breathing out

- passage of air
- windpipe
- lungs
- rib cage
- diaphragm
- intercostal muscles relax
- ribs move down and in
- diaphragm relaxes and bulges upward
- the volume of the chest cavity decreases

2 Breathing

Observe the breathing models.

a Which one is a model of deep breathing?

b Which one is a model of shallow breathing?

c What happens to the volume of your chest when you breathe in?

d What happens to the volume of your chest when you breathe out?

e Draw a diagram of the bell jar model. Label the parts of the model that represent the following parts of the human breathing system: *lungs, trachea, bronchi, rib cage, diaphragm*.

f Produce a summary of breathing, explaining the differences between what happens in deep and shallow breathing. Explain when and why we would breathe more deeply than normal.

g Try to think of some examples of breathing very forcefully. These are examples of when we would use the internal intercostal muscles.

- glass tube
- bell jar
- balloon
- rubber sheet

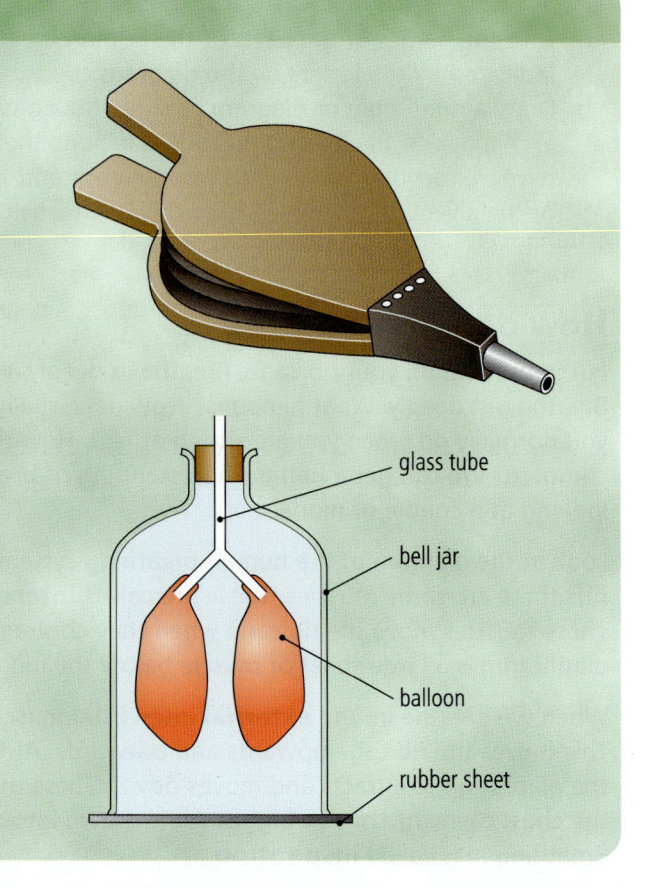

BIOLOGY   Fit and healthy

3 Model lungs

Try making your own set of model lungs. You could use a drinking straw, a plastic bottle, some plasticine, an elastic band and some balloons.

Points to discuss

1. How can we measure how much air you can breathe out in one breath?
2. What is the average sized breath?
3. How much air do you breathe in and out in a day?

Did you know

The average adult has a lung volume of about 4.5 litres.

The average resting adult breathes about 900 litres of air every hour.

In a lifetime we breathe enough air to fill about 50 000 000 party balloons.

There are about 300 000 000 alveoli in the lungs. If they were spread out they would cover the same area as a tennis court.

Points do discuss

1. Why do we cough?
2. Why do we yawn?
3. What causes hiccups?
4. What is the best way to get rid of hiccups?

Asthma

Asthma is a condition that affects the bronchioles. If you have asthma your bronchioles are sensitive. When you come into contact with something you are allergic to, or something that irritates your airways, the muscles of the bronchiole walls contract. The bronchioles become narrower, which makes it harder to breathe. The lining of the airways becomes inflamed and starts to swell and sticky mucus is often produced. This leads to the symptoms of asthma. Anti-inflammatory drugs can be used to reduce the symptoms of asthma. How do sufferers take these drugs?

4 Asthma

Use books, leaflets and the Internet to find out more about asthma.

Produce a scientific article about asthma. Include information such as causes of asthma, its symptoms and how it can be treated.

Aim your article at a parent who has just discovered that their child has asthma and wants to find out more.

Use a computer to produce a professional looking piece of work.

Include diagrams to show what actually happens inside the lungs of an asthma sufferer.

BIOLOGY   Fit and healthy

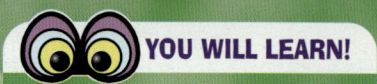

B3 Smoking

YOU WILL LEARN!
- that smoking causes many diseases
- that carbon monoxide, nicotine and tar all cause different kinds of damage
- that special ciliated cells in the epithelium of the lungs move fluid
- that our knowledge of how smoking causes disease has been built up over a number of years

You have already seen that healthy breathing and circulatory systems are essential to your body's overall health. Smoking causes damage to both of these vital body systems.

1 What's in cigarette smoke?

The apparatus shown can help us to investigate some of the effects of smoking.

Run the apparatus for five minutes without a cigarette.

Observe the temperature, the colour of the glass wool and the appearance of the lime water.

Repeat the experiment, this time with a cigarette.

Record your observations.

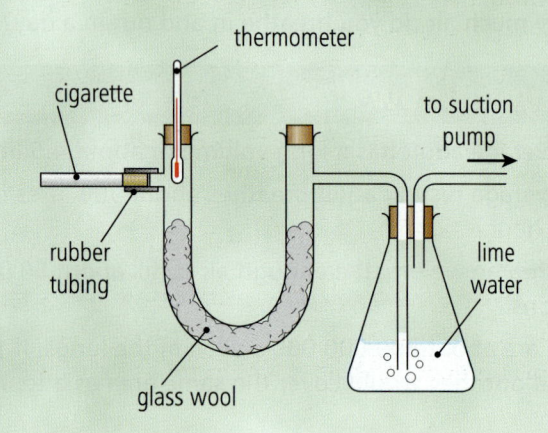

Dying for a smoke?

Cigarette smoke contains:

- **Nicotine** – this is a very poisonous substance. It affects your brain and is a stimulant. This means it makes you feel more alert. It also narrows your blood vessels and increases your heart rate. This increases your blood pressure. Your blood clots more easily due to the presence of nicotine. Nicotine is also **addictive.** Once your body has got used to it, it is hard to do without it.

- **Carbon monoxide** – this stops the cilia lining your bronchioles from working properly. This allows bacteria and dirt into your lungs, which can lead to **bronchitis**. Carbon monoxide is also absorbed into your blood. It reduces the amount of oxygen your blood can carry (see page 127). Carbon monoxide also contributes to narrowing of your arteries, including those that take blood to the muscle of the heart wall.

- **Tar** – this is absorbed by the cells lining the lungs. Tar is **carcinogenic**. This means that it causes cancer.

Did you know

Nicotine is as poisonous as cyanide.

Cigarette smoking increases the risk of having a heart attack by two or three times, compared with the risk to non-smokers.

About 200 people a year in the UK have a leg amputated as a result of smoking.

Tobacco use kills around 120 000 people in the UK every year. That's about 330 every day. Imagine if an aeroplane crashed every day and all of its passengers were killed.

BIOLOGY   Fit and healthy

2 Smoking and health

Read the information 'Dying for a smoke?'.

Find out more about what is in cigarette smoke using books, leaflets and the Internet.

Find out more about the effects of cigarette smoke on the body. (Topics 7B 'Reproduction' in *Ascent! Book 1* and 8B 'Respiration' in *Ascent! Book 2* have information that will help you.)

a Produce a report that shows what are the harmful chemicals in cigarettes and how these cause different diseases.
b Explain why people find it difficult to give up smoking.

Find out how much a packet of 20 cigarettes costs.

c Calculate the annual cost of smoking 20 cigarettes a day.
d Assuming the price of cigarettes rises by 5% a year, calculate how much someone who starts smoking now will have spent in ten years.

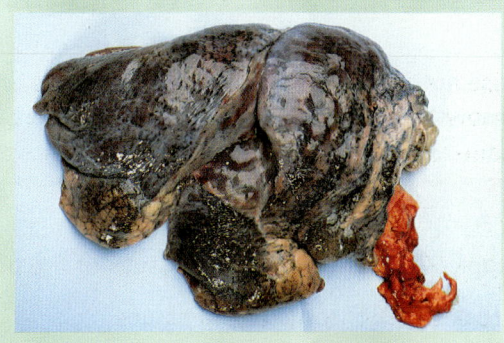

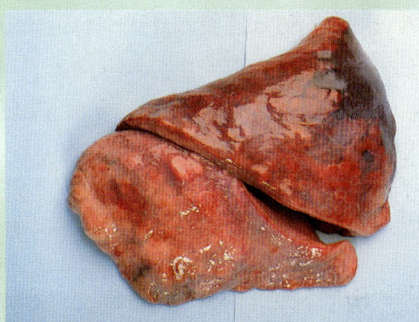

Lungs of a smoker and a healthy person

Point to discuss

If tobacco had not been discovered until now do you think people would be allowed to smoke it legally?

Passive smoking

Even people who do not smoke, take in all of the harmful substances from cigarette smoke if they are in the same room as a smoker. This is called **passive smoking**. Parents who smoke are more likely to have children who suffer from lung problems.

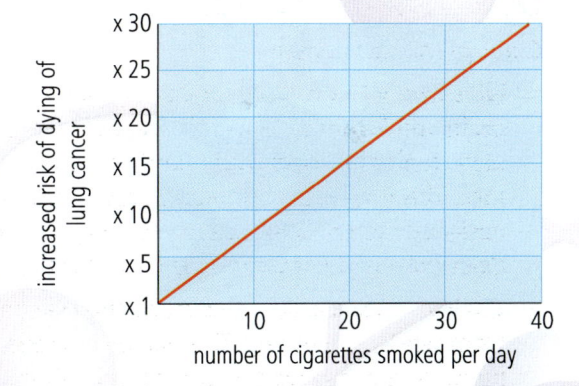

The effect of smoking on health

Point to discuss

Do you think smoking should be banned in all public places?

3 Smoking through the ages

50 years ago people did not know that smoking caused lung cancer.

Cigarettes were much cheaper then.

Advertisements for cigarettes were more widespread. Even many famous sportspeople used to smoke and some even advertised cigarettes.

There are fewer people smoking now than there were 50 years ago.

Why do you think our views on smoking have changed over the years?

Ed smokes about 30 cigarettes a day. He knows it is bad for him and he thinks he should give up. He doesn't know the details of what smoking can do to him.

Produce a one-page fact sheet to try to help Ed to give up smoking.

BIOLOGY   Fit and healthy

B4 A healthy diet

YOU WILL LEARN!
- that a balanced diet requires nutrients, including vitamins and minerals, in the correct quantities
- that certain diseases can be caused by a lack of a particular nutrient

We use nutrients to give us energy. Nutrients are also essential for the growth and repair of body tissues.

1 Review

In topic 7A you learned about tissues of the body.

a Make a list of some of the tissues.

In topic 8A you found out about what we mean by a balanced diet.

b List the nutrients that are required in a balanced diet.
c Explain why each nutrient is important.
d Give some examples of foods that are a good source of each nutrient you have listed.

A balanced diet is vital for good health

Minerals and vitamins

Minerals are elements or simple groups of elements that are needed in small amounts to keep the body working.

Mineral	Good source	Use in the body	Deficiency disease
Calcium	Milk, cheese, fish	Makes strong teeth and bones	Soft bones and teeth
Iron	Liver, red meat, cocoa	Healthy red blood cells	Anaemia
Iodine	Fish, drinking water	Makes thyroxine, a hormone	Goitre

Did you know?

The first vitamin to be identified was a type of chemical called an amine. The word vitamin comes from '**vit**al **amin**e'.

30

BIOLOGY — Fit and healthy

In the early 1900s a scientist called Sir Frederick Gowland Hopkins carried out an investigation on some rats. He gave them a special food mixture including everything thought important in a balanced diet – carbohydrate, protein, minerals and fats. After a few weeks all of the rats were dead. He then took a second group of rats and gave them the same diet but with a small amount of milk added. These rats were fine. We now know that milk contains vitamins. Vitamins are more complex molecules that are required in very small amounts in our diet. They are essential if we are to stay healthy.

Vitamin	Good source	Use in the body	Deficiency disease
A	Carrots, milk, butter, liver, eggs	Helps the eyes work properly	Night blindness
B group	Wholemeal bread, brown rice, liver, cereals, yeast extract, egg yolk	Healthy nerves, growth	Beri beri, pellagra
C	Fruit and vegetables	Repair of body tissues	Scurvy
D	Fish, butter, egg yolk, (also made in the body in sunlight)	Making healthy bones	Rickets

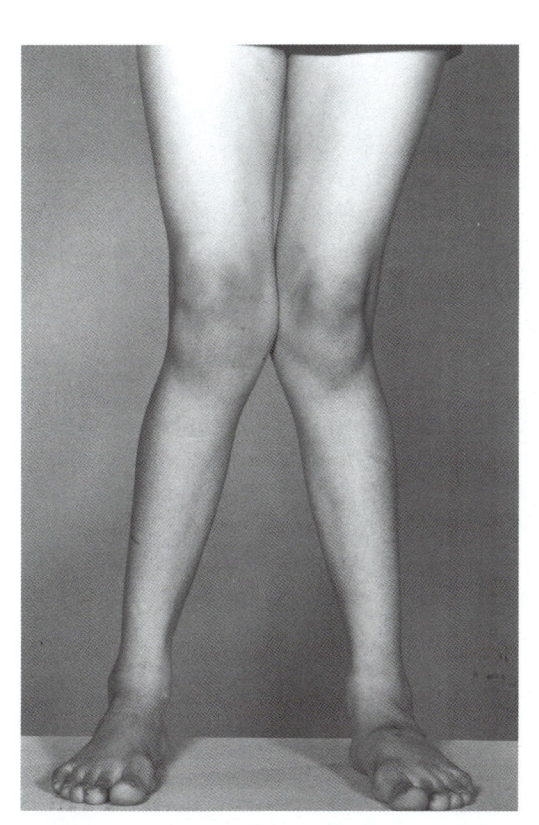

Rickets

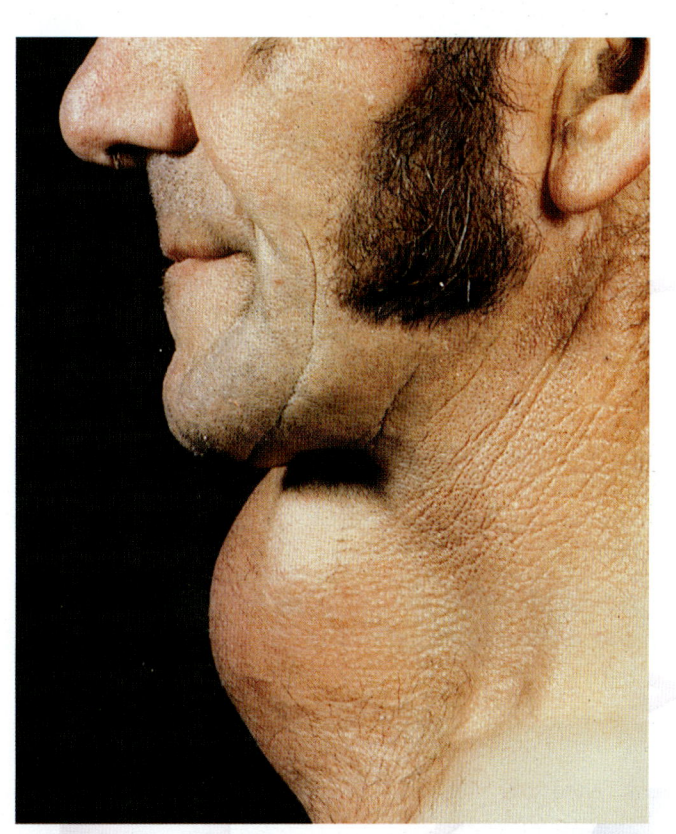

Goitre

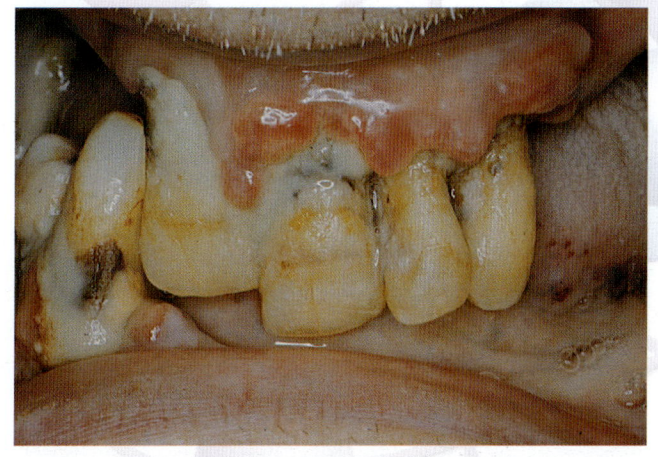

Scurvy

BIOLOGY   Fit and healthy

2 All about vitamins

Read the information on the previous page. Use other sources such as books and the Internet to find out more about vitamins and minerals.

a   Make a mind map about vitamins and minerals. Include information about how the body uses the vitamin or mineral, foods that are good sources, deficiency diseases.

Our knowledge of the importance of vitamins and minerals has been built up over many years. Many different scientists have contributed to our knowledge. These include Sir Frederick Gowland Hopkins, Joseph Goldberger, François Magendie and James Lind.

b   Write about the life and the scientific contribution made by one of these people. You can include them in a class book of famous scientists. Or you could do a computer presentation.

c   Find out about **folic acid**. Write an advice leaflet for pregnant women explaining the importance of folic acid.

d   Find out about **kwashiorkor**. What causes this type of malnutrition, what are the symptoms and how can it be treated and prevented?

3 Measuring vitamin C

We can use a chemical test to measure the vitamin C content of foods.

DCPIP (or dichlorophenol-indophenol) is a blue dye. It is decolourised by vitamin C.

Avoid skin contact with DCPIP.

1   Put 1 cm^3 of DCPIP in a test tube.
2   Measure 2 cm^3 of 0.1% vitamin C solution into a syringe.
3   Add a drop of vitamin C solution to the DCPIP. Shake the test tube to mix it.
4   Keep adding the vitamin C solution a drop at a time until all of the blue colour has disappeared.
5   Record how much vitamin C solution was needed to decolourise the DCPIP.

Now you know how much of a standard 0.1% vitamin C solution was needed to decolourise 1 cm^3 of DCPIP. You can use this to measure the vitamin C content of some samples of orange juice.

You could investigate:
- the vitamin C content of freshly squeezed orange juice and different brands of orange juice from a supermarket
- the effect of storage time on the vitamin C content of carton orange juice
- the effect of opening a carton of orange on its vitamin C content over a number of days
- the vitamin C content of orange juice and a range of other citrus fruits such as lemon, lime and grapefruit
- the vitamin C content of orange squash compared with fresh and carton orange juice.

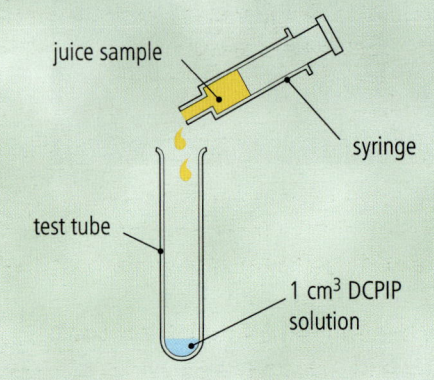

BIOLOGY   Fit and healthy

B5 Alcohol

YOU WILL LEARN!
- that alcohol affects behaviour
- that too much alcohol can affect the liver and damage the developing fetus

1 How much alcohol?

Look at the drinks in the picture:

- pint of lager
- pint of cider
- glass of wine
- small vodka
- bottle of alcopop

a The alcohol content of drinks is measured in units. How many units are there in each of the drinks shown?
b How many units a week is the safe limit for a man?
c How many units a week is the safe limit for a woman?
d At what age can you drink legally in the UK?
e At what age can you legally buy alcohol in the UK?
f Answer true or false to these statements:

Drinking black coffee will sober you up.

Having a sleep helps the effect of alcohol to wear off.

Drinking whisky warms you up.

People will find it easier to get on with you if you have a few drinks.

- Alcohol is a drug. In Britain people can drink alcohol legally. People can become **addicted** to alcohol. They are called **alcoholics**.
- Alcohol is a **poison**. Your liver is the organ of your body that breaks down poisons. Drinking too much alcohol over a number of years causes **cirrhosis** of the liver. The liver becomes damaged and cannot do its job properly.
- Alcohol can also cause stomach ulcers, brain damage, cancer of the mouth and stomach and heart disease.
- If a pregnant woman drinks, some of the alcohol will pass into the blood stream of the fetus. This can interfere with her baby's healthy growth and development.
- Alcohol is a **depressant** which means it can slow down your body's reactions by 10 to 30 per cent. It also reduces ability to perform two or more tasks at the same time and reduces the ability to see. Over half of the drivers killed in road accidents are over the drink driving limit.
- Alcohol reduces your **inhibitions**. That means you are more likely to do things you would not normally do. Alcohol is often involved in unwanted pregnancies.

2 It's your body

a Draw a diagram of the human body. Add information showing how different organs are affected by alcohol. Include the effects of alcohol on a fetus.
b Binzi is 15. She has started to go out drinking with her friend, Bev, who is a few years older. Make a leaflet, suitable for someone of Binzi's age, giving her facts about alcohol. Encourage her to realise that she has to make informed choices about drinking alcohol.

BIOLOGY   Fit and healthy

B6 Exercise and fitness

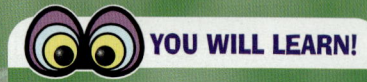

YOU WILL LEARN!
- how diet, smoking, alcohol and exercise can affect fitness and health
- how simple joints function
- that the wrong sort of exercise, or too much exercise, can damage muscles and weak or injured joints

Your body is a bit like a car. If you don't take care of it, it will not work properly and eventually it will break down. All of the cells of your body need a supply of blood to carry the oxygen and nutrients they need and to remove the waste they produce. A healthy heart is essential to maintain the blood supply.

Your heart beats about 70 times a minute throughout your life. It is made of a special kind of muscle called **cardiac muscle** which never gets tired. Muscle that works so hard needs a good supply of blood. This is carried to the heart muscle by the **coronary arteries**.

If these are blocked then the muscle cannot get the oxygen it needs.

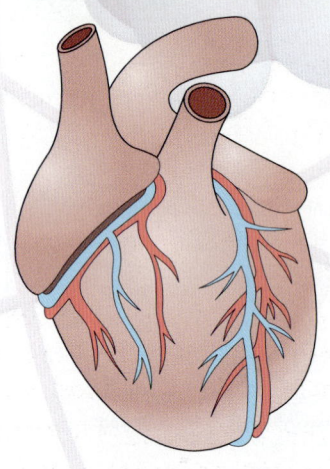

1 Looking at a heart

You may be able to examine a real heart from a sheep.

Find the coronary arteries which are on the surface of the heart. Draw the heart and show where the coronary arteries are found.

Your teacher will show you how to dissect the heart. Compare it with a diagram of a heart. (*Ascent! Book 8* section B2 has one you could use.) Try to find all of the parts marked on the diagram.

The human heart – showing coronary arteries and veins

How do arteries get blocked?

Cholesterol is a fatty substance, which can stick to the insides of the arteries. The arteries get narrower and the blood slows down. Cholesterol on the artery walls makes them rough. This makes the blood clot. A blood clot can block an artery. This is called a **thrombosis**.

If a thrombosis occurs in a coronary artery the result is a **heart attack**. Even a partly blocked coronary artery means that the heart muscle cannot get all of the food and oxygen it needs. This causes a severe chest pain called **angina**.

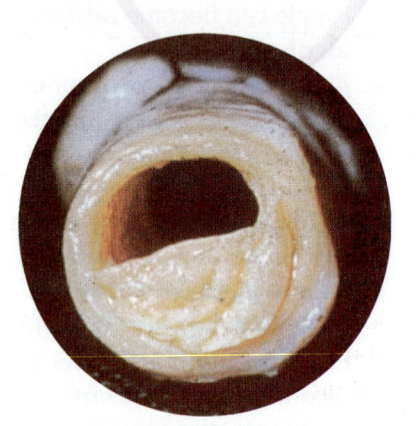

Cholesterol can block arteries

2 Preventing heart disease

Diet, smoking, drinking alcohol and a lack of exercise all contribute to heart disease.

Use secondary sources such as books, leaflets and the Internet to find out more about the effect of these.

a How do diet, smoking, drinking alcohol and lack of exercise lead to heart disease?

b Find out about the causes of high blood pressure.

c What is arteriosclerosis?

d Produce an advice sheet to help people reduce their chances of developing heart problems.

Exercise and your skeleton

Your skeleton contains over 200 bones. It has four main jobs:
- **support** – it supports your body

BIOLOGY   Fit and healthy

- **protection** – it protects your vital soft organs such as the heart, lungs and brain
- **making blood cells** – blood cells are made in marrow inside your bones
- **movement** – it has joints where muscles pull on bones to move them.

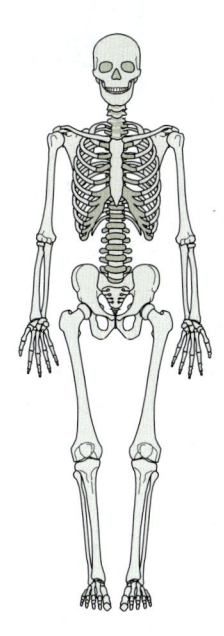

3 The skeleton

a Identify the bones which protect organs. Which organs do they protect? Make a table to show this information.
b On a diagram of the skeleton, mark joints where movement occurs.

Synovial joints allow movement to take place easily by reducing friction.

The **synovial membrane** holds **synovial fluid** between the bones. This is a lubricant like oil in a car engine. It lets the bones move smoothly against each other.

The ends of the bones are covered by a layer of **cartilage**. This protects the bones by acting as a shock absorber.

Ligaments hold the bones together.

Tendons connect muscles to bones.

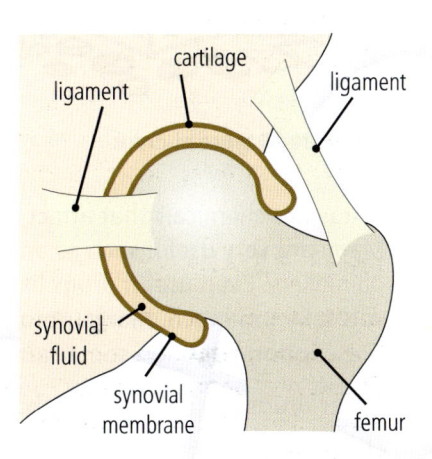

The human skeleton

4 Joints

a **Annotate** a diagram to show the functions of the different parts of a joint.
b What problems could occur with joints?

Joints work well most of the time but they can become damaged. This can be as a result of injury or just due to wear and tear. As we get older, joints don't work as well.

Arthritis is a disease of the joints. There are two types of arthritis – **rheumatoid arthritis** and **osteoarthritis**. In osteoarthritis the cartilage at the ends of the bones is worn away and bones rub together painfully. Osteoarthritis can be treated by replacing the damaged joint with an artificial one.

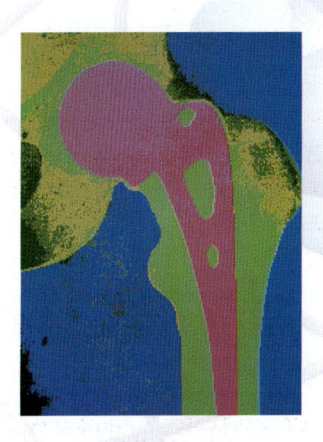

Hip joint

5 Injured and damaged joints

a Find out about rheumatoid arthritis. Write a report on its causes and symptoms.
b Science often involves the work of many different people. Which different scientists are involved in the replacement of a damaged hip joint? Present your findings as a flow chart.
c Find out about sports injuries. Produce a report about the different types of injuries, how they are caused, how they can be treated and how injuries can often be avoided.

An artificial hip joint

35

BIOLOGY   Fit and healthy

B7 Drugs

YOU WILL LEARN!
▶ that a drug is a substance that changes the way the body or mind works

Points to discuss

Look at the list below. Which of the substances in the list are drugs?

Aspirin, cannabis, alcohol, coffee, ecstasy, antiseptic cream, penicillin, heroin, tobacco, amphetamines, caffeine, paracetamol, insulin, glue.

These are all types of drugs

Drugs are chemicals that affect the way your body or mind works. Many are very useful such as antibiotics, anaesthetics and painkillers. Even useful drugs like these can be very dangerous if you take too much. Many useful drugs are only available on prescription although some can be bought 'over the counter'.

Other drugs are not useful. Tobacco and alcohol are two examples. They are often called **recreational** drugs. Many people commonly use them. As we have already seen, they can cause serious health problems. You can only buy alcohol and tobacco when you are over a certain age. Other recreational drugs are illegal. These include cannabis, ecstasy, LSD, cocaine, amphetamines and heroin, although a doctor can prescribe some.

1 Classifying drugs

a Sort useful drugs into those only available on prescription and those that can be bought over the counter.
b Sort recreational drugs into those that are legal and those that are illegal. Which of the illegal ones can be prescribed by a doctor?

Some drugs slow down the nervous system. They are called **depressants**. Alcohol and heroin are depressants. Other drugs speed up the nervous system. They are called **stimulants**. Amphetamines are stimulants. Other drugs make you see things that are not really there. These are called **hallucinogenic** drugs. LSD is a hallucinogen.

BIOLOGY   Fit and healthy

Drugs can be taken in different ways. Some, such as ecstasy, are swallowed as tablets. Others, like cannabis, can be smoked. Cannabis is usually mixed with tobacco, which leads to all of the health risks of cigarettes. Some drugs, like heroin, are injected. People who share needles risk being infected with hepatitis and HIV.

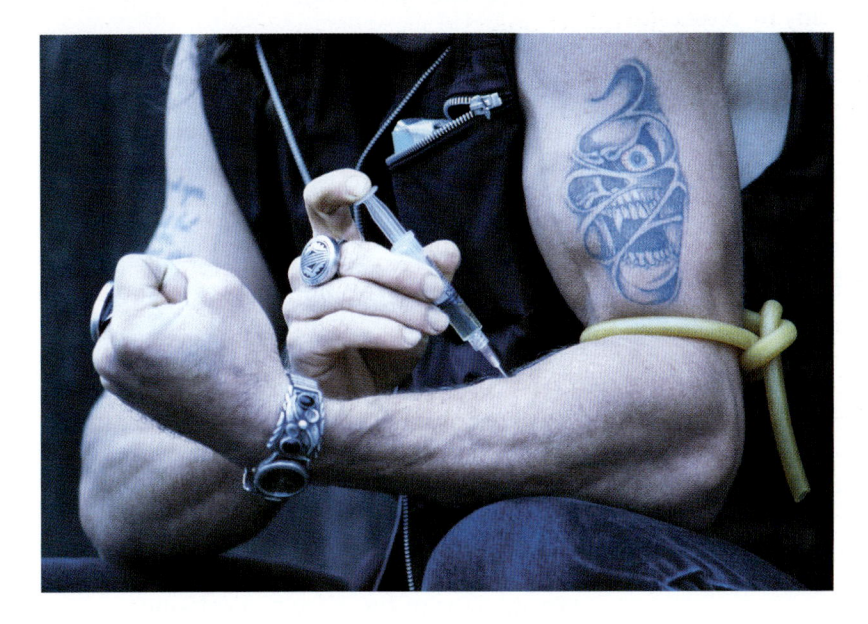

A person's body can get used to taking a drug. The person has to take more of the drug to get the same effect. This is called **tolerance**. Some drugs are **addictive**. This means that the person has to take the drug to avoid feeling unwell. It is very difficult for an addict to stop taking a drug. The person suffers from **withdrawal symptoms**, which make them feel very ill.

Drugs usually cost a lot of money and people often turn to crime to pay for their drugs.

Taking too much of a drug can cause an **overdose**. This can cause permanent damage to the body, or even death. It is impossible to know how strong illegal drugs are, so it is easy to take an overdose.

2 All about drugs

Use secondary sources to find out more about drugs and solvent abuse.

For each drug, find out:

- type of drug (e.g. depressant, etc.)
- what does it look like?
- what else is it called?
- how is it taken?
- how does it affect your body?
- what are the health risks?
- is it legal?

Display what you find out as a chart or mind map.

BIOLOGY   Fit and healthy

3 Investigating caffeine

In *Ascent! Book 2* page 22, you looked at 'high-energy drinks'. These contain a lot of sugar. They are aimed at sports people, who need the extra sugar to give them energy. Many of these drinks also contain **caffeine**. Caffeine is a stimulant. It is supposed to make people more alert and to make their reactions quicker.

Some other soft drinks, as well as coffee, also contain caffeine.

Your task is to investigate whether caffeine really does speed up your reactions.

The diagram shows a simple way of measuring your reaction time with a ruler.

Drinking is not normally allowed in science laboratories, so take special care.

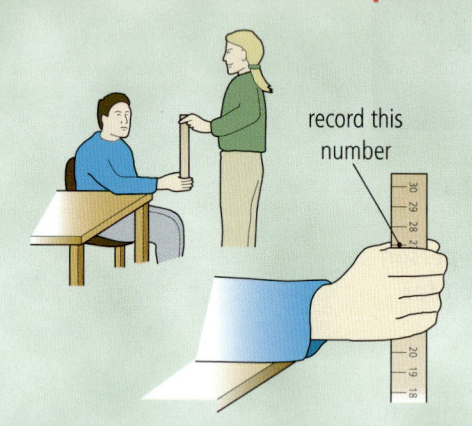

1 Hold your arm in front of you.
2 Your partner holds the ruler with the zero end level with your finger.
3 Your partner lets go of the ruler.
4 You have to catch it as quickly as possible.
5 Read off the number level with your finger to give a measurement of reaction time.

Alternatively, you can use a computer program that will help measure your reaction time.

You will need to make sure the investigation you carry out is fair, reliable and ethical.

- Only volunteers should take part.
- Some people are sensitive to caffeine and should not take part.
- The people who take part should not know if they have taken caffeine as they could behave differently based on their expectations of the effects of caffeine.
- How long after taking caffeine will it start to take effect?
- How long will the effect (if any) last?

Try to find out about **double-blind trials** and the **placebo effect**. You may need to make use of this information in planning your investigation.

These drinks contain caffeine

38

BIOLOGY   Fit and healthy

Summary

Fitness means that your body systems are working properly. Your body needs energy to work. We get our energy from food when it reacts with oxygen in **respiration**. It is important that our **respiratory**, **digestive** and **circulatory** systems are working well.

We breathe in by making our lung volume bigger. We breathe out by making our lung volume smaller. Movements of the rib cage and the diaphragm control our lung volume. Asthma is a condition that can prevent the lungs from working well. Smoking can cause many diseases of the lungs and do permanent damage. Tobacco smoke contains a number of harmful chemicals such as **tar**, **nicotine** and **carbon monoxide**.

A balanced diet should include **vitamins** and **minerals**. These are substances, needed only in small amounts, which are essential to keep the body working properly.

Alcohol is a drug. It can affect the way your mind works. It can also cause long-term damage to organ systems of your body.

Exercise is an important part of a healthy lifestyle. Regular exercise helps to keep your heart and lungs working well. Inappropriate exercise can do damage to our **skeletal** and **muscular** systems.

A **drug** is a chemical that changes the way your mind or body works. Many drugs can damage your health and are illegal.

Key words
alcohol
asthma
carbon monoxide
circulatory system
diaphragm
digestive system
drug
mineral
muscular system
nicotine
respiration
respiratory system
rib cage
skeletal system
tar
vitamin

Summary Questions

1. **a** What are the fitness S-factors?
   b Draw up a fitness programme suitable for a 14 year old. It should help her to develop her S-factors and should take about 45 minutes each day.

2. **a** Make a list of the main chemicals found in cigarette smoke.
   b Explain how each of these chemicals is harmful.

3. Write what each of these words means:
   Stimulant, depressant, addictive, carcinogen, hallucinogen, passive smoking, cirrhosis, thrombosis, angina, arthritis.

4. Do you think you are healthier than your great-grandparents were when they were your age? Write about the differences in lifestyle then compared with now. Which factors make you healthier than they were? Which factors made them healthier than you?

5. Being a healthy adult partly depends on your lifestyle and choices you make when you are younger.
   a Draw up a ten-point set of rules to help ensure that you will be a healthy adult.
   b For each of your ten points explain the scientific knowledge it is based on.

End of unit Questions

1. A person who has asthma finds it difficult to breathe. An inhaler helps the person breathe more easily.
   The diagrams show a cross-section of one of the small tubes (bronchioles) in the lungs.

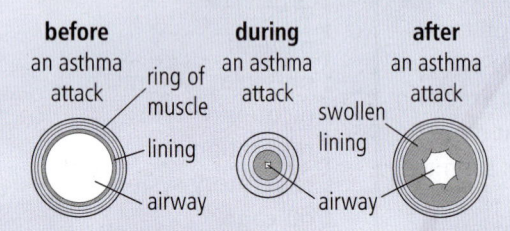

   a Describe the way the airway changes when the inhaler is used, and how this change makes it easier to breathe.
   2 marks

   b The wall of the tube contains a ring of muscle. During an asthma attack, this muscle contracts and the airways become narrower.
   How does using the inhaler affect this muscle? *1 mark*

2. **a** Drinking large amounts of alcohol every day can damage the liver. The type of damage is called cirrhosis, and it can kill a person quickly. The graph below shows the number of people dying from cirrhosis of the liver, in Paris, between 1935 and 1965.

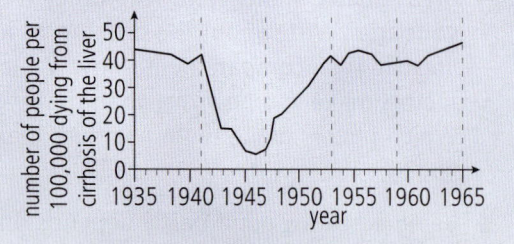

   During which period of time, P, Q, R, S or T, was it difficult to get alcohol?
   1 mark

   b Alcohol is a drug. Which property makes alcohol a drug? Choose from the list below.
   - It is soluble in water.
   - It is a chemical.
   - It can provide energy.
   - It affects the nervous system. *1 mark*

   c Look at the graph below.

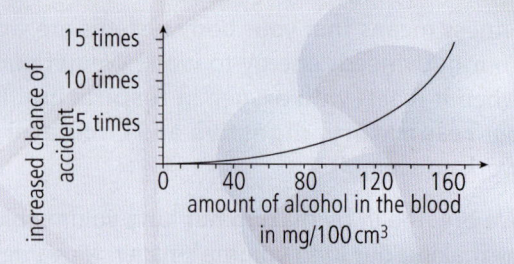

   i Using the graph, describe how increasing the amount of alcohol in the blood affects the chance of having an accident. *2 marks*

   ii Which of the following statements could be used to explain why alcohol in the blood can cause accidents? Choose from the list.
   - Alcohol cools the body.
   - Alcohol increases the time a person takes to react.
   - Alcohol is a stimulant.
   - Alcohol makes a person happy. *1 mark*

3. The diagram shows two types of cell in the lining of the windpipe.

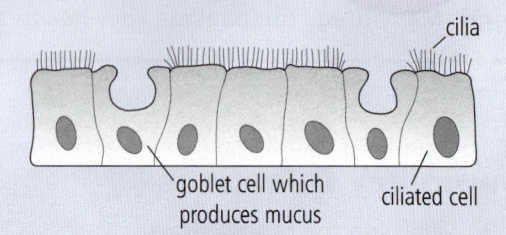

   a i These cells work together to keep the lungs free from bacteria and dust particles. What word describes a group of similar cells which work together? *1 mark*

   ii Mucus is a sticky substance. Describe how mucus and cilia keep the lungs free from bacteria and dust particles. *2 marks*

   b When a person breathes in cigarette smoke, the goblet cells produce extra mucus and the cilia are damaged. What will be the consequences of this? *2 marks*

   c Give the names of two harmful substances in cigarette smoke. In what way is each one harmful? *2 marks*

9C Plants and photosynthesis

Introduction
In this unit you will build on work about food chains from year 7. You will use your knowledge of chemical reactions as you investigate how green plants make food from simple substances during photosynthesis.

You already know
- the main parts of a plant e.g. leaf, root, stem, flower
- what plants need to help them grow well
- that respiration releases carbon dioxide
- that plants' roots take in water
- that plants' leaves help them to make food

In this topic you will learn
- that photosynthesis is the key process for plant growth
- that carbon dioxide from the air and water absorbed through the roots are the raw materials for photosynthesis
- that chlorophyll, the green substance in leaves, enables plants to use light energy in photosynthesis
- that leaves are adapted to carry out photosynthesis
- that photosynthesis is essential for all animals

1 What can you remember?

Look at the picture. What are the essential things that plants need to help them grow?

Humans use many products from plants. How many can you see in the picture?

How many more can you think of?

BIOLOGY — Plants and photosynthesis

C1 Building our knowledge of photosynthesis

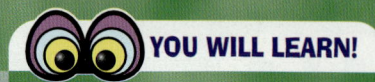

YOU WILL LEARN!
- that green plants do not absorb 'food' from the soil
- that green plants use carbon dioxide and water to produce biomass
- that the raw materials for photosynthesis are taken from the environment around the plant

Aristotle was a Greek philosopher, who lived over two thousand years ago. He wondered how plants could grow and make food for themselves and animals without eating anything. He knew that animals and plants died and decomposed in the soil. He knew that plants' roots went deep into the soil. He concluded that plants absorb decomposed material from the soil and use it for their own growth. Aristotle based his hypothesis on **observation**. He never tested it by **experiment**.

Jan Baptista van Helmont was a Belgian scientist who lived from 1580–1644. He carried out an experiment to investigate the growth of a plant.

'I took an earthen vessel, in which I put 200 pounds of earth that had dried in a furnace, which I moistened with rainwater, and I implanted therein the trunk or stem of a willow tree, weighing five pounds. And at length, five years being finished, the tree springing from thence did weigh 169 pounds and about three ounces. … Lest the dust that flew about should be mingled with the earth, I covered the lip or mouth of the vessel with an iron plate covered with tin and easily passable with many holes. … I again dried the earth up in the vessel, and there was found the same 200 pounds, wanting about two ounces. Therefore, 164 pounds of wood, bark, and roots, arose out of water only.'

1 Van Helmont's experiment

Read van Helmont's own account of his experiment. The language is rather old fashioned to us.

Rewrite his account using the sort of scientific language we use today.

Put his results in a table.

Write a conclusion.

Write an evaluation of the experiment. Could you improve van Helmont's experiment? Explain why you would make these improvements.

You may have learnt about Joseph Priestley in *Ascent! Book 1* unit F7 and will find out how he discovered oxygen in unit H7. (See page 139.) He found that a flame would quickly go out in a sealed container of air. A small animal would die. He wanted to find out why this did not happen to the whole atmosphere. Priestley carried out an experiment.

Priestley concluded that the plant had purified the air. If all plants could do this then the atmosphere would never be damaged by burning or by animals breathing.

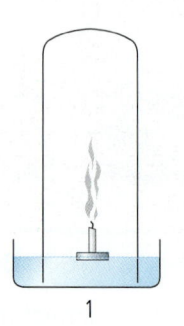

Priestley's experiment

2 Priestley

Find out more about Joseph Priestley. Write about his life and discoveries in your class book of famous scientists.

BIOLOGY   Plants and photosynthesis

C2 How do plants make food?

YOU WILL LEARN!
- that green plants use carbon dioxide and water to produce biomass
- the meanings of the words 'photosynthesis' and 'biomass'
- that light and chlorophyll are needed for photosynthesis
- how to test a leaf for the presence of starch
- how to heat a flammable liquid
- that the raw materials for photosynthesis are taken from around the plant

Jan Baptista van Helmont concluded that a plant grew by making new material from water. He was partly correct, but at the time he did his experiment not much was known about gases. We now know that carbon dioxide from the air is also involved in plant growth.

All of the plants shown in the photographs have grown from seeds. They have made leaves, fruits, roots and wood. We call this living material **biomass**. Biomass is the total amount of material in a living thing except for water.

You will carry out some experiments to investigate how plants make new biomass.

To do most of these experiments you need to be able to test a leaf for starch. (You used iodine as a test for starch in foods in *Ascent! Book 2* A1.)

Houseplant

Giant redwood

Pumpkin

Points to discuss

Why do you think water is not counted as part of the biomass of an organism?

43

BIOLOGY   Plants and photosynthesis

1 How to test a leaf for starch

1. Take a leaf from a plant that has been in a sunny place.
2. Put the leaf in a beaker of boiling water for about one minute. This will soften the leaf and allow iodine to pass into the cells.
3. **Turn off your Bunsen burner and make sure all other Bunsens in your area are also turned off. Ethanol is flammable.**
4. Put the leaf in a test tube of ethanol. Stand the test tube in your beaker of hot water.
5. Leave it until all the green colour has come out of the leaf. This will take a few minutes.
6. Rinse the leaf in cold water.
7. Spread out the leaf on a white tile.
8. Cover the leaf with iodine solution.
9. A blue-black colour shows that starch is present.

a Why did you turn off your Bunsen burner before you heated the ethanol?

b Why did you remove the green colour from the leaf before you added the iodine?

Avoid skin contact with iodine

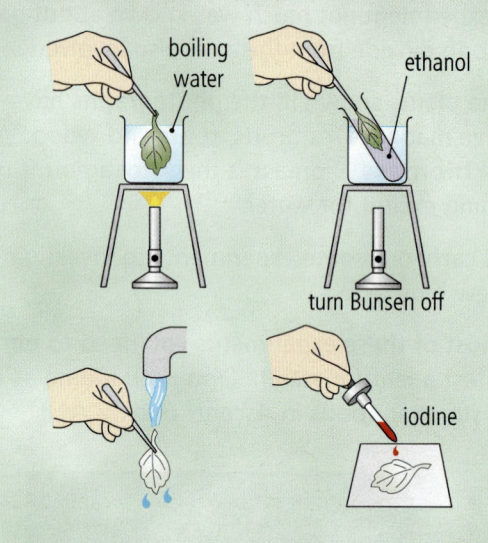

Testing a leaf for starch

What do plants need to make starch?

The green colour in a leaf is due to the presence of a substance called **chlorophyll**. In some plants, only part of the leaf has chlorophyll. These are called **variegated** leaves.

We will use a plant that contains no starch at the start of the experiment.

Variegated leaves

2 Do plants need chlorophyll for photosynthesis?

1. Take a **variegated** plant that has been kept in a dark place for two days.
2. Leave the plant in a sunny place for a few hours.
3. Take one leaf from the plant and do a drawing to show which parts are green and which are white.
4. Test the leaf for starch using the method in Activity 1.

a Draw what the leaf looks like after you added the iodine. Compare this with the drawing you made in 3.
b What conclusion can you make from the results of your experiment?

BIOLOGY — Plants and photosynthesis

3 Do plants need light to make starch?

1. Take a plant that has been kept in a dark place for two days.
2. Cover part of a leaf with some aluminium foil or black paper.
3. Leave the plant in a sunny place for a few hours.
4. Test the leaf for starch using the method in Activity 1.

a. Draw what the leaf looks like after you add the iodine. Compare this with the shape of the cover you put on the leaf.
b. What conclusion can you make from the results of your experiment?
c. What could you use as a control in this experiment?

4 Do plants need carbon dioxide to make starch?

Soda lime is a chemical that absorbs carbon dioxide.

1. Take a plant that has been kept in a dark place for two days.
2. Put a small dish of soda lime on top of the soil.
3. Put a plastic bag over the whole plant and secure it with a rubber band.
4. Leave the plant in a sunny place for a few hours.
5. Test the leaf for starch using the method in Activity 1.

a. What conclusion can you make from the results of your experiment?
b. What could you use as a control in this experiment?

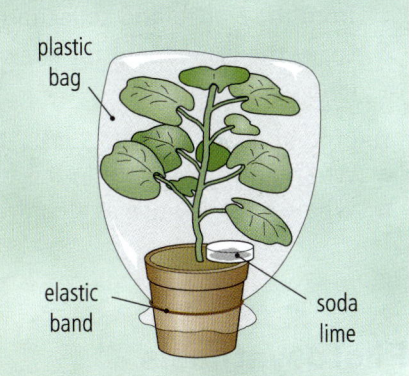

Points to discuss

Gardeners often use a paraffin heater to keep a greenhouse warm in winter. Apart from the temperature, how else will this help the plants?   (HINT: Combustion.)

Does a plant need water to make starch?

In the previous three experiments we have made sure that a plant has all it needs to make starch except for one factor in each experiment. It is more difficult to find out if a plant needs water. If we deprive it of water it will die anyway as all of the processes happening in a plant need water.

Scientists have shown that water is involved in making starch. You should remember that the formula of water is H_2O. Scientists use special molecules of water, which are **labelled** with **heavy oxygen**. This is a kind of oxygen atom that can be identified by a special test. Experiments show that during photosynthesis water is split up into hydrogen and oxygen atoms. The hydrogen becomes part of the starch. The oxygen goes somewhere else.

BIOLOGY   Plants and photosynthesis

What do plants make in the light?

You have already seen that plants in the light can make starch from carbon dioxide and water. In fact they make **glucose**, which is turned into starch to be stored in the leaves.

What else do they make? Look at the results of Joseph Priestley's experiment. What gas is essential for animals to breathe? What gas allows a candle to burn?

5 Do plants make oxygen?

1. Put some *Elodea* (Canadian pondweed) in a beaker.
2. Cover the *Elodea* with a glass funnel.
3. Put a test tube full of water over the funnel.
4. Put the beaker in bright sunlight.
5. After a few minutes you should see bubbles of gas coming from the *Elodea* and collecting in the test tube.
6. Leave the experiment for a few days and you should have enough gas to test.

You found out in *Ascent! Book 7* how to test for oxygen.
a. What did you find out in this experiment?
b. What could you use as a control?

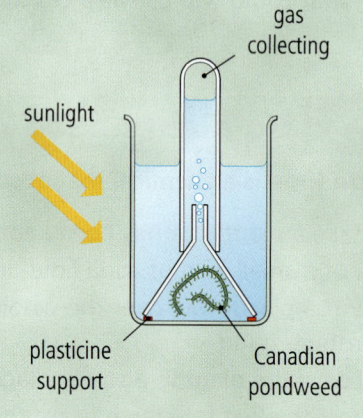

Collecting gas from a photosynthesising plant

Photosynthesis

The experiments you have carried out and read about tell us that plants need carbon dioxide and water, light energy and chlorophyll in the leaves. Plants make starch and oxygen. The starch is made from glucose. We can put this all together to make a chemical equation:

$$\text{carbon dioxide} + \text{water} \xrightarrow[\text{chlorophyll}]{\text{light energy}} \text{glucose} + \text{oxygen}$$

We call this process photosynthesis.

This can be written as a symbol equation:

$$6\,CO_2 + 6\,H_2O \longrightarrow C_6H_{12}O_6 + 6\,O_2$$

See page 80 to find out why the symbol equation has three large number 6s in it.

Did you know

The word photosynthesis comes from Greek. **Photos** means light, **syn** means together and **thesis** means putting. So the whole word means 'using light to put together'.

46

BIOLOGY   Plants and photosynthesis

C3 Measuring photosynthesis

YOU WILL LEARN!
- to measure the rate of photosynthesis
- to control variables
- to present results in tables and graphs, identifying anomalous results

Elodea produces bubbles of oxygen that can be seen. This provides us with a good opportunity to investigate factors that affect how fast *Elodea* photosynthesises.

1 Measuring the rate of photosynthesis

Think about Activity 5 on the previous page. As *Elodea* photosynthesises it gives off bubbles of oxygen. Counting the number of bubbles given off in a minute is a way of measuring the rate of photosynthesis.

Your task is to use this method to investigate how **light intensity** affects the rate of photosynthesis.

You will need to make sure your experiment is a fair test.

What other factors might affect the rate of photosynthesis? The temperature of the water? The amount of carbon dioxide available in the water? The size of the piece of *Elodea* you use?

If you are going to vary the light intensity, how will you do this? What if it becomes sunnier or more overcast outside your school laboratory while you are doing the experiment? If the light intensity changes, does it take time for the plant to adapt?

If you are going to count the number of bubbles, how can you be sure they are all the same size?

Plan your investigation. You could use secondary sources to help you to solve some of the problems outlined above. Show your teacher your plan then carry it out.

Record your results and plot them on a graph. Are there any **anomalous** results (ones that do not seem to fit in with the rest)? Can you explain why you got them? Can you repeat them to check your results?

What happens to the oxygen made by plants?

While plants are making glucose in photosynthesis they are using some of it in respiration at the same time. The same is true of the oxygen they make. As soon as it is made, some of it is used up again by the plant.

Remember that plants need light to photosynthesise. During the day they usually make more oxygen than they use. They are **net producers** of oxygen. At night, however, they are **net consumers** of oxygen. At certain times during the day they will produce exactly the same amount of oxygen as they use. When do you think that will be? Overall, do you think plants produce more oxygen or less oxygen than they use? How do you know?

Did you know

Elodea produces a lot of oxygen. People who keep fish in ponds call it **oxygenating** weed.

BIOLOGY — Plants and photosynthesis

C4 The leaf

YOU WILL LEARN!
- that leaves are adapted to photosynthesise efficiently
- how leaf cells close to the upper surface are adapted for photosynthesis

Leaves are the site of photosynthesis in plants. They are perfectly adapted to carry out this task efficiently.

1 Looking at leaves

Take a leaf from a plant and examine it closely, looking at both sides.

Compare the colour of each side.

Draw a diagram of the leaf. Annotate your diagram to explain ways in which the leaf is adapted for its job.

Look at a plant such as a bush or shrub. Can you see how the leaves are arranged so that all of them get light?

You need to examine a section of a leaf through a microscope so you can find out more about how its structure makes it suited for photosynthesis.

2 Microscopic structure of a leaf

Take a prepared slide of a leaf.

Examine it under a microscope at low power magnification.

Try to find the parts shown in the diagram and the photograph.

a In which layer of the leaf does most photosynthesis take place?
b Why is the upper surface a darker shade of green than the lower surface?
c What is the name of the green substance found in the chloroplasts?
d Why is the upper epidermis transparent?
e What is the function of the stomata in the lower epidermis?
f What is the purpose of the spaces in the spongy mesophyll?
g What role do the veins have in photosynthesis?
h Why is it important that leaves are thin?
i Why is it important that leaves have a large surface area?

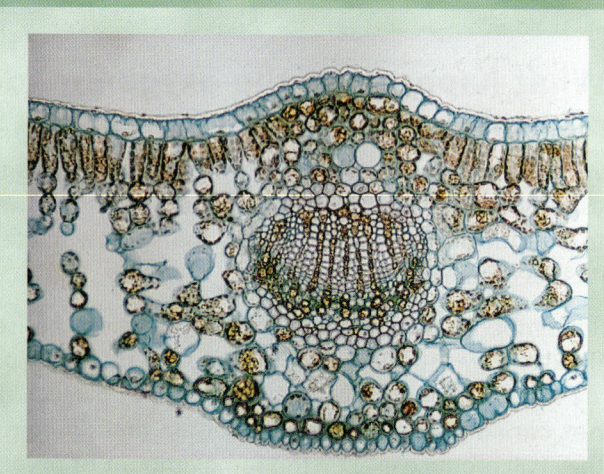

Cross section through a leaf

48

BIOLOGY   Plants and photosynthesis

C5 What happens to the glucose produced in leaves?

YOU WILL LEARN!
- that plants store starch
- that new materials made from glucose produced in photosynthesis lead to an increase in biomass
- that the glucose made in photosynthesis provides energy for all living processes in the plant

Look at these pictures. They all show products that come from green plants.

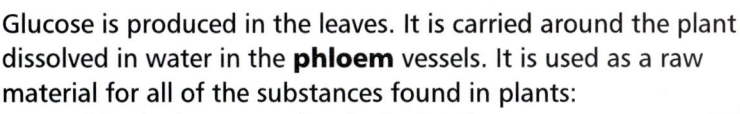

Glucose is produced in the leaves. It is carried around the plant dissolved in water in the **phloem** vessels. It is used as a raw material for all of the substances found in plants:
- used in the leaves to give the leaf cells energy
- converted to starch to store in the leaves
- carried to other parts of the plant to use as energy
- converted to starch in other parts of the plant and stored there
- converted to **cellulose**, which is used to make plant cell walls
- reacted with nitrogen to make **amino acids**. Amino acids are used to make proteins
- converted into **fats** and **oils**
- converted to **lignin**. Wood is made of lignin and cellulose.

All of these substances make up the **biomass** of the plant.

1 Products from plants

Look at the photographs and read the information above.
- **a** Match up the photographs with the substances made by plants.
- **b** Try to think of some that are not shown in the photographs.

Plants are economically very important.
- **c** Make a display to show the many different industries that make products from plants. Show some of the items made from these products. Find out which countries grow these different plant products.

BIOLOGY   Plants and photosynthesis

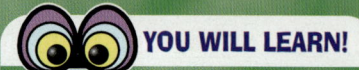

C6 Plant plumbing

YOU WILL LEARN!
- that roots are adapted to take in water and that this is used in photosynthesis
- that plants use water in many ways
- that roots require oxygen for respiration
- that plants need nitrogen and other elements in the form of minerals
- that a lack of minerals hinders plant growth

You know that plants take in water through their roots. But what do they use the water for? Obviously some is used in photosynthesis. But plants take in a lot more water than they use in photosynthesis. So what else is it used for?

- What happens if you forget to water a houseplant? At first it will wilt. Water is needed to keep the cells firm, giving the plant support.
- How is glucose carried around the plant? It is dissolved in water.
- How do plants get minerals like nitrogen? They take it in as nitrate, dissolved in water in the soil.
- Think about biting into a juicy orange. Fruits are full of water.
- What do you do when you are too hot? You sweat. Water passing out of the leaves helps to keep plants cool.

Did you know
A single winter rye plant can produce over 620 km of roots!

A wild fig tree in South Africa had roots that grew down into a cave 120 m below ground level.

How do roots work?
Normally, if you pull a plant from the soil you tear off most of its roots. To see the full root system you must grow a plant without soil.

1 Looking at roots

Either
Soak some mung beans in water and leave them on a damp paper towel in a petri dish. After a few days roots will grow.

Or
Use a pin to suspend a clove of garlic over a test tube of water. Again, you will see roots growing after a few days.

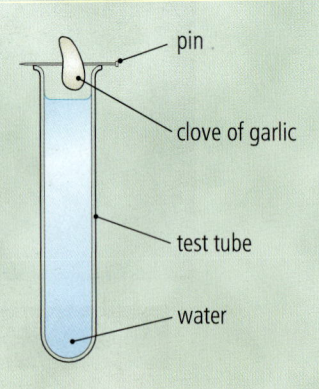

a Describe the roots on your plant.
b How are they adapted to take in large amounts of water?

pin
clove of garlic
test tube
water

Root hairs

Roots are very long and often branched. Near the tip they have thousands of root hairs. These give the root a very large surface area through which to absorb water. Dissolved in the water are minerals, which are essential if a plant is to grow properly. These minerals include **nitrate**, **phosphate** and **potassium**.

BIOLOGY   Plants and photosynthesis

Roots also help to anchor plants in the soil. They stop them from being pulled out by the wind, animals or gardeners trying to get rid of weeds!

Water is carried up the stem in vessels called **xylem**. Along with the phloem tubes, these make up the veins or **vascular bundles** of the plant.

Did you know

Many brands of fertiliser have the letters NPK on the pack. These are the chemical symbols for essential elements. What are they?

2 Up the stem

1. Take a stick of celery, preferably with the leaves left on.
2. Cut off the bottom 1 cm of the stem.
3. Stand it in a beaker of red dye.
4. Leave it overnight.
5. Examine the stem.
6. Cut a slice through the stem and look at the cut surface.

a. Describe what you see.
b. Draw your observations.

Try to remove a strip of the red-dyed xylem vessel.

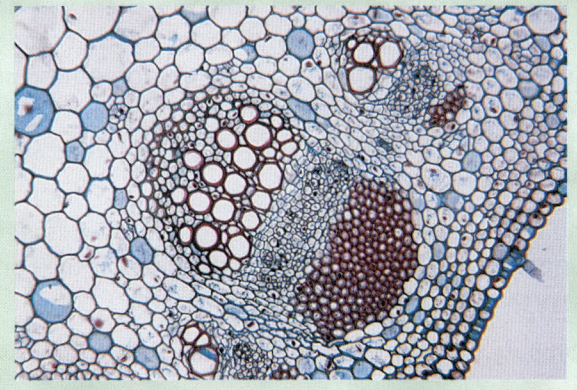

Vascular tissue in a plant stem

Xylem vessels go from the root, up the stem and into the veins of the leaves. You saw them in C4 when you looked at the structure of a leaf. Water passes out of the plant through the stomata that you also saw in C4.

3 Moving water

Use a diagram like that on the right to summarise the movement of water through a plant, from the roots to the leaves.

Most plants will die if they are in waterlogged soil for a long time even though they have plenty of water and minerals. Can you explain why?

4 Plants and minerals

What are the main minerals needed by plants?
Use secondary sources to investigate the effect on a plant of a deficiency of each of these in the soil.

I'M TRYING TO GET TO THE ROOT OF THE PROBLEM

Did you know

Plants found in areas lacking in minerals are sometimes insectivorous. They catch and 'eat' insects to get minerals. Venus fly trap is an example from America but there are others found in the UK.

BIOLOGY   Plants and photosynthesis

C7 Green plants in the environment

YOU WILL LEARN!
▶ that photosynthesis removes carbon dioxide from the air and produces oxygen

The Earth's atmosphere is a mixture of several gases, which include:

Oxygen	20.93%
Nitrogen + argon	79.03%
Carbon dioxide	0.04%

When the Earth first formed, however, there was no oxygen and there was a lot more carbon dioxide. So what made it change? Look at the chemical equation for photosynthesis shown below. Green plants arrived early in the life of the Earth. How did they change its atmosphere? Where did most of the carbon atoms from the carbon dioxide go?

The Earth's atmosphere changed gradually. It is well suited to support the animals and plants that inhabit the Earth. Let's hope it stays that way!

Compare the chemical equations for photosynthesis and respiration:

Photosynthesis

    carbon dioxide + water → glucose + oxygen

Respiration

    glucose + oxygen → carbon dioxide + water

What do you notice? Many millions of years ago there was more carbon dioxide in the atmosphere. Plants gradually used this up. It was converted into biomass. Animals ate some of the plants and carbon became part of their biomass. Huge amounts of this biomass became converted to coal, oil and gas. This locked the carbon away underground.

In the last few hundred years, humans started to use these as fossil fuels. This releases more carbon dioxide into the atmosphere. At the same time, humans are cutting down forests to clear the land for other uses.

Power stations produce carbon dioxide

BIOLOGY   Plants and photosynthesis

Car exhausts produce carbon dioxide

Deforestation

1 Deforestation

Read the information above and topic G6 'The issue of global warming'.

Use secondary sources to investigate the subject further.

Think about the following questions:

a Who benefits from deforestation?
b What problems can be caused by deforestation?
c What are the long-term effects of increasing the amount of greenhouse gases?
d What can be done to reduce deforestation?
e What can be done to reduce the effects of deforestation?

Organise a class debate or role-play. Different members of the class can take the parts of different people affected by this issue: a poor farmer, the chairman of a logging company, a medical researcher, the president of a country where deforestation is taking place, etc.

BIOLOGY   Plants and photosynthesis

C8 Reviewing your work

YOU WILL LEARN!
▶ how ideas about photosynthesis relate to a particular organism

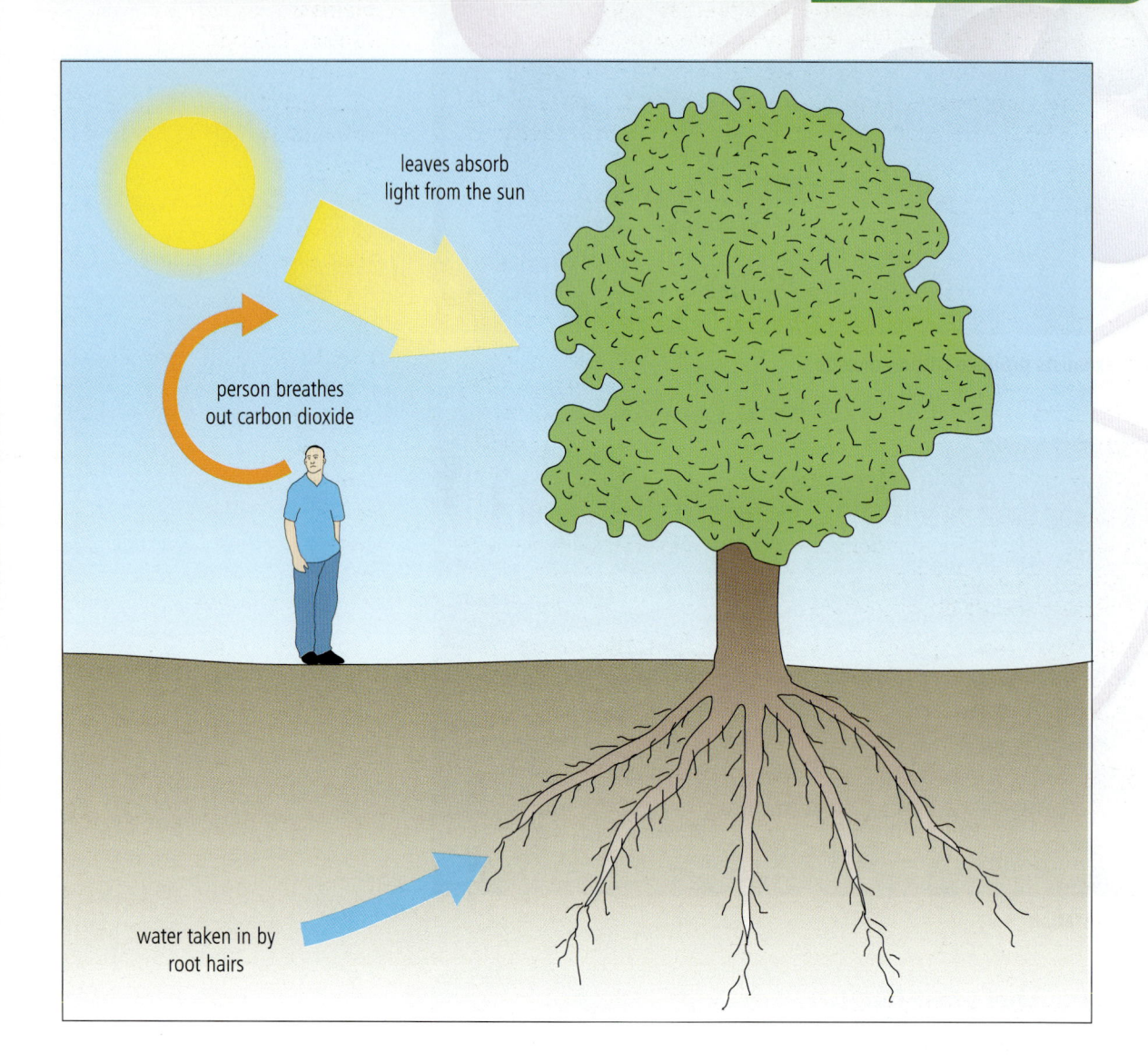

leaves absorb light from the sun

person breathes out carbon dioxide

water taken in by root hairs

1 Reviewing photosynthesis

Use the picture above as the basis of a flow chart showing what you have learnt in this unit.

Make sure you include relevant chemical equations.

Draw a similar picture showing how things would be different at night.

54

BIOLOGY — Plants and photosynthesis

Summary

Plants make food for themselves in a process called **photosynthesis**. They use **carbon dioxide** and **water** as the raw materials. They use **light energy** from the Sun. The green substance, **chlorophyll**, in their leaves is used to 'capture' the Sun's energy. The products of photosynthesis are **glucose** and **oxygen**.

Photosynthesis can be summed up in the equation:

$$\text{carbon dioxide} + \text{water} \xrightarrow[\text{chlorophyll}]{\text{light energy}} \text{glucose} + \text{oxygen}$$

Much of the glucose made by plants is used as a source of energy by the plant. Some is converted to **starch** and stored in the leaves. Other glucose is transported to different parts of the plant and used as a source of energy or converted into other substances like **cellulose**, **protein** and **fats** and **oils**. These substances make up the **biomass** of the plant.

Photosynthesis mainly takes place in the leaf. This is well adapted to its function being broad and thin, with a network of vascular bundles and many cells containing chlorophyll in structures called **chloroplasts**.

Vascular bundles spread throughout the plant. They consist of **xylem** vessels and **phloem** vessels. Xylem carries water and minerals from the soil. Phloem carries other substances, such as glucose, through the plant. Roots spread out through the soil to obtain water. They have **root hairs** to help increase their surface area.

Key words

- biomass
- carbon dioxide
- cellulose
- chlorophyll
- chloroplast
- energy
- fat
- glucose
- light energy
- minerals
- oil
- oxygen
- phloem
- photosynthesis
- protein
- root hair cell
- starch
- water
- xylem

Summary Questions

1. **a** Write out the chemical equation for photosynthesis using symbols.
   b Write out the chemical equation for respiration using symbols.
   c How do these normally stay in balance?

2. **a** Find out about the structure of glucose and starch molecules.
   b How are these so readily converted from one to another?
   c Find out about the structure of cellulose.
   d What are the similarities and differences?

3. **a** What **minerals are needed** by plants?
   b What happens if they do not get enough?

4. The graph shows how concentration of carbon dioxide in a field of wheat changes during the day.

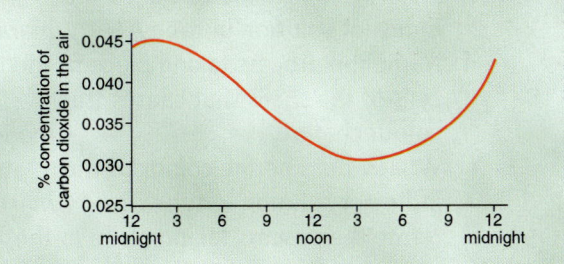

   a At what time was the concentration at its lowest?
   b Which process caused the concentration to decrease?
   c Where did the carbon dioxide go when it was taken from the air?
   d In which period did the concentration rise fastest?
   e What caused this rise?

End of unit Questions

1 Hydrogencarbonate indicator solution changes colour when the amount of carbon dioxide dissolved in it changes. This is shown in the table.

Colour of indicator solution	amount of dissolved carbon dioxide
reddish orange	same amount of carbon dioxide as in the air
yellow	more carbon dioxide than in the air
purple	less carbon dioxide than in the air

Five test tubes were set up as shown below. Air was bubbled through hydrogencarbonate indicator solution, which was then poured into each tube.

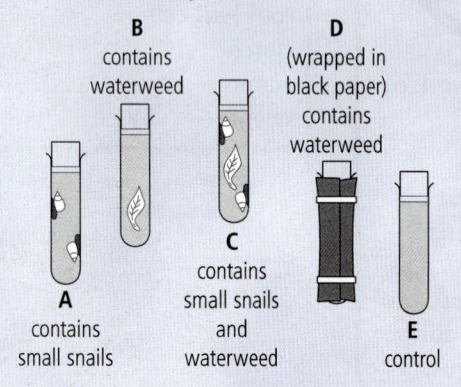

B contains waterweed
D (wrapped in black paper) contains waterweed
C contains small snails and waterweed
A contains small snails
E control

The test tubes were left in sunlight for two hours.
  a i What would be the colour of the indicator solution in tube A? *1 mark*
   ii Name the process taking place in the cells of the snails that causes this colour change. *1 mark*
  b i What would be the colour of the indicator solution in tube B? *1 mark*
   ii Name the process taking place in the cells of the waterweed which causes this colour change. *1 mark*
  c The colour of the indicator solution in tube C did not change. Explain why. *1 mark*

Tube D is wrapped to keep the light out. It contains waterweed but no snails.
  d i After 24 hours in the dark what would be the colour of the indicator solution in tube D? Choose from the list:
   reddish orange   yellow   purple *1 mark*
   ii Explain your answer. *1 mark*

2 In the 17th century, a Belgian scientist, van Helmont, planted a young willow tree in a tub of dry soil.
During the next five years he watered the plant with rainwater but he did not add anything else to the soil.

at the start   five years later

After five years van Helmont removed the willow tree from the tub and weighed the tree. He also dried and weighed the soil. Results from van Helmont's experiment are shown in the table.

	mass of willow tree, in kg	mass of dried soil, in kg
at the start	2.3	90.6
five years	76.7	90.5

  a Van Helmont concluded that the increase in mass of the willow tree was only due to a gain in water.
   i What **two** pieces of evidence did van Helmont use to reach his conclusion? *2 marks*
   ii We now know that van Helmont's conclusion is not correct.
    Explain why the mass of the willow tree increased by such a large amount. *2 marks*
  b Van Helmont believed that a plant would always grow faster if it was given more water. We now know this is **not** true.
   Give two environmental conditions that can slow down the growth of a plant, even when it has plenty of water. *2 marks*
  c The fresh mass of a plant includes water. To measure plant growth accurately, scientists calculate the increase in the dry mass rather than the increase in the fresh mass of a plant.
   Why is finding the increase in fresh mass not a reliable way to measure growth? *1 mark*

9D Plants for food

Introduction
In this unit you will build on Unit 8D 'Ecological relationships' and 9C 'Plants and photosynthesis'. You will learn about the production of food for humans. This will include the use of fertilisers and pesticides and weedkillers and how they can have an effect on the environment.

You already know
- about food webs and food chains
- about photosynthesis
- about the life processes common to living things, e.g. movement, growth, reproduction, nutrition

In this topic you will learn
- that humans are part of a complex food web
- about factors affecting plant growth
- how management of food production has many implications for other animal and plant populations in the environment
- about some of the issues involved in sustainable development of the countryside

1 What can you remember?

a Make a list of the different foods available in the restaurant.
b For each food, name the animal or plant it comes from.
c Link all of these animals and plants in a food web with humans at the top.
d Identify the producers, consumers, herbivores and carnivores in the food web.
e What is the source of **all** of the energy in the food web?

BIOLOGY — Plants for food

D1 Where does our food come from?

YOU WILL LEARN!
- that different parts of plants are food sources of different kinds
- that some parts of plants are starch stores
- about the products of photosynthesis
- how plants respire

We use many different parts of plants as foods.

1 Edible parts

Look at the pictures above.

a Make a table to show what part of the plant is actually eaten in each case, e.g. root, leaf, fruit, seed, etc.
b Try to think of other examples and add them to your table.

We eat these plant parts because they contain nutrients. In many cases the main nutrient is starch. Where does the starch come from? Think about the work you did in Unit 9C.

58

BIOLOGY   Plants for food

2 Which parts contain starch?

Get a variety of different plants and parts of plants. Use iodine solution to find out which parts contain starch.

Put your results in a table.

Avoid skin contact with iodine solutions.

You will have seen that many parts of plants contain starch. These are often the parts we eat. So why do plants make and store starch? **It is not for people and animals to eat** (although we do take advantage of them as a source of nourishment).

Remember that plants **respire** 24 hours a day. They need a source of carbohydrate to use in respiration. During the day there is no problem as they make glucose in photosynthesis. What about at night? Most plants make more glucose than they need during the day. Some of the glucose they do not need is stored as starch in the leaves. They use this during the night. Do you remember the experiments you did in C2? Leaving a plant in a dark place for a couple of days made sure it was **destarched**.

What about starch stored in the roots? Think back to the work in *Ascent! Book 1* about how plants survive the winter. Find out about **perennial** plants. There are also some plants called **biennials**. These grow one year, producing a **storage organ** below the soil and when winter comes the leaves die off. The next spring the plant grows very quickly and produces flowers and seeds. Carrots, parsnips and turnips are biennials, growing in two-year cycles.

3 Storage organs

a Explain why plants make storage organs.
b Give some examples that we can use as food.
c Why are they mostly found under the ground?
d Why do many of them, like onions, have a very strong smell and taste?
e Draw a diagram to show the life cycle of a perennial plant such as a potato.
f Draw a diagram to show the life cycle of a biennial plant such as a carrot.

The diagram of the life cycle of an annual should give you an idea of what to do.

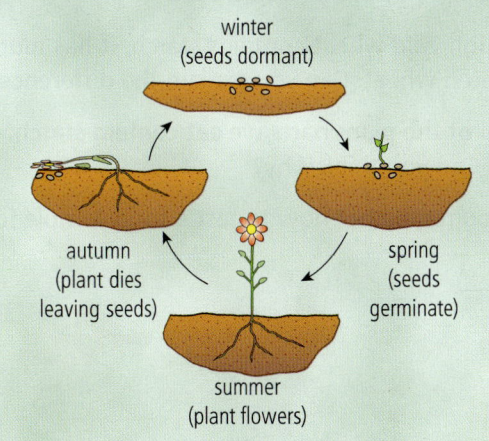

winter
(seeds dormant)

autumn
(plant dies leaving seeds)

spring
(seeds germinate)

summer
(plant flowers)

Life cycle of an annual plant

Did you know

Trees store starch in their roots. In the spring they use this starch when they start to grow. The starch is converted back into sugar and carried up the phloem vessels to the new buds. By cutting into the bark, some of this sugar solution, or sap, can be collected. This is the basis of maple syrup.

BIOLOGY   Plants for food

4 Looking at starch

1. Cut open a potato to show the white part.
2. Scrape some of the white part onto a slide.
3. Add a drop of iodine solution.
4. Put a coverslip over the top.
5. Examine the slide under a microscope.

Avoid skin contact with iodine solution.

a Can you see the starch grains?
b Draw a diagram.
c How many starch grains are there, on average, per cell?

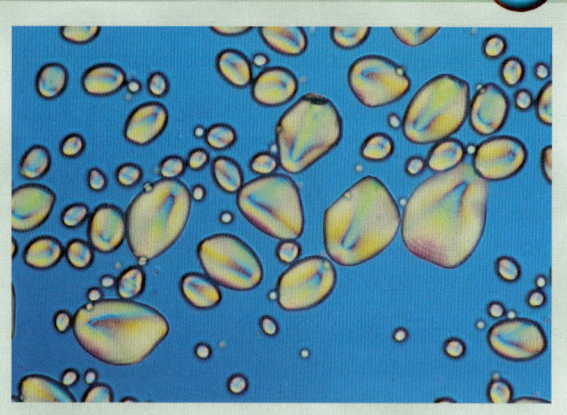

Starch grains in plant cells

5 Seeds

A lot of the parts of plants we eat are seeds.

a Why do seeds contain a lot of starch?

Some seeds contain oil as well as starch.

b Why do they contain oil?
c What is the advantage to the plant of storing oil instead of starch?

Points to discuss

Although wild wheat contains starch, it has much less than cultivated wheat. Can you explain the difference? (Look at 9A.)

Not all of the plant parts we eat contain starch. Some contain sugar. Can you think why?

Can you remember how to test a food sample for sugar?

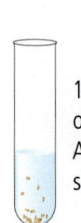

1. Put a small amount of food in a test tube. Add some water and shake it up.

2. Add about 1cm depth of Benedict's reagent

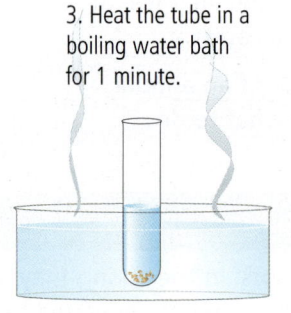

3. Heat the tube in a boiling water bath for 1 minute.

4. Red indicates a lot of sugar. Orange, yellow or green indicate less sugar.

Testing for sugar

BIOLOGY   Plants for food

6 Testing for sugar

Test some of the plants from Activity 2 for the presence of sugar.

a Which examples contained most sugar?
b Which is tastier to eat, sugar or starch?
c Are fruits designed to be eaten? Why? Think about what is inside fruits.

Did you know

Tomato plants are a common sight growing around the edges of the 'sludge lagoons' in sewage works! They grow really well.

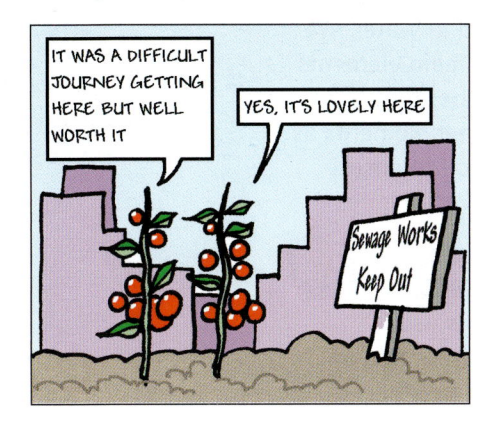

7 Review

Use what you have learnt so far in this unit and in 9C 'Plants and photosynthesis' to make a mind map.

'The Sun' would be a good starting point. You can show how photosynthesis, food chains and webs, energy, and the products of photosynthesis are all connected.

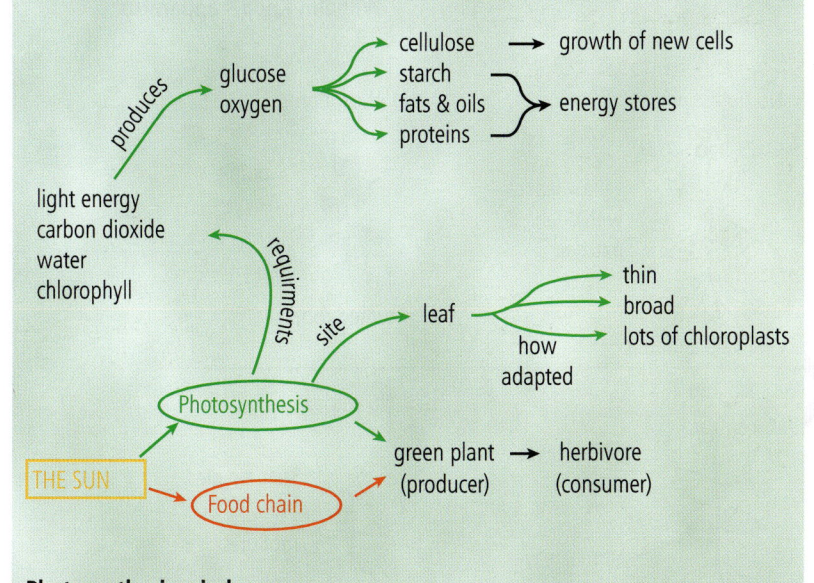

Photosynthesis mind map

BIOLOGY Plants for food

D2 Plants and fertilisers

YOU WILL LEARN!
- that plants need a range of minerals for healthy growth
- that fertilisers provide these minerals to crop plants

Plants need a range of elements. They need carbon, hydrogen and oxygen. These make up most of the biomass of a plant. Where do they get these elements? Look at the chemical equation for photosynthesis. Carbon and oxygen are taken in as carbon dioxide from the air. Hydrogen is taken in as water from the soil.

Other elements are absorbed from the soil, dissolved in water. We call these minerals. You should remember the three main elements that are essential for plants. What are they? Remember that they are sometimes called **NPK** fertilisers. Plants need other elements as well. Gardeners and farmers often add fertiliser to soil to ensure there are enough minerals for their plants.

A German scientist called Wilhelm Knop was one of the first people to realise that plants need minerals. In 1865, he carried out an investigation to find out how plants use these nutrients. He made a solution containing all of the minerals needed by plants. This was his **control**. Then he made other solutions, each lacking one mineral. He then put plant cuttings from the same plant in each solution. By comparing the cuttings that lacked a mineral with the control he worked out why each mineral was important.

Points to discuss

1 Why is the glass tube covered with black paper?
2 Why is oxygen bubbled into the solution every day?

Here are some results from an investigation into plant mineral requirements.

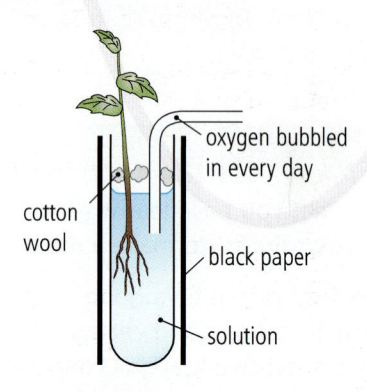

Wilhelm Knop's apparatus (oxygen bubbled in every day; cotton wool; black paper; solution)

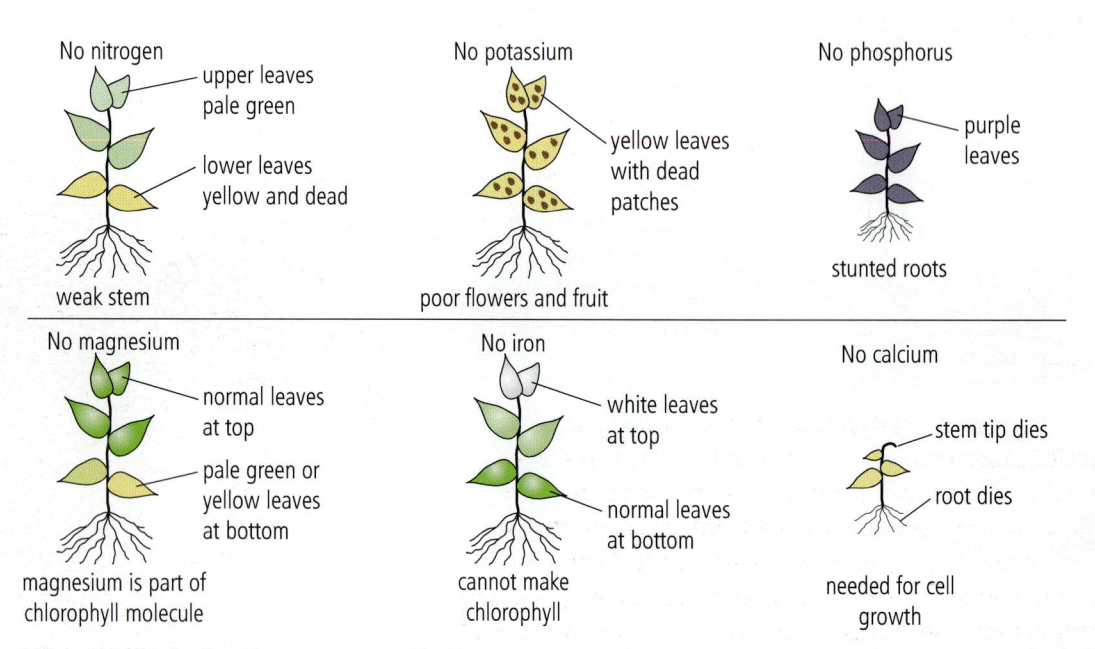

No nitrogen — upper leaves pale green; lower leaves yellow and dead; weak stem

No potassium — yellow leaves with dead patches; poor flowers and fruit

No phosphorus — purple leaves; stunted roots

No magnesium — normal leaves at top; pale green or yellow leaves at bottom; magnesium is part of chlorophyll molecule

No iron — white leaves at top; normal leaves at bottom; cannot make chlorophyll

No calcium — stem tip dies; root dies; needed for cell growth

Effect of lack of minerals on plant growth

62

BIOLOGY   Plants for food

1 Plants and minerals

You work for a company that is marketing a new fertiliser.

Your job is to design the packet that it will be sold in.

a Give the fertiliser a name that will attract customers.
b Make the packet bright and attractive.
c Most importantly, you need to make sure it gives the customer information about the benefits of using your fertiliser. You need to make sure it is scientifically accurate but can be easily understood by the average customer.

2 Costing fertilisers

a Find out the cost of some fertilisers.
b Find out the application rate. This means the amount of fertiliser to be used per unit of area.
c Calculate the cost of spreading fertiliser on 100 m² of a crop.

Compare some different fertilisers if possible.

d Put the information in a spreadsheet.
e Check which minerals are provided by each fertiliser you look at?
f Which fertiliser provides best value for money?

Applying fertiliser

So far we have looked at **artificial** fertilisers. Farmers and gardeners know exactly how much of each mineral there is in the fertiliser. Farmers use special machinery that measures out exactly the right amount of fertiliser. Artificial fertilisers can be easily **leached** away. This is when they are washed from the soil by rainwater and can end up in streams and rivers. (See page 120.) **Natural** fertilisers include compost and manure. Compost is made by allowing waste plant material to gradually rot away.

Muck spreading

Manure contains animal faeces, urine and straw. Both manure and compost add **humus** to the soil. Humus helps to hold the soil together. Natural fertilisers break down when they are spread on the soil and release nutrients slowly. A problem with natural fertilisers is that you do not know exactly how much of each nutrient they contain.

3 Natural or artificial?

Find out more about natural and artificial fertilisers.

a Draw a table to show the advantages and disadvantages of each.
b How do the costs of natural and artificial fertilisers compare?
c Try to find out about **green manure**. Add this to your table of advantages and disadvantages of different types of fertiliser.

Even though minerals are essential for plants they only need a very tiny amount of each one.

4 Testing fertilisers

There are many fertilisers available especially for houseplants. Some are liquids and others are powders. These are regularly tested to make sure that they actually help make houseplants grow faster, bigger and healthier. This sort of test will be done in a very large greenhouse with large numbers of plants. It will take several months to complete the test.

Your task is to find the best concentration of a fertiliser to increase plant growth. For the reasons outlined above you will not use houseplants. Instead you will use a tiny plant called duckweed. Duckweed is usually found floating on top of ponds. It grows very quickly, producing a pair of small leaves. With the right conditions it can completely cover the surface of a pond. In the laboratory you can grow many duckweed plants in a 250 cm^3 beaker.

a Plan an investigation to find the best concentration of fertiliser for the growth of duckweed.
b What concentrations of fertiliser will you use? (What is the recommended concentration?)
c What other factors will you have to control to make it a fair test?
d How many duckweed plants will you use? (Think about previous work on sample size.)
e How will you measure the growth of the duckweed?
f How long will your investigation last?

Show your plan to your teacher before you start.

BIOLOGY   Plants for food

5 The best concentration of fertiliser

Stewart wanted to find the best concentration of fertiliser for growing carrots. He divided his allotment into sections. He put different amounts of fertiliser on each section. He planted carrot seeds in each section. After six months he weighed the carrots he dug up.

Here are his results:

Amount of fertiliser (g)	Mass of carrots (kg)
0	3.0
20	5.5
40	7.5
60	8.5
80	8.0
100	7.5

a How would Stewart have made sure his experiment was a fair test?
b Plot a graph of his results.
c What was the best concentration of fertiliser?
d What are the disadvantages of using **more** than this amount of fertiliser?

In a natural environment, whenever a plant dies it will rot. The minerals in its cells are released back into the soil where they can be taken in by other plants.

When a farmer plants a field with crops the plants take in minerals from the soil. When the plants are harvested they are taken away so the minerals are removed from the soil. The soil will not contain enough minerals for plants to grow well. Farmers have to add fertilisers to replace the minerals that have been taken away.

One way that farmers can save money on fertilisers is by **crop rotation**. Some plants, like clover, peas and beans, have a bacterium called *Rhizobium* living in nodules on their roots. The plants are called **legumes**. These bacteria can take nitrogen from the air and turn it into nitrate in the roots. When the legumes are harvested the roots stay in the soil, leaving it enriched with nitrate. The following year the farmer can plant a crop such as oats, which needs a lot of nitrate.

Crop rotation also helps prevent plant diseases.

Point to discuss

How can crop rotation help prevent diseases of plants?

BIOLOGY Plants for food

D3 Competing plants

YOU WILL LEARN!
- that organisms living in a habitat compete with each other for resources
- how treating fields with selective weedkillers affects food webs

What do we mean by a weed? People often grow poppies in their garden. They look very nice! But when poppies grow in a field of wheat they are weeds. What are the problems caused by weeds growing in fields of crops? The answer is that the weeds **compete** with the crop for resources.

1 Competition

Ten allotment plots were cleared of weeds. Each plot was then sown with carrot seeds. Each plot was kept free from weeds for a different length of time. After 20 weeks the carrots were dug up and weighed. The results are shown in the table.

a How would the gardener ensure that this was a fair test?
b Plot a graph of the results.
c What pattern is shown by the results?
d Explain the results.
e What resources would the carrots and weeds be competing for?
f Would getting rid of the weeds have any effect on animals in the garden?

Number of weed-free weeks	Weight of carrots (kg)
0	3.0
1	4.0
2	5.0
3	6.0
4	7.0
5	8.0
6	9.0
7	10.0
8	11.0
9	11.5
10	12.0

Farmers use weedkillers or **herbicides** to kill weeds. In fields of cereal crops **selective weedkillers** are used. These kill all plants except the cereal plant that is being grown. This increases the yield of the cereal plant but at what cost to the environment? Many harmless species of animals use the weeds as a food source. What effect might this have on the bird population? What effect would not using herbicides have on crop yields?

Did you know?

Selective herbicides are absorbed through the leaves. Grass plants have narrow leaves so they do not absorb enough weedkiller to cause any harm. Broadleaved weeds absorb more and are killed.

Herbicides can be dangerous

66

BIOLOGY — Plants for food

A survey in 1999 showed that numbers of birds had fallen in the previous 30 years. Tree sparrow numbers had fallen by 95% and song thrushes by 56%.

2 Protecting the environment

Use the Internet to find out about how other bird species have declined in the last three decades. Make a list of the worst affected species.

Find out how farmers can help protect birds while also getting good crop yields. In particular, find out about how **beetle banks**, **field margin management** and **hedgerow management** can help birds.

Choose one of the ideas shown in bold. Make a wall display to explain how it works and the benefits it gives to birds and other wildlife.

How much effect does it have on crop yields?

Hedgerows are good habitats for birds

3 Surveying a habitat

Your school governors are concerned about the image of your school. They say that a lawn in front of the school is 'full of weeds' and 'is a disgrace'. Your task is to survey the lawn and write a report to the governors.

(You may not have a lawn at the front of your school but any grassy area will do.)

You used **quadrats** in 'Ecological relationships' in *Ascent! Book 2*. You should remember why it is important to make sure your sample is **random**.

Measure the area you are going to sample. Use the length of each side, in metres, as co-ordinates. Each pair of co-ordinates represents a square on the ground. You then pick a pair of co-ordinates at random. You can use tables of 'random numbers' to choose the co-ordinates. For example if your numbers are 6 and 3 you measure 6 metres along the edge of your area then 3 metres into the area.

Collect information about the type and number of weeds in the 'lawn'. You may find it useful to have books to help you identify the weed species.

Write a report for the governors. Tell them how many weeds and what types there are. Use information about weedkillers to suggest a type that could be used. Tell them how much it will cost to keep the weeds under control.

What are the disadvantages of killing weeds in this area? What are the effects on the wildlife around the school? Perhaps you could suggest a better solution, perhaps by developing it as a 'wildlife area'. Tell the governors of your plans.

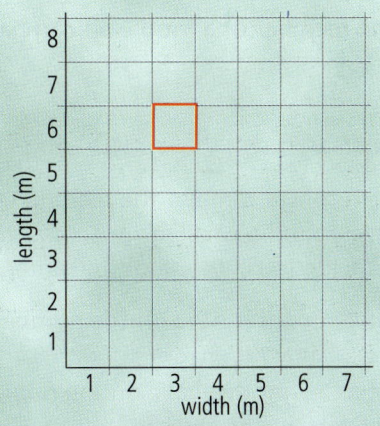

YES SIR, THIS IS OUR WILDLIFE GARDEN

BIOLOGY   Plants for food

D4 Plants and pests

YOU WILL LEARN!
- that the organisms living in a habitat compete with each other
- to represent feeding relationships using pyramids of numbers
- that the numbers of a population of predators influences the number of prey organisms
- that toxins enter a food chain when plants take them in or are in contact with them
- that toxins can accumulate at each stage in a food chain
- about the advantages and disadvantages of using pesticides

Many animals eat food crops as they grow. These animals are competing with humans for food. Not surprisingly farmers want to get rid of these pests.

1 Pests

a Try to find out what these pests eat: fieldmouse, cabbage white butterfly, aphid, snail, slug. Which of these are crops intended for humans?
b Draw a food web including humans, as well as these pests.
c Draw pyramids of numbers to represent some of the food chains within this food web.

Farmers and gardeners often use **pesticides** to kill these animals. **Insecticides** are chemicals specifically designed to kill insects.

2 Pesticides

Have a look at some pesticide packets.

Make a table to summarise what they are intended to kill, what chemicals they use and how dangerous they are.

Wash your hands after handling packets.

Removing one member of a food web can have effects elsewhere in the web.

Snails are pests

3 Upsetting the balance

The food web shows some of the feeding relationships around a small farm. The farmer is going to use a pesticide to kill the slugs and caterpillars.

a What effect might it have on the number of robins? Explain your answer.
b What effect might this have on the number of rabbits? Explain your answer.
c How might the insecticide affect the field vole population? Explain your answer.
d Use the Internet to find out about the effect of pesticides on bird populations.

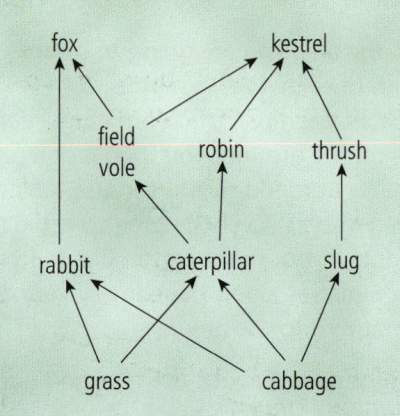

DDT is an insecticide. It was first discovered in 1939. In the 1940s and 1950s it was widely used to kill insects. It was used during the Second World War to kill lice and fleas that spread diseases.

Later, it was used to kill garden and farm pests. Probably its widest use was to kill mosquitoes which spread malaria. By killing mosquitoes it was probably responsible for saving millions of lives.

68

BIOLOGY   Plants for food

However, it was found to cause serious problems.
- When sprayed on insects it would kill most of them but a few would survive. These had a natural **resistance** to DDT. This resistance would pass on to the offspring. Eventually, most of the insects in a population were resistant to DDT.
- DDT was shown to be harmful to humans.
- DDT is **persistent**. This means it is not broken down in the soil or in animals' bodies and so, if an animal has DDT in its body it will pass on to any other animal that eats it. This can have very serious consequences.

Did you know
The full name of DDT is **dichlorodiphenyltrichloroethane**!

4 Clear Lake, a case study on DDT

DDT was used to kill midges around Clear Lake in California. Within a few months many grebes, (a species of water bird), were found dead. When they were examined it was found that they had very high levels of DDT in their bodies. Scientists studied the food chains in the lake. They found this food chain:

Microscopic plants → small crustaceans → small fish → large fish → grebe

a Draw a pyramid of numbers for this food chain.

DDT was found in the microscopic plants in very small amounts, about 0.015 ppm (parts per million).

Each small crustacean eats thousands of microscopic plants. The small crustacean cannot break down the DDT, nor can it excrete it.

b How will the concentration of DDT in the small crustaceans compare with that in the microscopic plants?
c What will happen as you go along the food chain to the grebes?

The diagram opposite sums up what happened in Clear Lake. It is an example of **bioaccumulation**.

5 Bioaccumulation

Another example of a problem with DDT happened in the UK. In the 1960s and 1970s the numbers of birds of prey fell. Peregrine falcons were particularly affected. It was found that the birds had DDT in their bodies. This was not enough to kill them but it caused them to lay eggs with very thin shells. These eggs usually broke before hatching. This was one of the reasons why DDT is now banned in most countries.

Write a news report on this story for a radio broadcast. Include the word bioaccumulation.

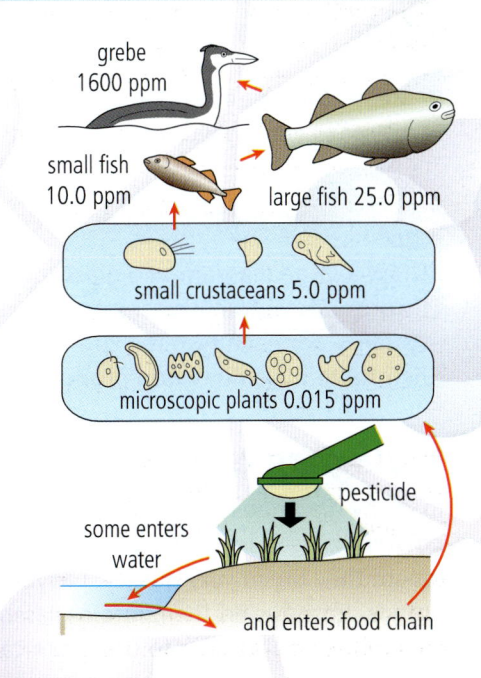

grebe 1600 ppm
small fish 10.0 ppm
large fish 25.0 ppm
small crustaceans 5.0 ppm
microscopic plants 0.015 ppm
pesticide
some enters water
and enters food chain

BIOLOGY   Plants for food

D5 What is the perfect place for growing plants?

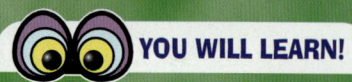

YOU WILL LEARN!
- about environmental factors that influence plant growth
- to consider the advantages and disadvantages of a controlled environment for growing crops

Think about what you have learnt in topics 9C and 9D. What conditions are needed for plants to grow? Light, water, warmth, minerals and carbon dioxide are all needed. Competition from other plants should be avoided. So where is the perfect place to grow plants? Spain is warm and sunny but is there enough water? The UK has plenty of rain but is it warm enough?

Forty years ago, greengrocers and supermarkets sold different products at different times of the year. Strawberries were only seen in the summer (or were very expensive having been flown to Britain from abroad). Lettuces were a summer crop, as were cucumbers and tomatoes. Nowadays we can buy these products all year. The winter price is only a little bit higher than the summer price. So where do they come from?

They are grown in glasshouses. A commercial glasshouse is a huge version of a greenhouse in a back garden but with a few extra features. In the most modern glasshouses sensors continually monitor conditions, which can be automatically modified.

- **Light** – glass lets in plenty of natural light. Artificial light can be used when the sensors detect that the light intensity has fallen.
- **Temperature** – energy from the Sun keeps the glasshouse warm in summer. If the temperature falls, paraffin heaters are used to raise the temperature. These also give out carbon dioxide. If it gets too warm then the windows can be opened to cool the glasshouse.
- **Carbon dioxide** – this can be kept at an optimum level by pumping carbon dioxide gas into the atmosphere if it falls too low.
- **Water** – plants can be given exactly the right amount of water by using automatic sprinklers and humidifying sprays.
- **Pests and weeds** – being in an enclosed space it is much easier to keep weed seeds and pests out of the glasshouse.

1 Design a glasshouse

Draw a large diagram of a glasshouse. Incorporate automatic sensing and control systems. For each system explain why it is helpful to maximum crop production.

Why is most of our food still grown out of doors in the traditional manner?

Biological control

In many glasshouses, the use of pesticides is avoided. **Biological control** is used instead. Aphids can be a major pest in glasshouses where they breed very quickly. Ladybirds are a natural predator of aphids. Introducing them into a glasshouse keeps the aphids under control without having to use chemicals.

BIOLOGY — Plants for food

Summary

We eat many different parts of plants including roots, leaves, stems, seeds and fruits. Most of these store nutrients for the use of the plant. Fruits contain sugar. Fruits are made so that animals will eat them. This helps to disperse seeds as they pass through the animal's digestive system.

Plants need a range of elements for healthy growth. These are taken in as minerals from the soil. They include **nitrogen**, **potassium** and **phosphorus**. Gardeners can add extra minerals to soil in the form of **fertilisers**. **Natural fertilisers** include **manure** and **compost**. **Artificial fertilisers** are made on a large scale and are usually easier to measure out and apply.

Plants need light, water, minerals, carbon dioxide and warmth to grow well. They **compete** with each other for these factors. **Weeds** are plants that grow where they are not wanted and compete with crops. Weeds reduce the yield of crops grown for food. **Herbicides** are chemicals that kill weeds. The use of herbicides increases crop yields but can kill plants that are an essential part of food chains.

Animals also cause damage to crops. Animals can be killed by the use of **pesticides**. Some pesticides, such as DDT, are **persistent**. They are not broken down in the soil and stay in animals' bodies. They pass from animal to animal, becoming more concentrated in animals at the top of the food chain. This is called **bioaccumulation**.

Key words
- artificial fertiliser
- compost
- fertiliser
- herbicide
- manure
- natural fertiliser
- nitrogen
- persistent
- pesticide
- phosphorus
- potassium
- weed

Summary Questions

1. Some pesticides, such as derris, are **biodegradable**.
   a. What does biodegradable mean?
   b. What is the advantage of this type of pesticide compared with DDT?

2. a. What does **organic farming** mean?
   b. What products would not be allowed on an organic farm?
   c. What methods of farming could be used to replace them?

3. Draw a table to show the ways in which plants use different minerals.

4. Why are tomato plants commonly seen around sewage works?

5. a. Why do some farmers remove hedgerows that separate their fields?
   b. What are the advantages to wildlife of **not** removing hedgerows?

6. Choose one of these people:
   - A farmer in Africa. Last year your crops were partly destroyed by locusts.
   - A conservationist in Africa. You are responsible for protecting an endangered species of eagle.

   Write a short speech saying whether you should be allowed to use DDT. Explain how you reached your decision.

BIOLOGY — Plants for food

End of unit Questions

1. Some pupils grew carrot plants for a project on plant growth. At the end of the summer they dug up the carrots. The drawings show two of their carrots.

   plant A   plant B

   Plant A came from a part of the garden which was covered with weeds. Plant B came from a part of the garden which had been kept free of weeds.

   a Suggest **two** ways in which the weeds may have stopped plant A from growing as large and healthy as plant B. *2 marks*

   b Explain why the pupils' plants produced bigger roots when they received more light. *3 marks*

2. Mango trees are grown in hot, dry countries where the soil can be hard and tightly compacted. Farmers water the mango trees by spraying water onto the soil around them.

   a i Only a small amount of the water actually reaches the roots of the trees. Suggest one reason why. *1 mark*

   ii Suggest one other reason why mango trees do not grow well in soil which is hard and tightly compacted. *1 mark*

   b Give two reasons why mango trees and other plants need water. *2 marks*

   c There is a new method of watering mango trees. Trenches are dug between the trees and filled with small pieces of rock. Plastic pipes with small holes in them are placed on top of the pieces of rock and water is pumped along the pipes.

   hard, tightly compacted soil   trench loosely filled with pieces of rock   plastic pipe with small holes in it

   Mango trees watered by this method produce 15% more fruit.

   i Suggest one reason why pieces of rock are placed in the trenches under the pipes. *1 mark*

   ii With the new method, farmers can also add nitrates to the water in the pipes. Give one reason why plants need compounds which contain nitrogen. *1 mark*

3. DDT is an insecticide that was discovered in 1939. In the 1950s and 1960s it was sprayed from planes over fields and lakes. Its use was banned in the 1970s.

   a The table shows the concentration of DDT in the tissues of two types of bird from the same area.

Type of bird	Concentration of DDT in the bird's tissues, in parts per million	bird's diet
heron	14.0	mainly fish
moorhen	0.2	mainly water plants

   Explain why DDT builds up in an animal's tissues and why herons had higher concentrations of DDT in their tissues than moorhens did. *2 marks*

   b Red scale insects are pests which feed on lemon trees in California. Ladybirds eat red scale insects. The graph below shows the effect of spraying lemon trees with DDT.

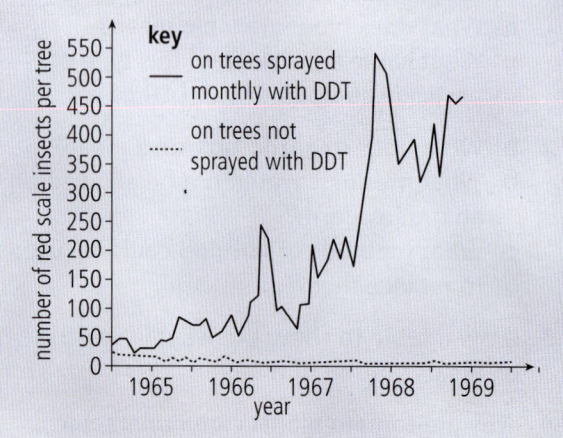

   key
   —— on trees sprayed monthly with DDT
   ······ on trees not sprayed with DDT

   Explain why the number of red scale insects on lemon trees which had been sprayed with DDT increased and why the number on untreated trees stayed nearly constant. *3 marks*

9E Reactions of metals and their compounds

Introduction

In this unit we will look at some chemical reactions of metals and the compounds they form. You will be familiar with some of these reactions from your previous work, but this time we will consider them in more detail using chemical formulae and symbol equations. This will involve 'balancing equations' to make sure that we have the same number of atoms shown before and after a reaction.

You already know

- the names and some properties of metals that are elements
- that atoms join (bond) together in different ways when chemical reactions take place
- the chemical symbols for some elements and the formulae of some compounds
- that chemical reactions can be represented by word and symbol equations and by particle diagrams
- how to test for hydrogen and carbon dioxide

In this topic you will learn

- the properties of metals and non-metals
- the similarities in the way that most metals, metal carbonates and metal oxides react with dilute acids
- how to represent the reactions above by word and symbol equations

1 What can you remember?

a List the names and symbols of five metallic elements.
b i Which metal compound are the workers collecting in the picture above?
  ii What is the chemical formula of this compound?
  iii Explain how the workers collect the compound.

CHEMISTRY   Reactions of metals and their compounds

E1 Properties of metals and non-metals

YOU WILL LEARN!
- that metals are good conductors of heat and electricity
- that most non-metallic elements are poor conductors of heat and electricity
- about the range of metals, their uses and where they are found
- to use and combine data from a variety of information sources
- to organise facts, ideas and information into an appropriate sequence

Metals

Life without metals would be difficult to imagine. We find their properties incredibly useful for a wide variety of functions.

Points to discuss

1. How many metals have you used today?
2. Which do you think is the most important property of metals – the property we would miss most, if suddenly metals were no longer good electrical conductors/good thermal conductors/etc.?
3. Where do you think we get metals like iron, zinc or copper from?

Look at the general properties of metals below:

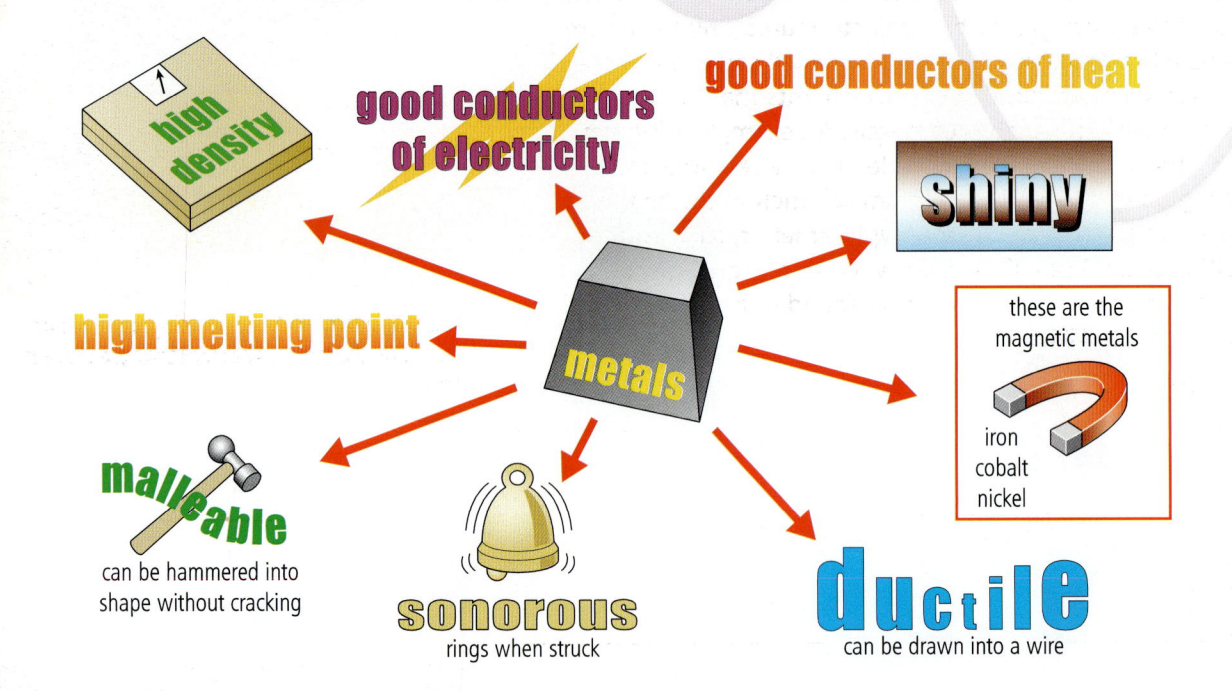

- high density
- good conductors of electricity
- good conductors of heat
- shiny
- these are the magnetic metals: iron, cobalt, nickel
- high melting point
- malleable — can be hammered into shape without cracking
- sonorous — rings when struck
- ductile — can be drawn into a wire

1 Useful metals

a. Take each property of the metals and link it to a use of metals that relies on that particular property.
b. Find out what alloys are and write a technical information card about one example of an alloy. You can use books, posters, videos, CD ROMs and the Internet to gather your data. Present your information in bullet points. (See next page for some ideas.)

CHEMISTRY   Reactions of metals and their compounds

Here is some information about a metallic element you are familiar with – gold.

- Name: gold
- Symbol: Au
- Type of element: metal
- Appearance: shiny, yellowish metal
- Melting point: 1064 °C
- Boiling point: 2850 °C
- Density: 19.28 g/cm^3
- Chemical reactivity: low

- Uses:
  Jewellery;
  Gold coated electrical connections in computers;
  Telecommunication and home appliance industries;
  Gold plated shields and reflectors to protect equipment on satellites;
  Reflectors to concentrate light energy in lasers used for eye operations and to kill cancerous cells;
  Gold coated contacts in the sensors that activate air bags in cars.

Gold bars in Fort Knox, USA

Strange metals

All metals are good electrical and thermal conductors. They all have free electrons within their structures which can carry charge (electrical current) or heat energy through the metal. However, there are some metallic elements that do not share the other usual properties of metals. An example is lithium, from Group 1 in the Periodic Table. It has a relatively low melting point of 180 °C. So lithium will melt in the heat of a Bunsen flame, whereas more typical metals, such as iron (melting point 1540 °C), will glow red hot but won't melt. Iron is one of the transition metals found in the central block of the Periodic Table.

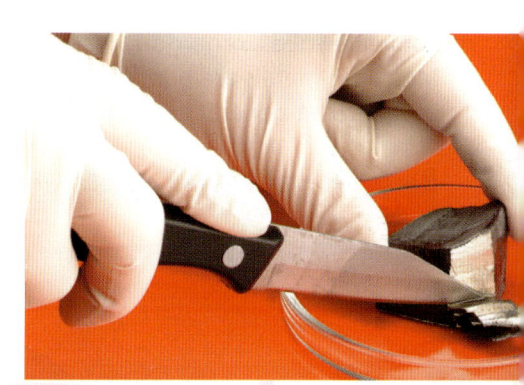

Reminder:

Li		
	Fe	

Lithium is a soft metal. It is shiny beneath its black coating. It is so reactive that we store it under oil.

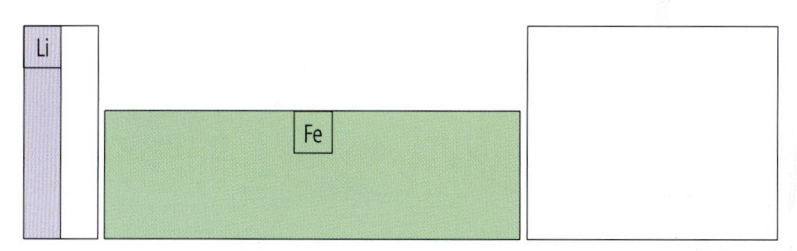

Lithium also has a density of just 0.53 g/cm^3 – the lowest density of all the metallic elements. Any substance with a density below 1 g/cm^3 (the density of water) will float in water. Compare that to iron with a density of 7.87 g/cm^3. Another difference is the hardness of the two metals. Iron is a hard metal, but you can cut through a piece of lithium with a kitchen knife.

The other metals in Group 1 of the Periodic Table share lithium's unusual properties. You will meet sodium and potassium in Unit 9F. These metals are much more reactive than most metals.

Iron is a more typical, hard metal, with a high melting point

CHEMISTRY   Reactions of metals and their compounds

Non-metals

Less than a quarter of the elements are non-metals.

Some are solids, others are gases and one is a liquid at 20 °C. Most non-metals are poor thermal and electrical conductors. Look at their general properties below:

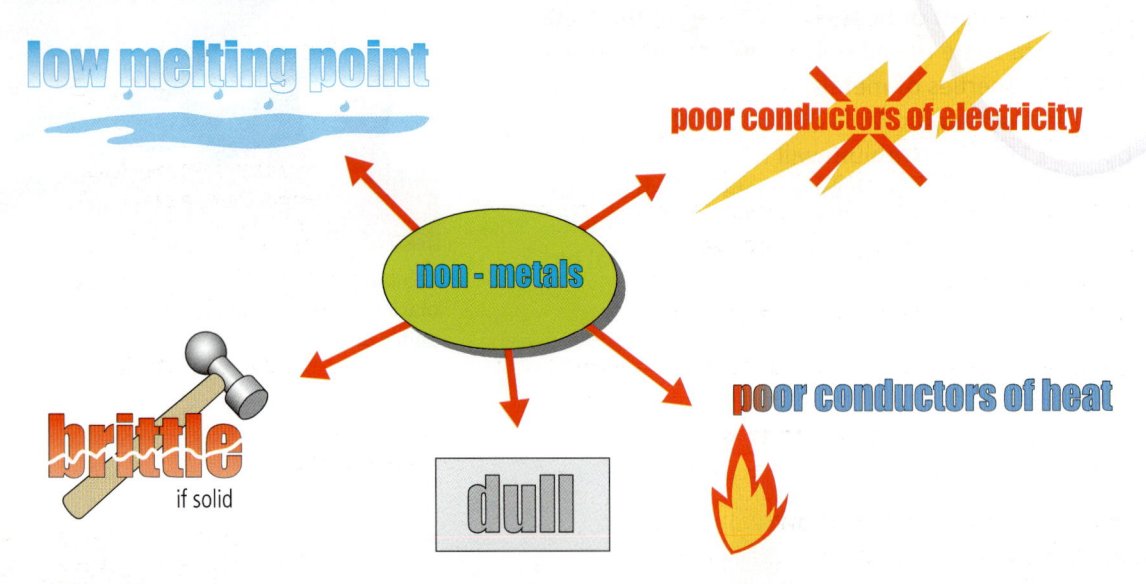

- low melting point
- poor conductors of electricity
- poor conductors of heat
- dull
- brittle if solid

2 Finding out about non-metals

Using books, posters, videos, CD ROMs and the Internet, try to find the answers to these questions:

a Name the non-metallic element that is a liquid at room temperature (20 °C).
b Make a pie chart showing the proportions of non-metals that are solid, liquid or gas at 20 °C.
c List the elements known as halogens.
d Which is the most chemically reactive non-metallic element?
e What type of element can be classified as a metalloid?
f Name three metalloids.

CHEMISTRY   Reactions of metals and their compounds

Strange non-metals

Did you notice that we said earlier that '*Most* non-metals are poor conductors of heat and electricity'? The exception to the rule is one form of the element carbon, called graphite. You will use graphite most days at school – it is mixed with clay in your pencil 'lead'.

It is a dark grey, shiny solid which sublimes at 3720 °C. (Sublimation is the process whereby a solid turns directly into a gas when heated – missing out the liquid state.)

Graphite is a form of carbon

The surface of graphite feels slippery when you touch it. That's because its carbon atoms are arranged in giant sheets of interlocking hexagons. The bonds between carbon atoms are very strong, but there are only weak forces between the layers. So the layers slip past each other easily (as you see by the trail of carbon atoms left on the paper when you use a pencil!).

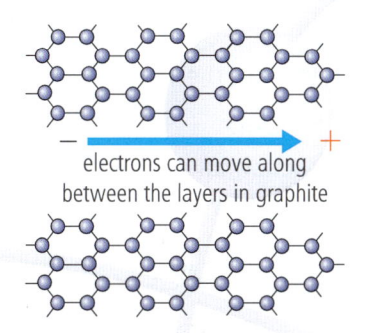

However, it is graphite's ability to conduct electricity that is really unusual for a non-metal. There are free electrons between the layers in its structure and these can drift through the graphite as it conducts electricity.

Another form of carbon you will know is diamond. Like graphite, it takes a lot of energy to break the bonds between the carbon atoms in the giant structure of diamond. It melts at 3550 °C. However, it is a typical non-metal as it is an electrical insulator. And yet, like graphite, it also has its surprises. It is used in the electronics industry as a 'heat sink' to conduct away heat energy in circuits. Weird, because most non-metals are thermal insulators.

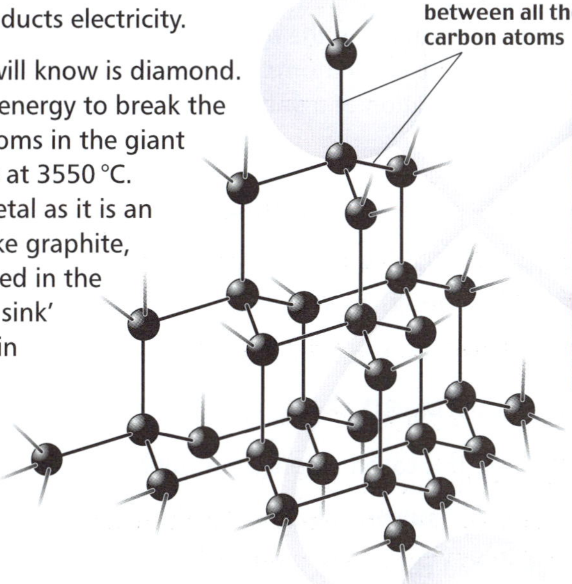

Graphite is mixed with clay in pencils. The less clay mixed in, the softer your pencil and the darker its lines (but you do have to sharpen it more often).

electrons can move along between the layers in graphite

Graphite conducts electricity

strong bonds between all the carbon atoms

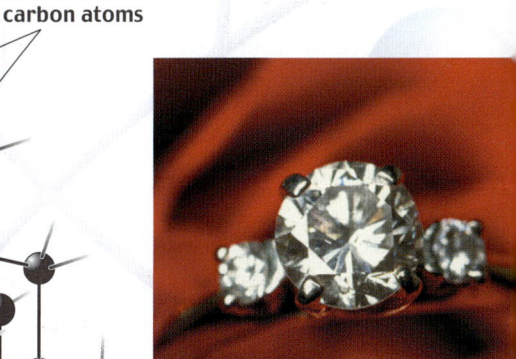

Diamond is another form of carbon

The giant structure of diamond – the world's hardest substance

CHEMISTRY   Reactions of metals and their compounds

E2 Metals reacting with acids

YOU WILL LEARN!
- that some metals react with dilute acids to form salts and release hydrogen gas
- to represent the reactions of metals with acid by word equations and balanced symbol equations
- to identify patterns in reactions between metals and dilute acids
- to use patterns in reactions to make predictions about other reactions

We first met the test for hydrogen gas in *Ascent! Book 1*. Can you remember how we made the hydrogen and how we tested it? If you need reminding, carry out Activity 1.

1 Making and testing hydrogen gas

Add a small piece of magnesium ribbon to a 2cm depth of dilute sulphuric acid in a test tube.

Hold a boiling tube upside down above the test tube.

Hydrogen is less dense than air, so it will displace air from the boiling tube.

Test the gas collected in the boiling tube by holding a lighted splint at the mouth of the tube.

Does it pop?

Now repeat the experiment above but instead of using dilute sulphuric acid, use dilute hydrochloric acid.

Do you get the same result?

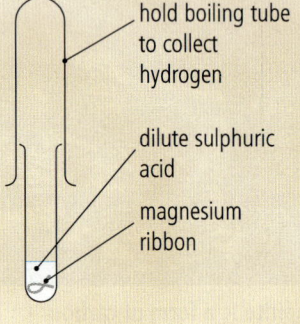

- hold boiling tube to collect hydrogen
- dilute sulphuric acid
- magnesium ribbon

If a reaction takes place between a metal and any dilute acid, it produces hydrogen gas (in the bubbles we see as fizzing).

Look at the formulae of the three acids we commonly use in school:

Can you see the element that each acid contains?

Acid	Formula
hydrochloric acid	HCl
sulphuric acid	H_2SO_4
nitric acid	HNO_3

In fact, **all acids contain hydrogen**. It is released as a gas (H_2) if a metal reacts with the acid.

But what happens to the rest of the atoms in the reactants? We have the metal, of course, and the other atoms in the acid. These are left in the test tube as a solution of a **salt**.

In general we can say:

$$\text{acid} + \text{a metal} \rightarrow \text{a salt} + \text{hydrogen}$$

A salt is a compound formed when the hydrogen of an acid is replaced (partially or wholly) by a metal.

So, in the reaction between magnesium and sulphuric acid we have:

$$Mg + H_2SO_4 \rightarrow MgSO_4 + H_2$$

The formula of the salt is $MgSO_4$. It is called magnesium sulphate.

So sulphuric acid makes salts called **sulphates**.

Hydrochloric acid makes salts called **chlorides**, and the salts we make from nitric acid are called **nitrates**.

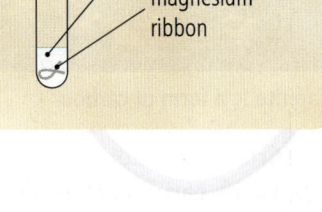

CHEMISTRY   Reactions of metals and their compounds

This is summarised in the table below:

Acid	Salts made	Formula ends in …	Example
hydrochloric acid	chlorides	…Cl	magnesium chloride, $MgCl_2$
sulphuric acid	sulphates	…SO_4	sodium sulphate, Na_2SO_4
nitric acid	nitrates	…NO_3	potassium nitrate, KNO_3

Look at the examples of the names of salts in the table.

Can you see that a salt gets its 'first name' from a metal and its 'surname' from an acid?

Salts are crystalline compounds. Their particles line up in regular patterns with water molecules bonded into their giant structures. Here are some examples of crystals of salts:

I'M CHARGING YOU WITH COMMON ASSAULT ON MR. SODIUM CHLORIDE. LET'S GET THIS STRAIGHT. YOUR SURNAME IS NITRATE, FINE – BUT THIS FIRST NAME, 'COPPER' – ARE YOU TRYING TO BE FUNNY SIR?

Crystals of zinc nitrate. Which metal and acid would you use to make this salt?

Crystals of iron chloride. Which metal and acid would you use to make this salt?

2 Preparing a sample of magnesium chloride

Now you can prepare some crystals of one of the salts formed in Activity 1.

1 Place 15 cm³ of dilute hydrochloric acid in a small beaker.
2 Add magnesium powder slowly until no more will react and you have some left undissolved in the solution.
3 Filter the mixture into an evaporating dish.
4 Heat the solution in the evaporating dish on a water bath until you see the first signs of crystals at the edge of the solution.
5 Leave the solution to evaporate at room temperature until next lesson.
   a What gas was given off in the reaction in step 2 above?
   b Give two ways in which you could tell that the reaction was complete.

CHEMISTRY   Reactions of metals and their compounds

Balancing equations

In the previous activity we carried out this reaction:

magnesium + hydrochloric acid → magnesium chloride + hydrogen

$$Mg + 2HCl \rightarrow MgCl_2 + H_2$$

Notice the number 2 in front of the HCl in the symbol equation.

It means we have 2 molecules of HCl in the equation.

This is called a **balanced chemical equation**.

We need to balance chemical equations to make sure that we have the same number of atoms before and after a reaction. Remember that no new atoms can be created or destroyed in a reaction – they just swap partners. (See pages 134 and 135.) We do this by inserting numbers in front of formulae in equations if necessary.

So why was it necessary in the reaction between Mg and HCl?

> ### 3 Balancing a chemical equation
>
> Write out the symbol equation for the reaction between magnesium and hydrochloric acid, but leave out the 2 in front of the HCl.
>
> a Now count the numbers of each type of atom on the left hand side of the equation (the reactants) and write down your answer.
> b Now do the same with the atoms on the right hand side of the equation (the products). Write down your answer.
> c Explain why we need to insert a 2 before the HCl in the equation. How many atoms of each element do we have on either side of the equation now?

IT'S VERY IMPORTANT TO BALANCE YOUR ATOMS ON EITHER SIDE, YOU KNOW

We can show the particles of reactants and products using a model that represents atoms as circles. This helps us to count the atoms on each side of the equation:

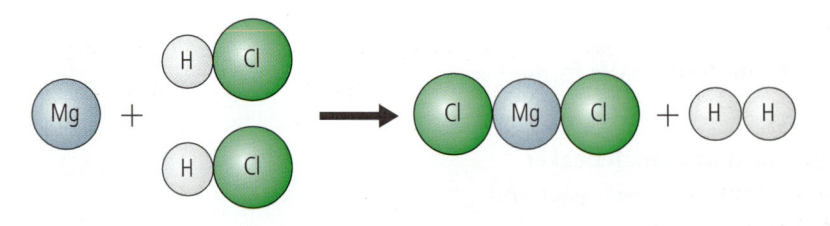

$$Mg + 2HCl \longrightarrow MgCl_2 + H_2$$

You can never change the formula of reactants or products in a reaction just to make an equation balance. Remember from *Ascent! Book 2* that each atom has a combining power and this determines the formula of the compounds it forms. So you can't change the formula of magnesium chloride from $MgCl_2$ to $MgCl$, or change hydrogen gas from H_2 to H, just to help you balance an equation!

CHEMISTRY   Reactions of metals and their compounds

Points to discuss

1. What do you think would happen to the mass of an open reaction vessel containing dilute acid and magnesium ribbon from the start of the reaction to its completion? Why?
2. What difference would you expect in the mass before and after the reaction above if you monitored the mass in a closed steel vessel? Why?

Now let's look at some other reactions of metals and acids.

4 Predicting reactions

a. Predict the products formed when you react zinc with sulphuric acid.
b. Plan how you could test the gas produced and collect crystals of the salt formed.

Now try the reaction in a test tube and test the gas given off. Do not put the lighted splint inside your tube of gas.
Make sure that the zinc is in excess.

c. How can you tell if all the acid has been used up?
Leave the solution formed to evaporate on a watch glass until next lesson.
d. Predict what you will see next lesson.
e. Write a word equation for the reaction between calcium metal and dilute hydrochloric acid.

Now watch your teacher react a small piece of calcium metal with dilute hydrochloric acid.

f. The formula of calcium chloride is $CaCl_2$. Write a balanced symbol equation for the reaction between calcium and hydrochloric acid.
g. Draw pictures of the particles involved in the equation, explaining why we can describe the equation as being 'balanced'.
h. In what ways are the reactions in this activity similar, and in what ways are they different?

Did you know

Although we use a model in which circles represent atoms when balancing equations, the particles in a salt are not really atoms; they are called ions, which are charged particles. The metal ion in a salt always carries a positive charge. The size of the charge equals its 'combining power', so sodium has a 1+ charge (shown as Na^+). The non-metal part of the salt from the acid carries a negative charge (for example, Cl^- or SO_4^{2-}).

Salts have giant structures in which millions of these oppositely charged ions arrange themselves in giant three-dimensional lattices that make up their crystals.

In just 6 grams of sodium chloride, there are over 60 000 000 000 000 000 000 000 Na^+ and Cl^- ions strongly attracted to each other! So, although when balancing equations we might represent NaCl as:

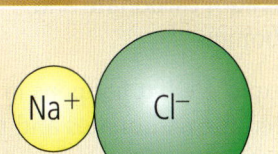

It is more realistically shown by part of its giant lattice (which will contain an equal number of Na^+ and Cl^- ions):

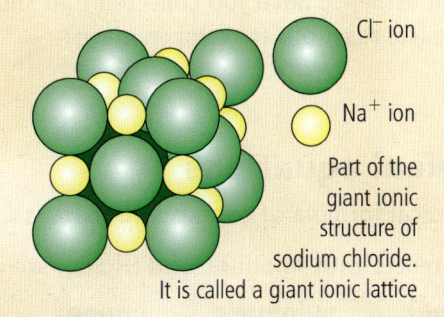

Part of the giant ionic structure of sodium chloride. It is called a giant ionic lattice

81

CHEMISTRY   Reactions of metals and their compounds

E3   Metal carbonates reacting with acids

YOU WILL LEARN!
- that acids react with metal carbonates to give a salt, water and carbon dioxide gas
- that the production of new substances and energy changes are evidence of chemical reactions taking place

In this topic you will investigate the reactions of metal carbonates with acids.

1 Investigating metal carbonates and acids

You are given the following apparatus and solutions:

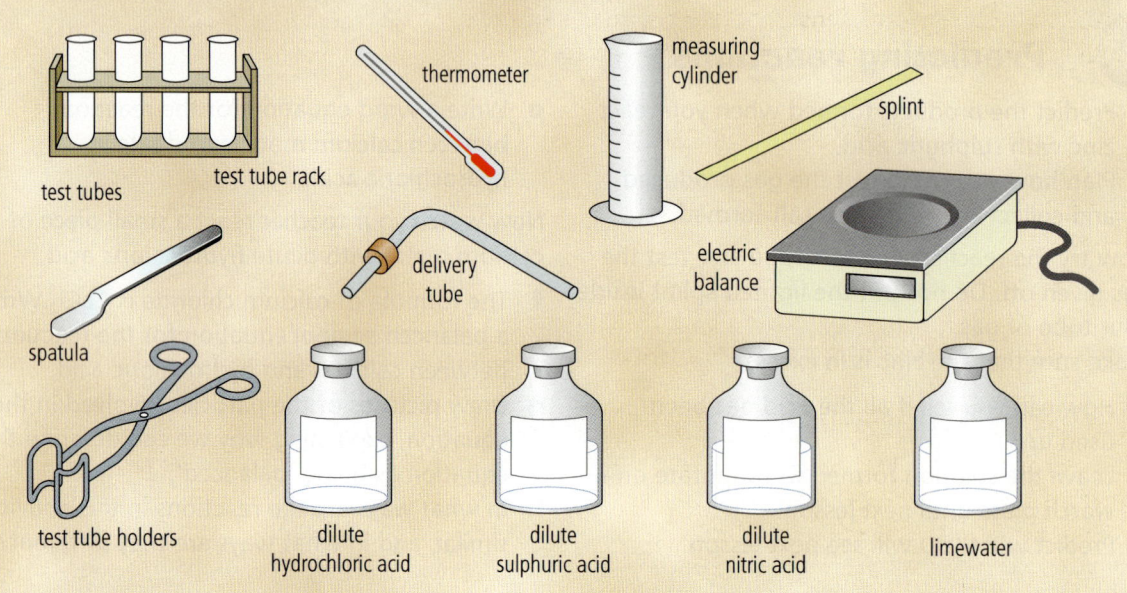

- test tubes
- test tube rack
- thermometer
- measuring cylinder
- splint
- delivery tube
- electric balance
- spatula
- test tube holders
- dilute hydrochloric acid
- dilute sulphuric acid
- dilute nitric acid
- limewater

You also have a range of different metal carbonates including copper carbonate, sodium carbonate, potassium carbonate and magnesium carbonate.

Your task is to explore what happens in reactions between the carbonates and the acids, recording similarities and differences systematically. Make sure you measure any temperature changes that take place.

Let your teacher check your plans before you try them out.

a What evidence have you collected that shows chemical reactions have taken place?

b Which gas is given off? How did you identify this gas?

c What do you think happens to the hydrogen present in the acids? (No hydrogen gas is produced.)

d What do you think happens to the metals from the original carbonates and the 'back end' of each acid?

e Write a general equation that describes what happens when a metal carbonate reacts with an acid.

f Plan an experiment to gather evidence for your answer to question d above.

Let your teacher check your plan before you try it out.

Chemical equations

The chemical formula of copper carbonate is $CuCO_3$.

When it reacts with sulphuric acid (H_2SO_4) we get:

copper carbonate + sulphuric acid → copper sulphate + water + carbon dioxide

$CuCO_3 + H_2SO_4 → CuSO_4 + H_2O + CO_2$

CHEMISTRY   Reactions of metals and their compounds

Count up the atoms on each side of the equation. Is this equation balanced?

When constructing balanced equations we need to know the formulae of the reactants and products. In *Ascent! Book 2*, we saw the combining power of several elements and how we can use this model to work out formulae. Remember that all the bonds must have atoms at each end (as if they are 'holding hands'!).

In the reactions of acids you have probably noticed groups of atoms, such as the SO_4 sulphate grouping, in the formulae of some salts. We can think of these groupings as having a combining power. The table below shows the common groupings we come across:

Grouping	Formula	Combining power
Sulphate	SO_4	2
Carbonate	CO_3	2
Nitrate	NO_3	1
Hydroxide	OH	1

Here are the combining powers of some metals:

Metal	Symbol	Combining power
sodium	Na	1
potassium	K	1
calcium	Ca	2
copper(II)	Cu	2
magnesium	Mg	2
zinc	Zn	2
aluminium	Al	3

So examples of salts are sodium sulphate, Na_2SO_4 and magnesium nitrate, $Mg(NO_3)_2$.

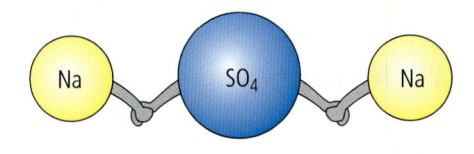

sodium sulphate – Na_2SO_4

WHY DO WE WRITE MAGNESIUM NITRATE AS $Mg(NO_3)_2$?

WELL, WITHOUT THE BRACKETS IT WOULD LOOK LIKE IT CONTAINS 1. MAGNESIUM, 1. NITROGEN AND 32. OXYGEN ATOMS!

Notice the brackets we put around groupings of atoms if there is more than one in a formula.

Try writing the formula of calcium nitrate.

2 Working out the formulae of salts and balancing equations

a Draw a table with the metals in the table above down the side, and sulphate, nitrate and chloride (combining power = 1) across the top, so that you can fill in the formulae of the salts for all the possible combinations.

b Write word equations and balanced symbol equations for the reactions of all the carbonates listed in Activity 1 with sulphuric acid.

CHEMISTRY — Reactions of metals and their compounds

E4 — Metal oxides reacting with acids

YOU WILL LEARN!
- that acids react with metal oxides, producing a salt plus water
- that production of the salt is evidence of a chemical reaction
- to represent the reactions of acids with metal oxides by word and symbol equations

Metal oxides are another important group of metal compounds.

Metal oxides tend to be basic (the opposite of acidic), so they react with acids in **neutralisation** reactions.

If the metal oxide dissolves in water, it forms an alkaline solution of a metal hydroxide. For example:

sodium oxide + water → sodium hydroxide (an alkali)

$Na_2O + H_2O → 2\ NaOH$

However, many metal oxides do not dissolve in water, but they will dissolve in dilute acid during a neutralisation reaction.

The metal oxide is called a **base**.

The general equation is:

acid + metal oxide → a salt + water

For example:

hydrochloric acid + zinc oxide → zinc chloride + water

$2\ HCl + ZnO → ZnCl_2 + H_2O$

Points to discuss

1. The combining power of oxygen is 2, so what is the chemical formula of copper(II) oxide?
2. Which salt will be made if copper(II) oxide reacts with dilute sulphuric acid?
3. Try to work out a balanced equation for the neutralisation reaction in question 2 above.

1 Preparing copper sulphate crystals

Now you can try out the reaction between copper oxide and dilute sulphuric acid and prepare a sample of crystals.

1. Pour 20 cm³ of sulphuric acid into a small beaker. Then add a spatula of black copper oxide.

2. Stir with a glass rod. Add more copper oxide, one spatula at a time, until no more will dissolve. To make sure all the acid is neutralised, you can warm the beaker **gently** on a tripod and gauze at this stage (but do not overheat). Add more copper oxide if necessary.

84

CHEMISTRY Reactions of metals and their compounds

1 continued

3 Filter off the excess copper oxide from the solution.

4 Pour the solution into an evaporating dish. Heat it on a water bath as shown below.

Stop heating when you see a few small crystals appear around the edge of the solution.

Leave the solution to evaporate at room temperature for a few days.

a Was any gas given off during the reaction in step 1 of your method? What happened to the hydrogen present in the sulphuric acid (H_2SO_4) in the reaction?

b How can you tell that a reaction took place?

c What do we call this type of reaction?

d Write a word equation for the reaction. Check back against the symbol equation you worked out in Points to discuss before you did the experiment. Was the equation correct? Correct it if necessary.

e How do you know when excess copper oxide has been added?

f How did you remove the excess copper oxide?

g Why is the solution left for several days at the end of the experiment?

h Draw a diagram to show the shape of your copper sulphate crystals.

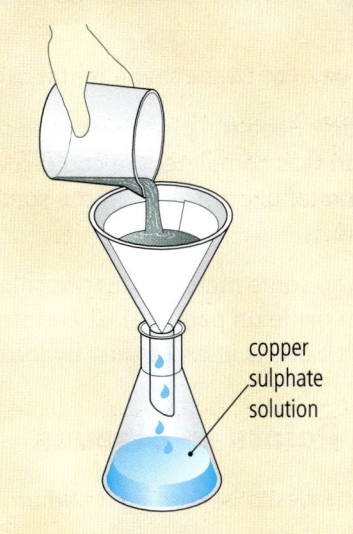

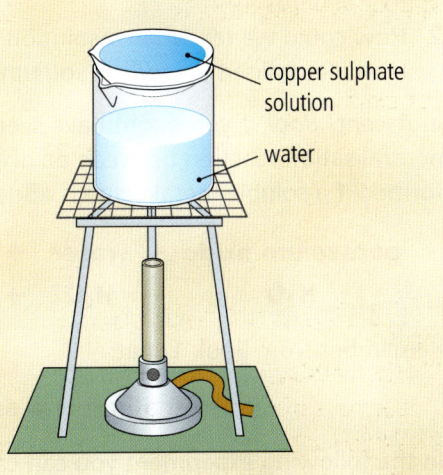

2 What's the equation?

Write word and symbol equations for the following reactions:

You can look back to page 83 to see the combining powers of different atoms and groups of atoms. Make sure your symbol equations are balanced.

a calcium oxide + sulphuric acid
b magnesium oxide + hydrochloric acid
c sodium oxide + nitric acid
d copper(II) oxide + nitric acid

3 Monitoring pH changes

a What do you predict will happen to the pH of an acid when a metal oxide is added? Repeat step 1 in Activity 1, but use a pH sensor to monitor the initial pH of the sulphuric acid and subsequent changes as you add small amounts of copper oxide until it is in excess.

b Check your data against your prediction. Evaluate your prediction.

CHEMISTRY — Reactions of metals and their compounds

E5 Neutralisation and salts

YOU WILL LEARN!
- that when an alkali is added to an acid, neutralisation takes place
- how to obtain a neutral solution from an acidic and an alkaline solution
- the hazards associated with alkalis
- that there are many different salts
- that many salts are useful compounds

In Activity 1 of E4 we saw a metal oxide (a base) neutralise an acid.

We didn't need the pH sensor used in Activity 3 to tell us when the reaction was complete. We could see because the insoluble copper oxide no longer dissolved in the solution once all the acid had been used up.

However, some metal oxides are soluble in water. (For example, sodium oxide on page 84). Therefore, we can't tell when the sodium oxide is in excess just by looking at the reaction mixture.

Points to discuss

1. What would be formed if sodium oxide was added to hydrochloric acid?
2. How could we tell when a solution of hydrochloric acid had been neutralised by adding sodium oxide powder?

In *Ascent! Book 1* you might have seen a **burette** used in a neutralisation reaction between an acid and an alkali. Alkalis are formed if a soluble metal oxide is added to water:

$$\text{potassium oxide} + \text{water} \rightarrow \text{potassium hydroxide}$$
$$K_2O + H_2O \rightarrow 2\,KOH$$

Remember from Book 1 that:

$$\text{acid} + \text{alkali} \rightarrow \text{a salt} + \text{water}$$

In the following experiment you can carry out a neutralisation reaction using a burette. The burette enables us to make very small additions of one solution to another. An indicator is usually used to tell us when the reaction is complete. The technique is called **titration**.

Did you know?

Strong alkalis are even more dangerous than strong acids of the same concentration if they get on your skin or in your eyes. Alkalis attack fats and oils breaking them down into soapy salt solutions. This reaction is used to make soaps from animal fats or plant oils.

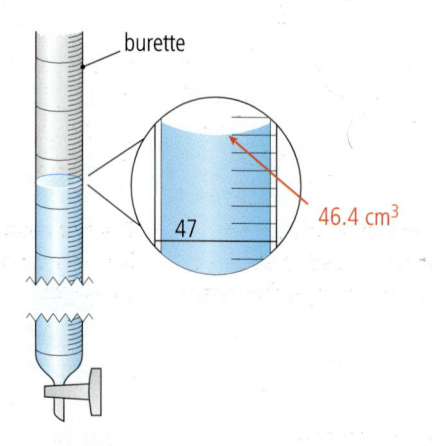

We can measure precise volumes of solution using a burette

CAN YOU HELP? HE'S HAD AN UNFORTUNATE ACCIDENT WITH SODIUM HYDROXIDE

CHEMISTRY   Reactions of metals and their compounds

1 Titrating acid and alkali

Collect 20 cm³ of potassium hydroxide solution in a conical flask.

Add a few drops of phenolphthalein indicator.

Fill a burette with dilute hydrochloric acid using a funnel.

Add the acid to the potassium hydroxide solution, swirling the flask as you proceed. (Your teacher will show you this technique.)

When the indicator shows signs of changing colour, add the acid from the burette a drop at a time. Stop when the solution just turns colourless.

This is difficult to achieve, so you will probably have to repeat the titration a few times.

Record how much acid is needed to neutralise the alkali.

a What is the pH of a neutral solution?

b How else could we have monitored when the reaction was complete? (We used this method in *Ascent! Book 1*.)

c Write the general equation for an acid reacting with an alkali.

d Write a word equation and symbol equation for the reaction between hydrochloric acid and potassium hydroxide.

e How could you go on to prepare a sample of crystals of the salt formed in the titration?

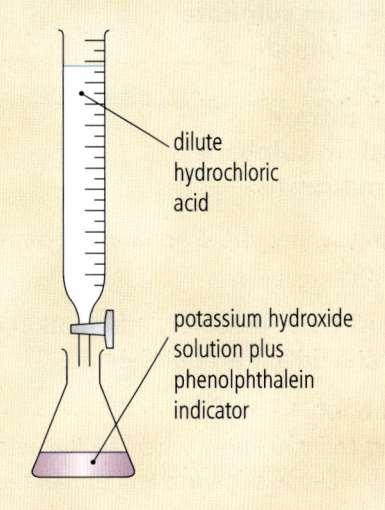

- dilute hydrochloric acid
- potassium hydroxide solution plus phenolphthalein indicator

Uses of salts

There are many possible combinations between metals and the 'back end' of an acid. In other words there is a wide variety of the compounds we call salts. Some of these salts have uses in industry or in our everyday lives. Here are a few examples:

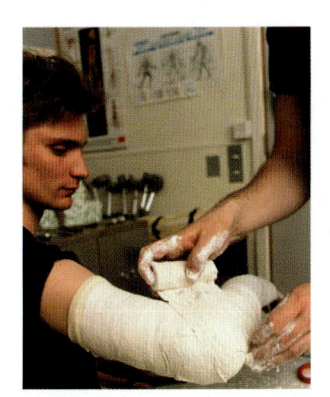

The insoluble salt calcium sulphate is used in hospitals to help set broken bones

The salt sodium fluoride is used in toothpastes to help prevent tooth decay

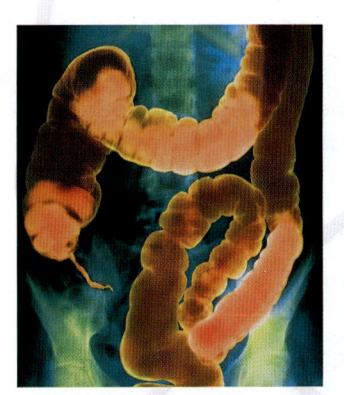

The insoluble salt barium sulphate is used to show up X-rays of the digestive system

The salt copper sulphate is used as a pesticide in vineyards

2 Useful salts

You have already found out about the uses of common salt, sodium chloride, in *Ascent! Book 1*. Try to find out the uses of one of the following salts:

aluminium sulphate; magnesium sulphate; sodium stearate; silver bromide

87

CHEMISTRY   Reactions of metals and their compounds

E6   Preparing salts

YOU WILL LEARN!
- to use preliminary work to find out if a planned approach is possible
- to use common laboratory equipment safely and effectively
- to evaluate the methods used in terms of the quality of the salt made
- to organise the write-up of your plan and method, including clear paragraphs that follow on from each other

To finish off this unit you can plan an experiment to make a salt.

1 Making your own salt crystals

Choose an example of a salt to prepare from the list below:

magnesium sulphate
copper chloride
zinc nitrate
copper nitrate
potassium sulphate
sodium nitrate

You can use any of the apparatus commonly found in the laboratory.

You must check the safety information on any reactants you plan to use and on any products made.

Think about:
- How will you know when all the acid has reacted?
- How will you separate any unreacted solids if necessary?
- What will you do to make well-formed crystals of your salt?

a Write down your plan in note form, including safety precautions.

Before starting any practical work, you must check your plans with your teacher.

Having made your salt:

b Write down an account of your experiment. Include any changes to your original plan, why you had to make them and whether they were effective in producing a good sample of your chosen salt.

WELL I THINK THAT EXPERIMENT WAS QUITE A SUCCESS!

CHEMISTRY Reactions of metals and their compounds

Summary

Metals that react with acid give off hydrogen gas and form a salt in the course of the reaction. The general equation is:

metal + acid → a salt + hydrogen

e.g. $Mg + H_2SO_4 \rightarrow MgSO_4 + H_2$

A salt is a crystalline compound in which a metal takes the place of all or some of the hydrogen in an acid. The common acids form these salts:

Acid	Salts made
hydrochloric acid	chlorides
sulphuric acid	sulphates
nitric acid	nitrates

Examples of salts include:
potassium chloride, KCl,
copper sulphate, $CuSO_4$, and
sodium nitrate, $NaNO_3$.

Other general equations for the reactions of metal compounds with acids that you should know are:

metal carbonate + acid → a salt + water + carbon dioxide

e.g. $CaCO_3 + 2HCl \rightarrow CaCl_2 + H_2O + CO_2$

metal oxide + acid → a salt + water

e.g. $CuO + H_2SO_4 \rightarrow CuSO_4 + H_2O$

metal hydroxide + acid → a salt + water

e.g. $NaOH + HNO_3 \rightarrow NaNO_3 + H_2O$

We can prepare crystals of the salts formed in these reactions by neutralising the acid with the metal or its compound (removing any excess insoluble reactant by filtration). Then evaporate the salt solution to the point of crystallisation and leave for a few days to allow well-formed crystals to come out of solution.

Key words

- balanced equation
- copper sulphate
- copper nitrate
- general equation
- neutralisation
- potassium chloride
- a salt
- sodium hydroxide
- sodium oxide
- symbol equation

Summary Questions

1. Draw a concept map using the words:

   acid; alkali; salt; base; carbonate; metal.

   Don't forget to label the connections you make.

2. **a** Write a word equation and a balanced symbol equation for the reaction between nickel(II) carbonate and sulphuric acid.
   b How could you positively identify the gas given off in the reaction in part **a**?
   c carbonate is insoluble in water. Write a 'step-by-step' method for preparing crystals of the salt formed in the reaction in part **a**.

3. Complete these word equations:
   a … + hydrochloric acid → zinc … + hydrogen
   b manganese oxide + … → … sulphate + …
   c … + nitric acid → magnesium … + … + carbon dioxide

4. Write down the reactants that could be used to safely prepare the following salts:
   a calcium chloride
   b sodium nitrate
   c potassium sulphate
   d zinc nitrate
   e iron(II) chloride
   f copper nitrate
   g Write a word and symbol equation for the formation of each salt in **a** to **f**.

CHEMISTRY   Reactions of metals and their compounds

End of unit Questions

1. A Japanese volcano erupted in 1936. Molten sulphur poured out of the volcano. When it cooled it formed rock sulphur.
   a. Sulphur is a non-metallic element. It is yellow and melts at 115 °C. Complete the sentences about sulphur.
      i. Sulphur is a poor conductor of ...... *1 mark*
      ii. At 115 °C sulphur changes from a .... into a .... *2 marks*
   b. Sulphur burns in air to form an oxide. What gas in the air reacts with sulphur when it burns? *1 mark*

2. Ben put a beaker weighing 50 g on a balance. He added 50 g of dilute hydrochloric acid and 2.5 g of calcium carbonate to the beaker.
   The total mass of the beaker and its contents was 102.5 g.
   a. The hydrochloric acid reacted with the calcium carbonate.
      How could Ben tell that a chemical reaction was taking place in the beaker? *1 mark*
   b. The word equation for the reaction which took place is:

   hydrochloric acid + calcium carbonate → calcium chloride + carbon dioxide + water

   When the reaction stopped, the total mass had decreased from 102.5 g to 101.4 g.
   Some water had evaporated from the beaker.
   What else caused the drop in mass? Use the word equation to help you answer the question. *1 mark*
   c. When the reaction stopped, Ben tested the contents of the beaker with universal indicator paper. The calcium carbonate had neutralised the acid.
   What is the colour of universal indicator paper in a neutral solution? *1 mark*
   d. Which **two** materials in the list below are mainly calcium carbonate? *2 marks*
   coal   marble
   glass   sandstone
   limestone

   e. Many metals react with acids. What gas is produced when a metal reacts with an acid? *1 mark*

3. a. Calcium burns brightly in oxygen, forming calcium oxide (CaO). Calcium oxide reacts with water, forming a compound with the formula $Ca(OH)_2$.
      i. Give the name of the compound with the formula $Ca(OH)_2$. *1 mark*
      ii. The compound, $Ca(OH)_2$, is slightly soluble in water. Would you expect this solution to be acidic, alkaline or neutral? *1 mark*
   b. i. Name the salt formed when $Ca(OH)_2$ reacts with dilute hydrochloric acid. *1 mark*
      ii. Write a word equation for the reaction in part **i**. *1 mark*
      iii. Write a balanced symbol equation for the reaction in part **i**. *2 marks*

4. The names and formulae of five compounds are listed in the table below.

name of compound	formula of compound
ammonia	NH_3
ammonium chloride	NH_4Cl
ammonium sulphate	$(NH_4)_2SO_4$
sodium hydroxide	NaOH
sodium sulphate	Na_2SO_4

   Ammonia and sulphuric acid react to give ammonium sulphate, $(NH_4)_2SO_4$.
   a. Balance the equation for this reaction. *1 mark*

   $NH_3 + H_2SO_4 \rightarrow (NH_4)_2SO_4$

   b. Complete and balance the symbol equation for the reaction between sodium hydroxide and sulphuric acid.
   $NaOH + H_2SO_4 \rightarrow$ ―― + ―― *3 marks*

5. a. Potassium nitrate (KNO_3) can be made by reacting 'potash' (K_2CO_3) with nitric acid (HNO_3).
      i. What is the chemical name for 'potash' (K_2CO_3)? *1 mark*
      ii. Write a balanced equation for the reaction of 'potash' with nitric acid. *3 marks*

90

9F Patterns of reactivity

Introduction

In this unit we will look more closely at the differences between the reactions of metals and use these to set about constructing an order of reactivity. We will link the uses and methods of extraction of metals to their position in this order of reactivity.

You already know

- the differences between elements and compounds
- that elements can be represented by symbols and compounds by formulae
- how to represent chemical reactions by word (and balanced symbol) equations
- the tests for hydrogen, carbon dioxide and oxygen
- that many metals react with oxygen to form oxides
- the general equation for the reaction if a metal reacts with dilute acid

In this topic you will learn

- that although metals react in a similar way with oxygen, water and acids, some react more readily than others
- how to arrive at a Reactivity Series for the metals
- to present more reactions by word and symbol equations

1 What can you remember?

a Look at the picture above: Which type of material makes up the bulk of each mode of transport?
b Give the names and chemical symbols of two chemical elements used in the bodywork of any of the objects in the picture.
c What would be the ideal properties of a material used to make the body of an aeroplane?

91

CHEMISTRY   Patterns of reactivity

F1 Tarnished metals

YOU WILL LEARN!
- that many metals are affected by air and water
- that different metals are affected in different ways
- that some metals are soft and can be cut

In the previous unit, 9E, we saw some strange metals from Group 1 in the Periodic Table. These soft metals can be cut with an ordinary kitchen knife. Look at the photos below showing some freshly cut lithium and potassium, and the same pieces of the metals a few minutes later.

Freshly cut lithium

The same piece of lithium a few minutes later

Freshly cut potassium

The same piece of potassium a few minutes later

Points to discuss

1. What happens to the freshly cut surface of the metals above when they are exposed to air?
2. Try to explain what happens to the surface.
3. Give one property of lithium and potassium that suggests that they are metals, and one property that is unusual for a metal.

When the atoms at the surface of a metal react with substances in the air, the metal loses its shiny appearance. We say that the metal becomes **tarnished**. Often the metal will form a dull coating of the metal oxide (although water vapour, carbon dioxide, pollutant

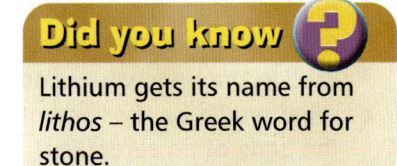

Did you know
Lithium gets its name from *lithos* – the Greek word for stone.

CHEMISTRY   Patterns of reactivity

gases such as sulphur dioxide, and even nitrogen can be involved in tarnishing some metals).

Here are some examples of other metals that tarnish in the air.

This roof contains copper, and the green colour arises from copper compounds which are formed as the copper tarnishes

A rusty bicycle chain. The red/brown rust is a compound of iron.

On the other hand, the metal gold does not tarnish in air. Gold coins found in shipwrecks, hundreds of years old, can still be found in mint condition.

1 To tarnish or not to tarnish?

Look at the metals in the photos above:

a Which of the metals above tarnish and which don't?
b Why do you think there is a difference between the three metals?
c Are there any problems associated with the reactions involved in the photos? What are they?

Collect a small strip of magnesium ribbon.

d Describe the appearance of magnesium.

Now rub the surface of the magnesium with some emery paper.

e What do you see now? Explain your observations.

Gold resists tarnishing

Rusting

The rusting of iron and steel (which contains a very high proportion of iron) costs millions of pounds each year. In the following activity you can find out what causes the corrosion of iron. Have you any ideas before you start?

CHEMISTRY   Patterns of reactivity

2 Corrosion of iron

Set up the experiment below:

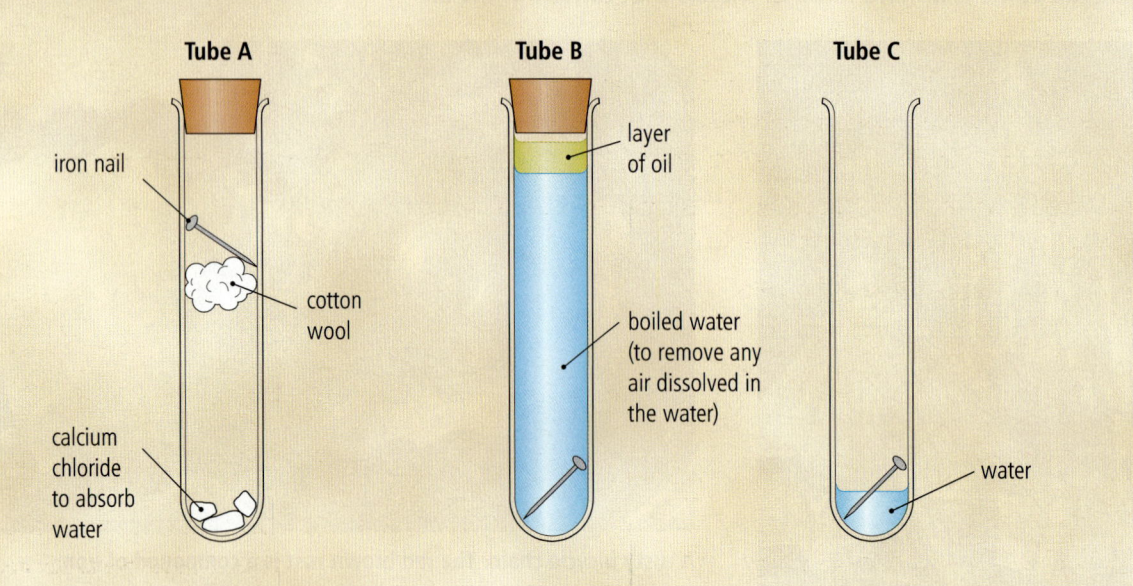

Tube A — iron nail, cotton wool, calcium chloride to absorb water

Tube B — layer of oil, boiled water (to remove any air dissolved in the water)

Tube C — water

Leave for a few days then record your observations in a table.

a In which tube(s) is there signs of rust?
b What are the conditions needed for iron to rust?

Metals react with oxygen and other substances in air at different rates, if at all. Some, such as lithium and potassium, react quickly, whereas others, such as copper, react slowly. Gold is so unreactive that it doesn't tarnish in air.

Iron needs both air (oxygen) and water in order to rust.

When iron corrodes it produces a form of hydrated iron(III) oxide. Hydrated iron(III) oxide is iron(III) oxide with water bound in its structure, which some people describe as iron(III) hydroxide. The rust is a crumbly substance that flakes away and exposes fresh iron to attack so that the iron can corrode completely. This presents us with problems because iron, often in the form of steel, is the most widely used metal in the construction industry. It is used as rods to reinforce concrete, for example.

Points to discuss

1. How do we protect iron from rusting? Think of at least three methods that we can use. How does each method work?
2. If a large proportion of the metal in steel sinks is iron, why don't steel sinks rust?
3. What will happen to reinforced concrete if the iron inside it rusts?
4. Work out the chemical formula of:
    a iron(III) oxide
    b iron(III) hydroxide
    (The combining power of oxygen is 2 and hydroxide (OH) is 1.)

Did you know

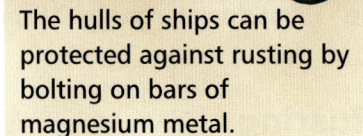

The hulls of ships can be protected against rusting by bolting on bars of magnesium metal.

CHEMISTRY   Patterns of reactivity

F2   Metals reacting with water

YOU WILL LEARN!
- that some metals react with cold water to produce hydrogen
- that some metals react more readily with water than others
- about the hazards associated with some metals

Most metals don't react vigorously with water.

Just imagine the chaos in your kitchen at meal times if they did! However, there is a great range in reactivity between different metals, as we saw in F1 when looking at metals tarnishing.

You have done plenty of experiments using magnesium metal – how do you think it reacts with water?

You can find out in the next activity.

Fortunately most metals do not react vigorously with cold water!

1 Magnesium and copper in cold water

Clean the surface of a strip of magnesium ribbon with emery paper.

Then place it in the apparatus shown below.

Repeat this with a piece of copper foil.

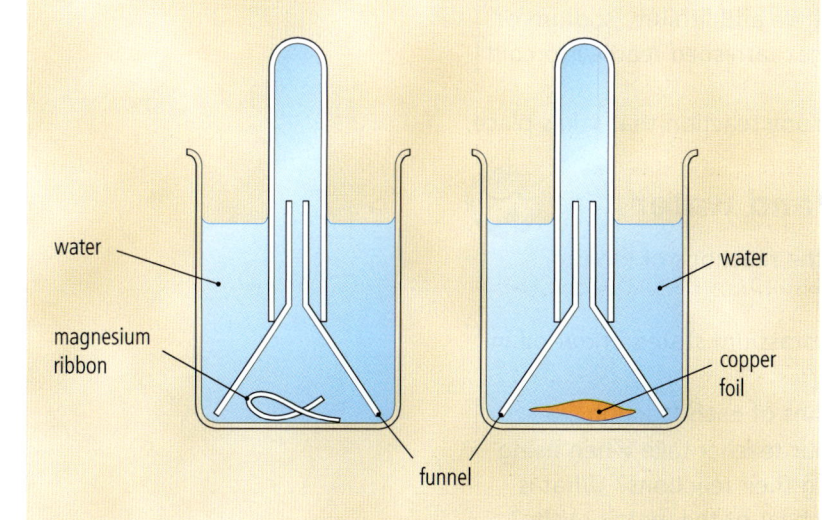

Leave the apparatus for a week.

a What do you observe after a week? Which metal shows no sign of a reaction?

Test any gas collected with a lighted splint.

b Which gas is produced?
c Where did this gas come from?
d Which of the two metals is more reactive with water?

The reaction between magnesium and water is very slow. We can make it go faster by reacting hot magnesium with steam.

Did you know?
Water pipes used to be made from the pliable metal lead. However, lead reacts slowly, forming toxic lead salts. Copper is less reactive than lead and has now taken its place in all modern domestic water pipes.

CHEMISTRY   Patterns of reactivity

2 Magnesium and steam

Watch your teacher demonstrate the reaction opposite:

a Describe what happens as the magnesium reacts with the steam.
b Which gas burns off at the end of the tube?
c The white solid left in the test tube is magnesium oxide (MgO).
   Write a word equation and a symbol equation for the reaction.

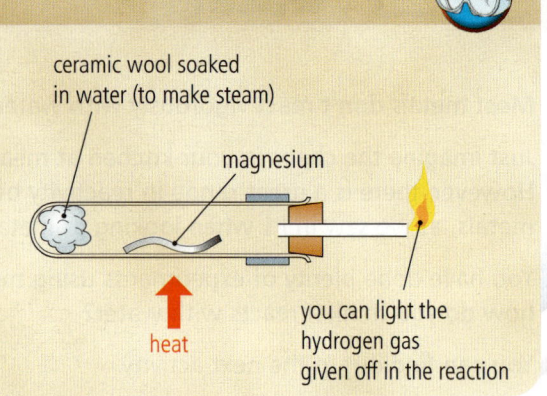

ceramic wool soaked in water (to make steam)

magnesium

heat

you can light the hydrogen gas given off in the reaction

Other metals that react very slowly with cold water but more readily with steam are iron and zinc.

For example:

zinc + steam → zinc oxide + hydrogen
$Zn + H_2O → ZnO + H_2$

Points to discuss

1 What do you think will happen if we add lithium, sodium or potassium (the metals from F1 that tarnished readily) to cold water?
2 Predict what might be formed in any reaction that takes place.

3 Group 1 metals and water

Watch your teacher demonstrate the reactions of lithium, sodium and potassium with water.

a Why are lithium, sodium and potassium stored under oil in their jars?
b Record in detail your observations of each reaction.
c What safety precautions did your teacher take when using these metals and demonstrating their reactions? What is the hazard warning sign on each jar of the metals? Why?
d How were the reactions similar?
e How were the reactions different?
f Put the metals in an order of reactivity with water, listing the most reactive one first.
g Alkaline solutions are formed as the metal hydroxides produced in the reactions dissolve in water. For example, lithium hydroxide, LiOH, solution is left after lithium's reaction with water.
   Write word and symbol equations for each reaction. The combining power of metals in the same group of the Periodic Table is the same, so each formula for the hydroxide will be in the same ratio, 1 : 1. Remember to balance your symbol equations. (This should be easy after you've done the first one.)

CHEMISTRY   Patterns of reactivity

Did you know

1807 was a great year for Sir Humpry Davy – it was the year that he discovered both potassium and sodium by electrolysing molten compounds of the metals.

Rubidium and caesium are two other metals from Group 1. Look at caesium's reaction with water, below:

Caesium (Cs) reacting with water

These highly reactive metals are too dangerous to store in schools, but the products of their reactions are similar to the other metals in Group 1:

rubidium + water → rubidium hydroxide + hydrogen
2 Rb + 2 H$_2$O → 2 RbOH + H$_2$

Now try applying the knowledge you have gained so far in the unit in the next activity.

4 Predicting reactions

Calcium is a metal that is more reactive than magnesium, but less reactive than lithium.

a Predict what you will see when a piece of calcium is added to half a beaker of water, and any products that might be formed.

Try out the reaction in a large beaker or trough of water. Have an inverted test tube full of water ready to collect any gas given off and test the solution left with universal indicator paper. Test the gas collected with a lighted splint.

Safety: Do not touch calcium metal or the solution formed in the reaction.

b Evaluate your prediction by comparing your observations with the ideas you had before trying out the experiment.
c Write a word and symbol equation for the reaction between calcium and water. (The combining power of calcium is 2 and hydroxide is 1.)
d Put the metals lithium, sodium, potassium and calcium into their order of reactivity with water.

...AND DO YOU SELL CAESIUM BY ANY CHANCE....?

CHEMIST

Did you know

Marguerite Perey (1909–1975) discovered Francium

The bottom element in Group 1 in the Periodic Table is called Francium (Fr). It was discovered in 1939 by Marguerite Perey whilst working at the Curie Institute in Paris – hence its name.

It is a radioactive element that only exists for a very short time before disintegrating into a series of new elements (changes associated with radioactive decay are very different from chemical changes!). In fact, nobody has actually seen this very unstable element and it has been estimated that there is likely to be less than 10 grams of Francium in the entire Earth's crust at any given time.

CHEMISTRY   Patterns of reactivity

F3 The reactivity of metals with dilute acids

YOU WILL LEARN!
- that some metals react more readily with acids than others
- to decide which observations or measurements help to answer our question
- to identify variables that need to be controlled in an investigation and decide how to do this
- to choose axes and scales for graphs
- to decide whether results that do not fit the pattern we expect arise from shortcomings in our experiments or are significant
- to explain results in the light of scientific knowledge and understanding

We have now seen how a range of metals react (or do not react) with water, and that we can use our observations of these reactions to place the metals into an order of reactivity. However, where the reactions are very slow, the task of ordering the metals is difficult. With these metals we can look at their reactions with dilute acid to arrive at an order of reactivity.

SORRY SIR, BUT HE'S BEEN WAITING THREE DAYS FOR THIS COPPER TO REACT WITH DILUTE ACID!

Points to discuss

1 From Unit 9E, what is formed, in general, when a metal does react with dilute acid? Think of a word equation for a specific example. How can we use the reaction between metals and acids to judge relative reactivity?
2 Which metals would you not try adding to acid? Why not?

1 Preliminary work with metals and acid

You are given coarse-mesh filings of the metals copper, zinc, iron and magnesium to put into an order of reactivity according to their reactions with either:
- dilute hydrochloric acid, or
- dilute sulphuric acid.

Plan a test to put the metals in order of reactivity based on your observations. Your plan should include the quantities of reactants you intend to use. (You will have access to a balance and measuring cylinders.)

Let your teacher check your plan before you start your tests.

a Give a brief outline of your method.
b Record your results in a suitable table.
c Put the metals in order of reactivity according to your observations.

Check your order with another group that used the alternative acid in their tests.

d Did you agree on the order of reactivity?

The strange case of aluminium

Aluminium fits into the order of reactivity you are building up between magnesium and zinc.

CHEMISTRY   Patterns of reactivity

Points to discuss

Predict the reactions you would expect between:
- aluminium and water,
- aluminium and dilute acid.

2 Reactions of aluminium

Try adding some aluminium foil to water first of all, then to dilute acid.

a What do you observe?
b How were your observations surprising?

Aluminium is protected on its surface by a **tough layer of aluminium oxide**.

Once the initial outer oxide layer has covered the metal, the aluminium atoms beneath do not come into contact with water or dilute acids – hence its apparent lack of reactivity.

That's why this fairly reactive metal can be used outside, for example in patio doors, without corroding.

3 Gathering quantitative data

In this investigation you should plan to collect more data to test out your order of reactivity. This time, measurement will play a big part in the results you record. This is called **quantitative data** (involving numbers) as opposed to the qualitative data that is based on observations.

You will be looking in more detail at the metals zinc, magnesium and aluminium and their reactions with dilute acid. So 'type of metal' will be your **independent variable** in this investigation.

Think about these questions to help your planning:
- What could you measure as each reaction proceeds? This will be your **dependent variable**.
- What equipment will you need?
- How will you make it as fair a test as possible? These will be your **control** variables.
- How will you make your results reliable?
- How will you record your results as the tests take place?
- How will you present these results graphically?

a Predict the graph you expect to get.

Let your teacher check your plan before you start your practical work.

b Write up your investigation to include your:
- completed results table;
- graph to display your results;
- a conclusion that refers to your prediction, comments on your graph and explains your results;
- an evaluation of the quality of the data you were able to collect and any ways in which it could be improved, giving your reasons.

Did you know

The statue of Eros at Piccadilly Circus is made of aluminium.

It was a very expensive metal when the statue was erected in 1893.

The statue of Eros is made from aluminium

99

CHEMISTRY   Patterns of reactivity

F4 Metals reacting with oxygen

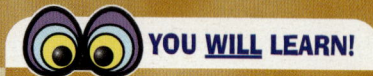

YOU WILL LEARN!
- to use a proposed Reactivity Series to make predictions
- to test predictions made
- that metals react with oxygen to produce oxides

A list of metallic elements in order of reactivity is called the **Reactivity Series**.

1 Constructing and using the Reactivity Series

a Look back through this unit and construct a list of metals in order of reactivity, starting with potassium at the top.

This is your Reactivity Series.

b You have tried out, and watched, different metals reacting in air and in oxygen gas as you worked through *Ascent! Books 1 and 2*.

Using your previous knowledge and your Reactivity Series, predict what you would expect to see if the following metals were heated then plunged into a gas jar of pure oxygen gas:

magnesium; **copper**; **calcium**; **zinc**; **sodium**; **iron**

Your teacher will show you some of these reactions.

c Compare your predictions with your observations of the reactions.

Were your predictions accurate? What could account for any unexpected results?

d Write word and symbol equations for each metal reacting with oxygen.
(The combining power of the metals in the oxides formed are: magnesium 2; copper 2; calcium 2; zinc 2; sodium 1; iron 3; and the combining power of oxygen is 2).

Potassium reacts vigorously in oxygen. The white smoke contains fine particles of potassium oxide.

Look up the names of any metal you don't know in this Reactivity Series

CHEMISTRY   Patterns of reactivity

F5   Displacement reactions

YOU WILL LEARN!

- that a metal will displace a less reactive metal from a solution of one of its salts
- to construct a table to show patterns clearly
- to identify patterns in observations
- to use a model to explain results
- that displacement reactions take place between metals and metal oxides and that this reaction can be useful

So far we have put the metals in order of reactivity on the basis of their reactions with water, dilute acids and oxygen. We can use the resulting Reactivity Series to predict the results of reactions when we put the metals 'into competition' with each other.

Try out the reactions below.

1 Metals in competition

Set up the boiling tubes shown below:

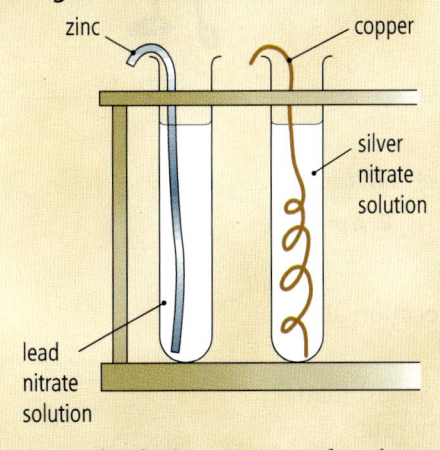

- zinc
- copper
- silver nitrate solution
- lead nitrate solution

Leave the metals and solutions to react for about 15 minutes.

a Record your observations.
b Think about the reactants in each tube and what they could form. (Remember that chemical reactions involve a rearrangement of the particles in the reactants to form the products.) Try to explain, in your own words, what might be happening in each reaction.

Safety: Wash your hands after the experiment as lead salts are toxic.

Most metallic elements become more stable once they have reacted to form compounds. If you give two different metals the chance to form a compound, then the more reactive of the two will take the opportunity. The less reactive metal will be left as the element; as the metal itself. Let's look at an example using a 'model' involving competition between metals.

If we have silver nitrate solution and copper, we set up a competition between silver and copper. Both copper and silver want to form a compound, but it is silver that starts off with the nitrate as a compound in solution. However, copper is more reactive than silver. It appears above it in the Reactivity Series. We can think of it as 'stronger' than silver. Therefore, it 'takes the nitrate' for itself, going into solution to join it. The silver is 'kicked out' of solution and left as the element itself.

Remember that this is just a model to help us visualise what is happening. The cartoon on page 102 might also help:

CHEMISTRY   Patterns of reactivity

> HEY NITRATES, FORGET SILVER! I'M THE MORE REACTIVE ONE

The word equation is:

copper + silver nitrate → copper nitrate + silver

$$Cu + 2\,AgNO_3 \rightarrow Cu(NO_3)_2 + 2\,Ag$$

We call this a **displacement reaction**.

Exam tip: In your SATs, when asked to explain the reaction above, an ideal answer would be:

Copper is **more reactive** (or higher in the Reactivity Series) than silver. Therefore it can **displace** the silver from silver nitrate solution, forming silver metal and leaving copper nitrate in solution.

If we had added silver to copper nitrate, there would have been no reaction. Silver is not reactive enough to displace copper from its solution.

silver + copper nitrate ⇸ no reaction

2 Predicting displacement from solution

You are given small samples of the metals magnesium, copper, iron and zinc, as well as access to solutions of magnesium sulphate, copper sulphate, iron(II) sulphate and zinc sulphate.

a Construct a table that is large enough to record your observations of the various combinations of each metal with the relevant sulphate solutions. The table should also have space for your predictions of whether you expect to see a reaction (✓) or not (✗).

You can observe the reactions on a spotting tile. Use the end of a spatula to add a small amount of the metal powders to the appropriate well.

b Were there signs of a reaction in all the combinations that you ticked?

c Select four ticks from your table and write word equations and symbol equations for these displacement reactions.

CHEMISTRY Patterns of reactivity

Displacing metals from their oxides

We can also carry out displacement reactions between metals and metal oxide powders. As both reactants are in the solid state, they need mixing thoroughly so that reacting particles can get next to each other. The mixture also needs to be heated to start off the reaction.

Points to discuss

What differences are there between the way reacting particles meet in displacement reactions that occur in solution and those between powders in the solid state? Explain your ideas.

3 Metals plus metal oxides

Watch your teacher demonstrate the following reactions in a fume cupboard.

Once the Bunsen burner has been placed under the tin lid holding the reaction mixture, it can be left until the reaction takes place.

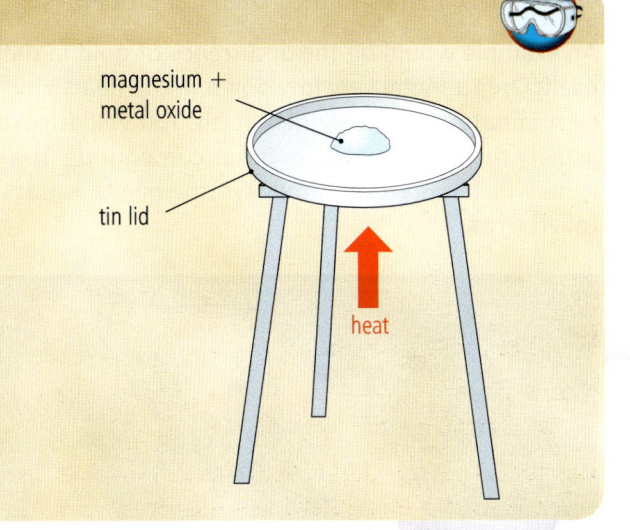

a Describe what happens and give a word equation and symbol equation for each reaction:
   magnesium + copper oxide
   magnesium + zinc oxide
   magnesium + lead(II) oxide
   zinc + copper oxide

4 Thermit reaction

a Predict the word equation for the reaction between aluminium and iron(III) oxide.

Watch your teacher demonstrate the spectacular reaction between aluminium powder and iron(III) oxide in a fume cupboard.

b How is the reaction started off?
c What is formed in the reaction?
d Why does the iron melt in the reaction?

Aluminium reacting with iron(III) oxide.

This reaction is used by railway workers to weld tracks together. The molten iron drips down into the gap and solidifies when it cools down. The iron can then be filed down to make a smooth joint.

103

CHEMISTRY   Patterns of reactivity

F6 Reactivity linked to the sources and uses of metals

YOU WILL LEARN!
- to identify what information is needed, and use different texts as sources
- to structure paragraphs to develop points, using evidence and additional facts
- to relate the occurrence, extraction and use of metals to their position in the Reactivity Series

In 9E on page 74 we looked at the properties of metals and linked these to the uses we can make of particular metals. These are called the **physical properties** of the metals (for example, their electrical conductivity or high melting points). In this unit we have looked at the **chemical properties** of the metals in more detail. In the next activity you can link some uses, sources and methods of extraction of metals to their chemical properties.

An example would be the occurrence of gold in nature as the metal itself. Only a metal very low down in the Reactivity Series could exist in nature as the element itself. You will discover in the next activity that most metals occur as compounds. The compounds from which it is economically worthwhile to extract the metal are called **ores**.

Gold can be found as the element itself because of its low reactivity

Gold has been used for thousands of years. Why?

1 Finding links with the Reactivity Series

Working as a group, collect together some examples of:
- uses of metals
- the occurrence of metals in nature
- the way we extract metals from their ores
- the date of their discovery

that depend on their position in the Reactivity Series.

You can use a range of source materials e.g. books, videos, CD ROMs, posters, leaflets, the Internet.

a Write an account to summarise your findings in each area, making sure you structure your work logically and use paragraphs to develop each idea.

Discovery of Group 1 metals

Lithium	1817
Sodium	1807
Potassium	1807
Rubidium	1861
Caesium	1860
Francium	1939

b Comment on the data above.

CHEMISTRY   Patterns of reactivity

Summary

Here is a table that summarises the reactions of some important metals.

Order of reactivity	Reaction when heated in air	Reaction with water	Reaction with dilute acid
potassium	burn brightly, forming metal oxide	fizz, giving off hydrogen, leaving an alkaline solution of metal hydroxide	explode
sodium			
lithium			
calcium			fizz, giving off hydrogen and forming a salt
magnesium		react with steam, giving off hydrogen and forming the metal oxide	
aluminium			
zinc			
iron			
tin	oxide layer forms without burning	slight reaction with steam	react slowly with warm acid
lead			
copper		no reaction, even with steam	no reaction
silver	no reaction		
gold			

This list of metals is known as the **Reactivity Series**.

A metal higher up the Reactivity Series can displace a less reactive metal from its compounds. For example, in solution:

zinc + copper sulphate → zinc sulphate + copper
Zn + $CuSO_4$ → $ZnSO_4$ + Cu

This is called a **displacement reaction**.

Another example is the thermit reaction (used by rail workers to weld track together):

aluminium + iron(III) oxide → aluminium oxide + iron
2 Al + Fe_2O_3 → Al_2O_3 + 2 Fe

Key words
- aluminium oxide
- displacement reaction
- qualitative observations
- quantitative data
- Reactivity Series
- tarnish
- thermit reaction

Summary Questions

1. Imagine that a new metal, given the symbol X, has been discovered. It lies between calcium and magnesium in the Reactivity Series.
   a. Describe its reaction when heated in air and give a word and symbol equation. (The combining power of X is 2.)
   b. Describe the reaction of X with dilute sulphuric acid and give a word and symbol equation.
   c. Why can't you be sure how X will react with water?
   d. X is added to a solution of copper nitrate. Explain what you would expect to happen.

2. Another new metal, Y, does not burn in air but does form a layer of oxide on its surface. It doesn't react with water or steam, but there is a slight reaction with warm dilute acid.
   a. Where would you place metal Y in the Reactivity Series?
   b. Explain what you would expect to happen if metal Y was added to magnesium sulphate solution.
   c. A sample of aluminium does not display the reactions as shown in the table above unless it has been freshly chemically cleaned. Why not?

CHEMISTRY   Patterns of reactivity

End of unit Questions

1 The table shows the observations made when four metals are added to cold water and to dilute hydrochloric acid.

metal	observations with cold water	observations with dilute hydrochloric acid
zinc	no reaction	bubbles of gas form and the metal slowly dissolves
platinum	no reaction	no reaction
potassium	the metal floats and then melts, a flame appears, and sometimes there is an explosion	(cannot be done safely)
nickel	no reaction	a few bubbles of gas form if the acid is warmed

a Write the names of these **four** metals in the order of their reactivity (most reactive first). *1 mark*

b i Give the name of another metal, **not** in the table, which reacts in a similar way to potassium. *1 mark*

ii What gas is formed when zinc reacts with dilute hydrochloric acid? *1 mark*

iii The experiment with potassium and dilute hydrochloric acid should **not** be done in school laboratories. Suggest why it is dangerous. *1 mark*

c A scientist set up two test tubes as shown below.

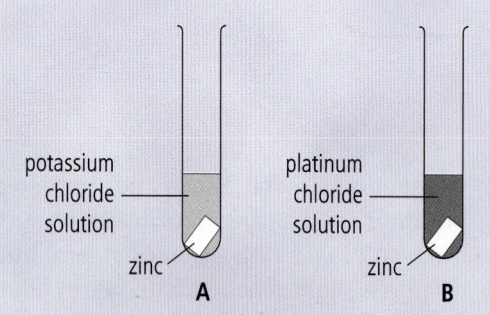

Test tube A: potassium chloride solution with zinc
Test tube B: platinum chloride solution with zinc

In test tube B the zinc strip was slowly covered with a grey deposit.
Nothing happened in the other test tube.

i What was the grey deposit in test tube B? *1 mark*

ii Why was this grey deposit formed in test tube B? *1 mark*

iii Explain why **no** reaction took place in test tube A. *1 mark*

2 Aisha placed small samples of four different metals on a spotting tile. She added drops of copper sulphate solution to each metal.

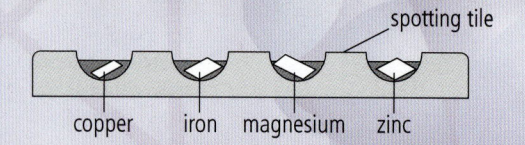

spotting tile with copper, iron, magnesium, zinc

Aisha repeated the experiment with fresh samples of the four metals and solutions of different salts. She recorded some of her results in a table.

✓ shows that a reaction took place
✗ shows that no reaction took place.

metals solutions	copper	iron	magnesium	zinc
copper sulphate	✗	✓	✓	A
iron sulphate	✗	✗	✓	✓
magnesium sulphate	✗	B	✗	C
zinc sulphate	✗	✗	✓	✗

a The four metals have different reactivities.

i Use the information in the table to put the four metals in a Reactivity Series starting with the most reactive. *1 mark*

ii Use the Reactivity Series to complete the table by deciding whether a ✓ or a ✗ belongs in boxes A to C in the table above. *2 marks*

b Copper reacts with silver nitrate solution.

i Complete the word equation for the reaction:

copper + silver nitrate → _____ + _____
2 marks

ii Platinum does **not** react with silver nitrate.
Put the metals platinum, copper and silver in the correct order according to their reactivity, starting with the most reactive. *1 mark*

c In many houses the hot water pipes are made from copper and the boiler is made from iron.
Which of these metals will corrode first? Explain your answer. *1 mark*

106

9G Environmental chemistry

Introduction
In this unit you will find out about different types of pollution – how they are caused, their effects and how we can reduce the problems they bring. This will include issues associated with acid rain and global warming.

You already know
- that there are differences between soils which relate to the rocks they were formed from
- how to find the pH of a solution, and how to relate the pH scale to the acidity of a solution

In this topic you will learn
- that rocks, soils and building materials have a variety of chemical characteristics
- that chemical weathering alters rocks and building materials over time
- how the atmosphere and water resources are affected by natural processes and the activity of humans
- how environmental conditions are monitored and controlled
- to distinguish between different environmental issues

1 What can you remember?
Look at the picture of the scene above:
a Name the sources of pollution you can see.
b The pH of rainwater in an unpolluted area can be as low as 5.6. What does this tell you about rainwater?
c Would you expect the pH of vinegar to be higher or lower than 5.6?

CHEMISTRY   Environmental chemistry

G1 Different types of soil

YOU WILL LEARN!
- that different soils have different characteristics, including pH ranges, and that this affects the plants that grow in them
- to locate information about plants and preferred soil types in secondary sources
- to use your knowledge of acids, alkalis and neutralisation to suggest ways of reducing the acidity of soils

In *Ascent! Book 2* you saw how rocks can be weathered (broken down), transported (moved from the place they were weathered), eroded (worn down) and then deposited as sediments. These sediments form the basis of soil.

Points to discuss

1. What will affect the different types of soil we find in different places?
2. What else, besides deposited rock fragments, do we find in soil?

We can classify soils into 6 main types:

- clay
- sandy
- silty
- peaty
- chalky
- loamy

The characteristics of each type of soil are determined by:

- the size of the rock fragments it contains,
- the chemical composition of the rock fragments, and
- the amount of organic materials mixed in it. This organic material is called **humus** and originates from living organisms.

For example, a clay soil contains very tiny particles of weathered rock. This means that there are few gaps between particles for water to drain through and the soil gets waterlogged. You can recognise clay soil as it is lumpy and sticky when wet but turns rock-hard when dry.

Compare this with a sandy soil, which feels gritty to the touch, and drains water quickly because of the larger rock particles present. The sandy soil does have a disadvantage in that heavy rain can wash away the soluble nutrients in the soil. We say that they are leached from the soil.

You can test the soil from different parts of the school to find out which type of soil you have.

There are different soil types and these are suitable for growing different plants

CHEMISTRY   **Environmental chemistry**

1 Which type of soil?

Do all the following tests to identify the soil type.

Touch test: Squeeze a handful of your soil sample gently then use the questions below:

1. Does it feel slimy and sticky, then stay in a lump when you open your hand?
   → It is clay soil.
2. Does it feel gritty and crumbly, then crumble apart when you open your hand?
   → It is sandy soil.
3. Does it feel spongy and springy?
   → It is peaty soil.
4. Does it feel smooth and keep its shape better than sandy soil, but not as well as clay when you open your hand?
   → It is a silty or loamy soil.

Safety: Wash your hands after this test.

Sedimentation test: Stir two large spatulas of soil in a beaker of water then leave it to stand for two hours:

1. Does the water look fairly clear and have a layer of sand on the bottom of the beaker?
   → It is sandy soil.
2. Is the water cloudy with a thin layer of particles on the bottom that took a long time to settle?
   → It is clay or silty soil.
3. Are there lots of bits floating on top of the water, with a little sediment on the bottom and a little cloudiness in the water?
   → It is peaty soil.
4. Is the water a pale greyish colour with a layer of white, gritty fragments on the bottom?
   → It is chalky soil.
5. Is the water fairly clear, with sediment which has formed in layers on the bottom – with the finest particles on top?
   → It is loamy soil.

Acidic soil

The pH of different soils can also vary. For example, peaty soil is acidic. You might recall from *Ascent! Book 1* that the remains of ancient bodies have been found remarkably preserved in peat bogs. This type of soil contains lots of organic material because it doesn't rot down in the acidic conditions. The bacteria that aid decomposition cannot thrive in the acidic soil. So although you might expect a peaty soil to be rich in nutrients because of animals and plants returning their nutrients to the soil, these tend to be 'locked up' in the organic matter as it doesn't decompose readily. Therefore, you need to add fertilisers, but then you have an excellent soil for growing plants as peaty soil holds moisture well.

You only find blue hydrangeas growing naturally in acidic soil

Alkaline soil

If you have a chalky soil you will find that its pH is 7.5 or above.

This is usually a stony soil that drains well. It is usually found above beds of chalk or limestone rock. The alkaline nature of the soil means that some essential elements needed for plant growth, such as manganese and iron, cannot be absorbed. This results in plants that have yellowing leaves (chlorosis) and poor growth. You can rectify this by adding fertilisers containing the missing nutrients.

Did you know?

The general name for the acids we find in peaty soil is humic acid. Can you see where this name originates from?

CHEMISTRY   Environmental chemistry

2 Testing the pH of soil

Test the soil samples to find out if they are acidic, alkaline or neutral.

Using deionised water, stir a spatula of soil in half a beaker of water.

Filter the mixture into a conical flask and test the filtrate (the clear solution in the flask) with narrow range universal indicator paper. Use a pH scale to find the pH value of the solution.

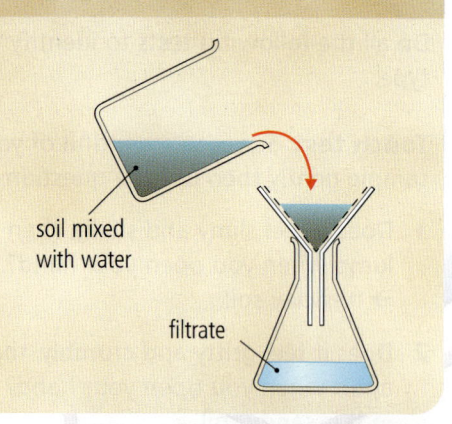

a Record your results, then rank them in order of acidity.
b Why did you add **deionised** water to the soil sample?

3 Neutralising acidic soil

Take a spatula of an acidic soil you tested in Activity 2 and mix in a spatula of powdered limestone. Repeat the method from Activity 2 to test the pH of the resulting solution.

a What is the pH of the soil mixed with limestone?
b Which is the main compound present in limestone?
c Write the general equation for a carbonate reacting with an acid.
d Lime (or calcium hydroxide) is also used to neutralise acidic soil.
    Write a general equation that could describe this neutralisation reaction.

Most plants grow best in soil with a pH value between 6.5 and 7.0 because their nutrients are most easily absorbed within this range. However, some plants prefer more acidic or alkaline conditions. Look at some examples in the table below:

Plants that grow well in acidic soil	Plants that grow well in alkaline soil
Heather	Some alpines
Camellia	Brassicas (cabbage family)
Rhododendron	Lilac tree
Azalea	Madonna lily

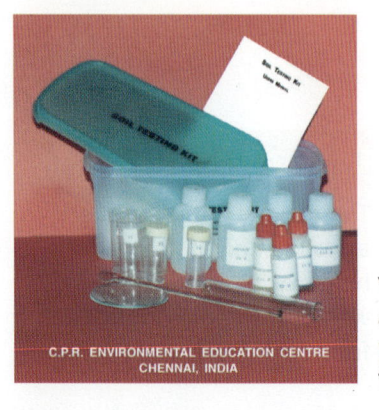

These plants prefer acidic conditions

You can buy soil testing kits from a garden centre. They can test your soil for vital minerals as well finding its pH value.

These plants prefer alkaline conditions

CHEMISTRY — Environmental chemistry

It is possible to adjust the pH of your soil to suit your plants. As you saw in Activity 3, we can raise the pH value of acidic soil by adding limestone or lime. Farmers do this on a large scale if they want to grow a crop that needs a higher pH range than their own soil has. However, it is more difficult to lower the pH of an alkaline soil for any length of time. Adding iron sulphate or vegetable compost can work, but the soil returns to its higher pH when the acids are washed away.

A low-cost soil testing kit is demonstrated to farmers in Thailand to help them operate more efficiently

4 Soil information sheet

Use secondary sources and the information in this unit to produce a fact sheet for a garden centre about growing plants in different types of soil.

If possible, use your ICT skills to ensure that your fact sheet includes images of plants and will attract customers to read the information.

CHEMISTRY   Environmental chemistry

G2 Weathering of rocks and building materials

YOU WILL LEARN!
- that rocks and building materials change over time
- about factors that affect the way in which materials change

Weathering is the breakdown of rock by physical or chemical means. In *Ascent! Book 2* you found out about the physical effects of changes in temperature and 'freeze-thaw'. You also looked at chemical weathering by the reaction of rocks with acidic rainwater. The process of weathering also affects building materials, such as brick, as well as rock we use directly to construct buildings, such as limestone.

Points to discuss

1 Look at the photos below and speculate on the type of weathering that has taken place.
2 Think about the factors that would make chemical weathering more rapid.

This statue and gravestone have been weathered over time

Bricks and mortar have been weathered in this old wall

Cleopatra's Needle in London

A similar obelisk that has stood in Egypt since it was built about 3500 yeas ago

Chemical weathering will take place more quickly if you have more concentrated acid, for example in areas affected by acid rain or in the ground beneath vegetation. High rainfall and high temperatures will also aid the breakdown of rocks by acidic solutions.

1 Weathering trail

Conduct a survey to find examples of weathering around your school grounds. Include the corrosion of metals and the decomposition of wooden structures.

Did you know?

Cleopatra's needle was built in Egypt in 1460BC. It was brought to London in 1878 on a specially designed ship. Six crew drowned during its very difficult voyage to England.

CHEMISTRY **Environmental chemistry**

G3 What causes acid rain?

YOU WILL LEARN!

▶ that the atmosphere contains carbon dioxide from natural sources and from the burning of fossil fuels, and that this can dissolve in rainwater causing it to be slightly acidic
▶ that dissolved oxides of sulphur and nitrogen increase the acidity of rain
▶ that oxides of sulphur in the air can arise from human activity and geological activity

Do you enjoy the slightly sharp taste of a sparkling mineral water? The tanginess comes from the dissolved carbon dioxide in the water that makes the solution weakly acidic. There is a small proportion of carbon dioxide in the air (just less than 0.04%) from natural processes, such as volcanic activity, respiration in living organisms and their eventual death and decomposition. This is enough to make rainwater naturally acidic, as we saw in G1. As we burn more and more fossil fuels, this also puts increasing amounts of carbon dioxide into the atmosphere. For example, when we burn natural gas, methane:

methane + oxygen → carbon dioxide + water
CH_4 + $2 O_2$ → CO_2 + $2 H_2O$

However, there are also impurities of sulphur present in fossil fuels. When we burn fossil fuels, especially coal in power stations, the sulphur is oxidised to sulphur dioxide:

sulphur + oxygen → sulphur dioxide
S + O_2 → SO_2

This is a major pollution problem because sulphur dioxide is the main cause of acid rain. The sulphur dioxide reacts with water and oxygen in the atmosphere to make sulphuric acid, which falls back to ground in rain, snow and fog. This acid reduces the pH value of rainwater below its natural level of about 5.6 and damages the environment. (See pages 115 to 117.)

1 Testing the pH of acid rain

Collect some rainwater and test its pH value.

Compare this with samples of deionised water, and solutions of carbon dioxide and sulphur dioxide in water.

Rank the samples in order of acidity and comment on your results.

As well as the combustion of fossil fuels, other industrial processes also result in sulphur dioxide emissions. These include the manufacture of sulphuric acid, smelting of ores to extract metals, making paper from wood pulp and the incineration of waste. The proportion of sulphur dioxide that can be traced back to each industry varies between countries. In some countries, such as Britain and the USA, power stations that burn fossil fuels are the main culprits, whereas in Canada, a larger part of its emissions result from smelting ores and other industrial processes.

Cars also contribute towards the problem of acid rain. Although we can now buy fuels that have a low sulphur content, cars give off oxides of nitrogen. These oxides react in the atmosphere to form nitric acid that eventually finds its way back to earth in rain.

In Britain, most of the sulphur dioxide we emit comes from burning fossil fuels in power stations

CHEMISTRY Environmental chemistry

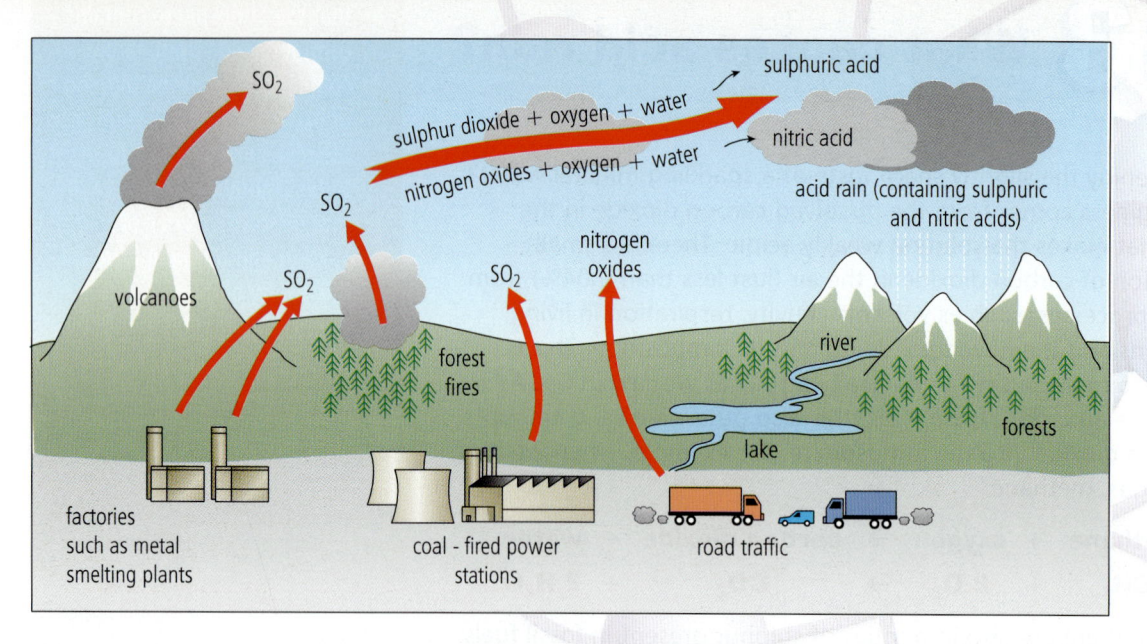

The sulphur dioxide in our atmosphere from volcanic activity is about 15% of the total made by human activity.

2 Summarising the sources of acid rain

a Summarise the information in the diagram above as a flow diagram.

b One oxide of nitrogen is nitrogen dioxide. What is its formula?

c Nitrogen dioxide reacts with oxygen and water in the air to make nitric acid (HNO_3). Write a word equation and a symbol equation to show this reaction.

Is it fair?

It is not always the countries that produce the largest amounts of acidic gases that suffer most from the consequences of acid rain. The oxides of sulphur and nitrogen can travel hundreds of miles in the atmosphere, blown by prevailing winds, so the acid rain affects neighbouring countries. For example, much of the pollution in the forests and lakes in Scandinavia originates from Britain. Pollutants from the USA affect large areas of Canada, and Japan suffers acid rain from gases given off by Chinese industry.

Countries meet to discuss setting targets for the reduction of pollutants

3 Tackling 'transboundary' pollution

We often hear that pollution is a global problem.

Find out about some conferences that have tackled issues on a global scale.

Which issues have they addressed?

What problems do they encounter?

Imagine you run a small hotel in the Swedish countryside.

Write a letter to the British prime minister expressing your concerns about your business as a result of acid rain.

(You may wish to refer to the effects of acid rain on pages 115 to 117.)

CHEMISTRY   Environmental chemistry

G4 The effects of acid rain

YOU WILL LEARN!

- about the effects of acid rain on rocks and building materials
- why acid rain will dissolve some building stones
- that acids in the environment can lead to corrosion of metals
- to make careful observations over time
- that acid rain damages living organisms
- about ways in which emissions of oxides causing acid rain can be reduced
- to use secondary information to find information about key questions related to acid rain

You can now apply the work you have done on acids to the issue of acid rain. You should be able to predict the type of rock and metals that will be attacked by acids, and suggest the products that will form.

1 Investigating attack by acid rain

You will be given a dilute solution of sulphuric acid or nitric acid to simulate the effects of the acids in rain on different structural materials. The materials you can investigate are:

- different types of rock (including sandstones and limestones);
- different types of metals (including zinc, iron, copper and lead).

You can also test mortar (what binds bricks to each other) and concrete.

This investigation will have to be carried out over several weeks as some of the chemical reactions will be slow. Make sure you set up control experiments using water instead of acid. You can work with other groups, then draw your results together at the end of the investigation.

Design a table in which you can record your observations carefully.

a From your knowledge of the reactions of acids, which metals would you expect to react with the acid rain solutions?

b Give a word and symbol equation for one metal that will react with dilute sulphuric acid.

c Name a metal that you would not expect to react with dilute acid.

d Which rocks would you expect to react with dilute acids? What would be formed?

As well as acid rain, buildings are also affected by dry deposits of acids that form more concentrated solutions on damp stone or metal. We have already seen how dilute acids react with carbonates and some metals, dissolving them away. Over time statues lose their fine features as the carbonate rock (such as marble, which contains calcium carbonate) is broken down and washed away.

Many ancient monuments, such as the Taj Mahal in India, the Colosseum in Rome and the Parthenon in Athens are showing advanced signs of attack by acid rain.

Metal structures need protecting with acid-resistant paint so that corrosion does not weaken them.

Effects on plants

Some soils can cope well with acid rain. In G1 we saw that alkaline soils are found on beds of chalk or limestone. Fragments of the rocks are mixed in with soil. These rock fragments contain

CHEMISTRY   Environmental chemistry

calcium carbonate, which will neutralise the acid rain. However, thin soils on top of granite or gneiss rock, cannot neutralise much acid and essential nutrients get washed from the soil. This affects the growth of plants. Not only that, but acid rain attacks the waxy coating on leaves that helps prevent water loss from a plant. The plants are also more prone to diseases and attack from insects.

Forests at high altitudes are particularly vulnerable to attack by acid rain as they spend long periods of time in contact with the tiny droplets of acidic solution in the clouds. For example, the spruce forests high in the Appalachian mountains in the eastern USA are now in decline, and half the trees in the famous Black Forest in Germany have been affected by acid rain and other pollution.

2 Acid rain and plant growth

In this activity you can look at the effect of sulphur dioxide on the germination and growth of cress.

Set up the experiment below. Add equal volumes of water to moisten the cotton wool in each gas jar.

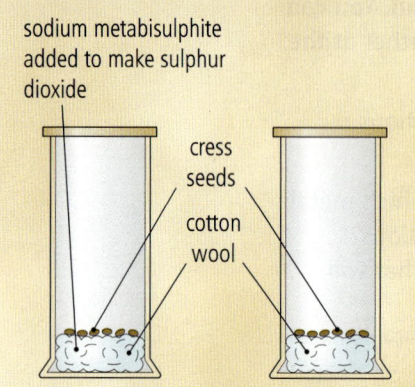

The sodium metabisulphite will give off sulphur dioxide gas.

Safety: Take care not to inhale sulphur dioxide.

Record your observations and conclusions in a suitable format.

These trees have been attacked by acid rain

Effects on wildlife

The most serious effects on wildlife are seen in lakes and rivers affected by acid rain. Some aquatic animals, such as mayfly, are very sensitive to changes in pH and cannot survive in water whose pH value drops below about 6. Others may be more resistant, but once one part of the food chain is broken the knock-on effects, for example on frogs, will follow.

In Norway, acid rain has affected all the major rivers, and populations of salmon and trout are falling. If the pH drops below 5, fish eggs will not hatch, and once it falls below 4.5, as it has in thousands of lakes in Scandinavia, no animal life survives.

CHEMISTRY   Environmental chemistry

Fighting the effects of acid rain

Some lakes have had to be neutralised by dropping powdered limestone into the water. This reacts with the acid and raises the pH of the water to a level where wildlife can be re-introduced.

We have also seen how acidic soil is neutralised by farmers, using powdered limestone or lime (calcium hydroxide) on their fields.

Powdered limestone is used to neutralise acidic lakes

Stopping acid rain

However, it is better to stop the acidic gases ever reaching the atmosphere in the first place.
There are three approaches to help with this problem:
- use less fossil fuels
- remove the sulphur from a fossil fuel before you burn it
- prevent the acidic gases, given off when a fuel burns, escaping into the atmosphere.

3 Researching acid rain

Use books, CD ROMs and the Internet to find more information about acid rain. Examples of questions you could find out are:

Which places are badly affected by acid rain? How has acid rain affected these places?

How do catalytic converters fitted to cars help reduce acid rain?

How are acidic gases removed from the flue gases in power stations and factories?

What are the alternatives to burning fossil fuels to generate electricity?

How can we all use less electricity?

Each member of your group can research a different aspect of the problem. Then collate your reports into a display to share with the rest of your class.

Did you know ?

Songbirds in the Netherlands are finding fewer snails to eat. The snails are being affected by acid rain. This is weakening the birds' eggshells as they now get less calcium in their diet.

Did you know ?

Catalytic converters fitted to car exhausts contain precious metals, such as platinum.

CHEMISTRY   Environmental chemistry

G5 Monitoring pollution

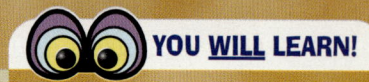

YOU WILL LEARN!
- how air or water pollution is monitored and controlled
- to decide what evidence should be collected
- to collect evidence to answer a question
- how to decide whether evidence is good enough to answer a question
- to appraise texts quickly for their usefulness
- to recognise the author's standpoint and how it affects the meaning

Points to discuss

Do you think that air pollution is worse now than 50 years ago?

Think of reasons to explain your opinion.

The industrial revolution in the 19th century resulted in lots of coal being burned in cities. Their populations increased as people flocked into towns for the new jobs created. Coal fires were the main source of heat in the workers' homes. Therefore, the smoke and sulphur dioxide gas released from factories and from domestic use became intolerable.

Look at the quotation below:

> 'It has often been observed that the stones and bricks of buildings crumble more readily in large towns where much coal is burnt … I was led to attribute this effect to the slow but constant action of acid rain.'

This was said by Robert Angus Smith, the scientist who first used the term 'acid rain', in 1856; and it was exactly a century later that the first Clean Air Act was passed in response to the Great London Smog of 1952. Other smoke reduction acts had been necessary in 1875 and 1926, but the suffocating smog (combination of smoke and fog) that clung to London in the winter of 1952 brought the problem of urban pollution to a head. About 4000 extra deaths were recorded in the city before Christmas that year. Look at the graph below:

The Great Smog of 1952. London had become famous for its terrible smogs (or 'pea-soupers' as Londoners called them).

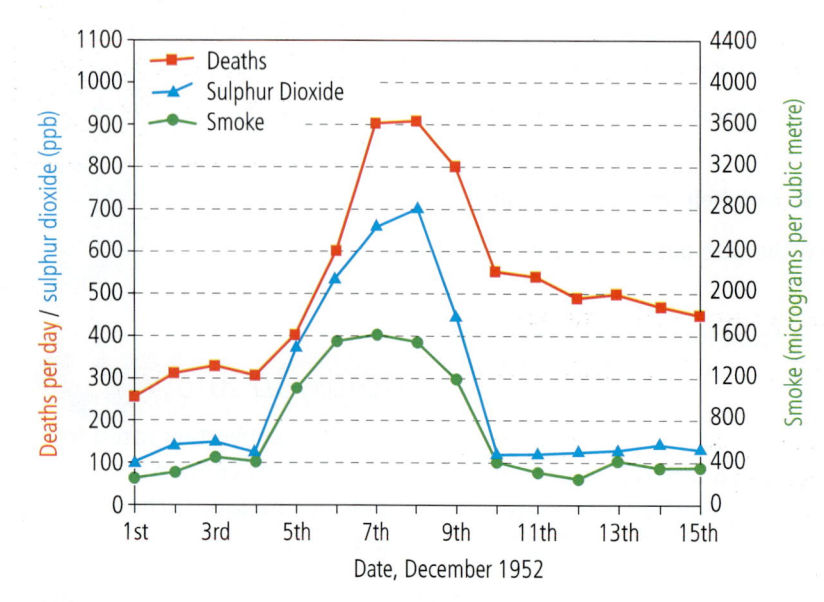

118

CHEMISTRY   Environmental chemistry

1 Patterns in data

Look at the graph showing the deaths in London during the early part of December, 1952.

a What pattern can you see in the data for the first half of December, 1952 in London?
b What caused the smoke and sulphur dioxide?
c What do you think were the kind of illnesses brought on by the Great Smog?
d Why didn't the death rate fall to its level before the Great Smog after it had dispersed?
e What kind of weather conditions allowed the smog to hang over London for almost a week?

The Clean Air Act, passed four years later, forced people to use 'smokeless' forms of coal. A later Clean Air Act, in 1968, also made industry discharge its gases from tall chimneys in built-up areas. However, we have seen in G3 that this just passes the pollutants on to another place.

Further pollution control measures followed these acts, and the quality of our air has improved in many respects, although the massive increase in cars that started in the 1980s remains a concern.

Local Authorities are now responsible for monitoring air and water quality in their areas and the figures are available for the public to inspect (for example on local and national environmental websites).

Nowadays we monitor air quality at about 1500 sites across the UK, using ever more sensitive equipment. The Environment Agency also uses sophisticated computer modelling to predict pollution levels.

However, this is not totally accurate because emission levels at a particular place are affected by unpredictable weather patterns. Some regions have their air quality reported on local TV stations as part of their weather broadcasts, for example Anglia Air Watch.

In the USA, air quality is monitored and standards are set by the Environmental Protection Agency. They check six major air pollutants:

- carbon monoxide,
- lead,
- ozone,
- nitrogen dioxide,
- sulphur dioxide, and
- **particulate matter** (tiny solid particles suspended in the air)

They have reported the following improvements in air quality from 1982 to 2001:

Sulphur dioxide has decreased by 52%, carbon monoxide by 62%, nitrogen dioxide by 24% and lead by 94%.

119

CHEMISTRY   Environmental chemistry

Points to discuss

1 Look at the figures on page 119 and comment on how such improvements could have been brought about.
2 What problems do you think there are in looking at long-term trends in pollution? What can you say about the data we have nowadays compared to that available 20, 50 or 100 years ago?
3 How do you think scientists today can get clues about the composition of the air as it was hundreds of years ago (or even longer ago in history)?

Did you know
About 95% of the rivers in the UK have had their chemical quality classified as good or fair by the Environment Agency.

Water pollution

Water is an excellent solvent for many substances. This is a very useful property, but also makes rivers and lakes susceptible to soluble pollutants leached from the land. Fertilisers get into the rivers and lakes causing **eutrophication**. Algae flourish, cutting off light to plants on the riverbed. The numbers of bacteria multiply as they feed on the algae, which eventually die. The bacteria use up the dissolved oxygen in the water, and fish and other aquatic animals effectively suffocate. Sewage and phosphate detergents cause similar effects in rivers.

Water is also used as a coolant in power stations. This can cause **thermal pollution** if water is put back into the river at a higher temperature. Oxygen gas is less soluble in warmer water, and the delicate balance of ecosystems is disturbed. Other river pollutants come from factories discharging waste. There are strict controls, but sometimes accidents occur and prosecution through the courts follows.

There are 7000 sites in rivers and canals that are monitored by the UK Environmental Agency for water quality. The good news is that tighter controls and monitoring are improving the quality of most of our waterways.

Pollutants in water upset the delicate balance of life in a river

Careful monitoring using sensitive instruments is improving the quality of rivers

2 Finding out more about air or water pollution

Think of a question that you would like to find out about concerning the quality of air or water.

Use books and the Internet to find information.

Look out for any bias in reports from particular sources and report on this, as well as other findings, to the rest of your class.

120

CHEMISTRY — Environmental chemistry

G6 The issue of global warming

YOU WILL LEARN!
- to use secondary sources to answer scientific questions
- how to decide whether evidence is good enough to answer a question
- to evaluate evidence put forward by others
- to discuss and evaluate conflicting evidence to arrive at a considered viewpoint

You've probably heard of the Greenhouse Effect and global warming, but do you know the main gas being blamed for increasing average global temperatures? Carbon dioxide, along with water vapour, is the main 'greenhouse' gas. The molecules of a 'greenhouse' gas absorb the heat given off by the Earth as it cools down at night – in effect trapping the heat in the atmosphere and warming the Earth. In fact, without carbon dioxide in our atmosphere, it has been estimated that the average temperature on Earth would be −19 °C!

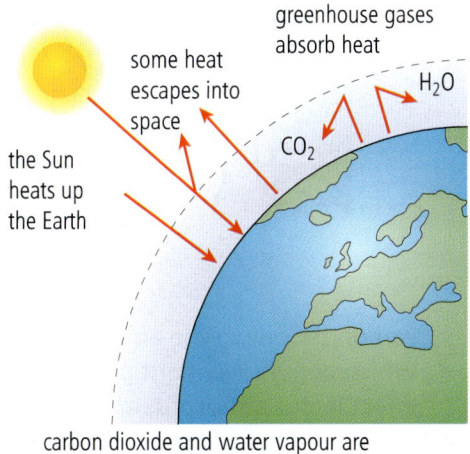

the Sun heats up the Earth; some heat escapes into space; greenhouse gases absorb heat (H_2O, CO_2); carbon dioxide and water vapour are the main 'greenhouse gases'

Did you know
The gases that have caused a hole to appear in our ozone layer – CFCs or chlorofluorocarbons – are also very effective 'greenhouse' gases. Fortunately, their levels are now decreasing, so ozone depletion is slowing down and the latest reports from Antarctica suggest the hole is actually shrinking.

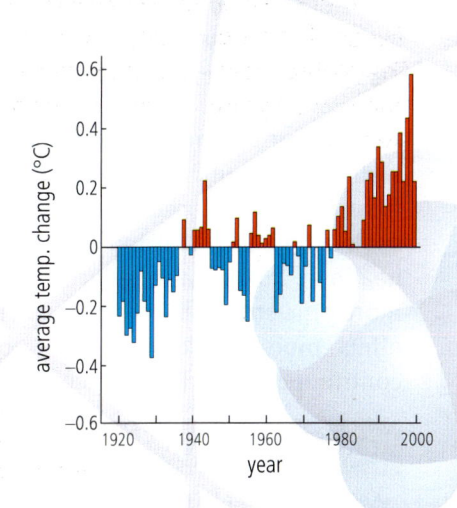

The problem of increased carbon dioxide levels arises because, as we mentioned in G5, the amount of fossil fuels we are using up has increased alarmingly in recent history. We have burned more fossil fuels in the last 200 years than the estimated total since humans first inhabited our planet. Remember that fossil fuels are made up of carbon compounds which react with oxygen to produce carbon dioxide when they burn. Not surprisingly, the proportion of carbon dioxide in the air has increased.

Look at the diagram opposite.

1 Temperature patterns

a Does the graph show a steady pattern?
b What is the general pattern in the data?
c Is this enough data to be certain that the Earth's average temperature is rising and will continue to do so if carbon dioxide levels keep rising? Explain your answer.

Many scientists agree that we are now seeing the start of global warming. For example, six of the ten warmest years ever recorded were in the 1990s and the other four were in the previous decade. But even on this point there is some disagreement.

CHEMISTRY Environmental chemistry

The main opponent of current theories on global warming is an American scientist called Richard S. Lindzen. He argues that the recent rises observed are due to natural variations in temperature that have happened throughout the long history of the Earth. The last major change was the Ice Age, about 12 000 years ago.

Despite advances in science, we cannot predict with certainty the effects of increasing carbon dioxide levels – even with the aid of our most powerful computers. Lindzen thinks that the computer models used are flawed and that data gathered on climate change over the last one thousand years is not reliable.

However, other leading scientists, who have deduced temperatures from before records began, from tree rings and samples of ice from deep within ice caps, are confident in their data. They believe we are at the start of a slippery slope whose effects could be:

- increased sea levels and flooding of low-lying areas
- changing weather patterns all over the world
- extinction of some species of animals.

2 What's your viewpoint?

Use books, CD ROMs and the Internet to gather more information about global warming. Here are some questions to investigate. Think up some of your own questions too.

- Which other gases, besides carbon dioxide and water vapour, are 'greenhouse' gases?
- How are governments tackling the problem?
- How can we help reduce the levels of carbon dioxide in the atmosphere by our own actions?
- What temperature rise would a doubling of carbon dioxide in the air bring with it?
- Which pollutants might produce a cooling effect in our atmosphere?
- Why are people worried about the destruction of the Amazon rainforest?

Consider for which questions you can be certain of the answers you find and which are open to debate. Why might some information be biased?

Listen to feedback from others in your group, then form your own conclusions about global warming.

At the moment, most of our electricity is generated in power stations that burn fossil fuels. So if we can use less electricity, less fossil fuel will be used up and less CO_2 will be released. We can also use our cars less. Walking and cycling will not only make us healthier, but will also reduce emissions. If we have to drive, it is more efficient to share lifts or use public transport. But to have any effect, more people must start to believe that we can all make a contribution to reducing pollution!

Did you know

As our climate in the UK gets warmer it has been predicted that more than a quarter of our species of butterflies will die out. They will be forced north to find cooler conditions, but their favoured habitats, such as heathland, will be impossible to find. We are already seeing the effect as mountain butterflies are moving to ever higher altitudes – but conservationists are worried that Britain's mountains aren't high enough for this to go on much longer.

The mountain ringlet butterfly is in danger of extinction

CHEMISTRY   Environmental chemistry

Summary

There are many different types of soil. The basis of all soils is the rock from which it was originally weathered. This, along with vegetation, affects the pH of the soil. Some soils containing limestone or chalk fragments are basic and can resist the lowering of pH caused by **acid rain**.

Acid rain is caused mainly by **sulphur dioxide** gas given off from the combustion of fossil fuels (especially coal), industry (such as the extraction of metals from sulphide ores), and natural sources (such as volcanic activity). In fossil fuels, the sulphur is present as an impurity which burns to give sulphur dioxide:

sulphur + oxygen → sulphur dioxide

This reacts with oxygen and water in the air to form **sulphuric acid**.

We can reduce the problem by removing sulphur before burning the fossil fuel, preventing the sulphur dioxide gas escaping (by neutralising the acidic gas) or by burning less fuel.

Nitrogen oxides from cars also cause acid rain (forming **nitric acid**). Catalytic converters on exhausts help remove this source of pollution.

Global warming is caused by 'greenhouse' gases, such as carbon dioxide, in the atmosphere. Once again, burning fossil fuels produces this gas. For example, when we burn natural gas:

methane + oxygen → carbon dioxide + water

There is some debate about whether the increasing temperatures noted in the last few decades are just natural variations and to what extent they are caused by human activity. However, most people agree that it is sensible to reduce the volumes of carbon dioxide produced.

Careful monitoring and controls on pollutants are helping to combat the effects of our industrialised societies on the environment.

Key words

- acid rain
- biased
- catalytic converter
- eutrophication
- global warming
- ozone depletion
- reliable
- thermal pollution

Did you know ?

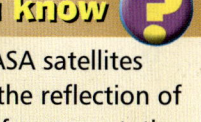

In 2001, NASA satellites measuring the reflection of green light from vegetation, noted that Europe has become 12% 'greener' since 1981.

This could be due to the increased carbon dioxide in the atmosphere favouring photosynthesis. This might help to slow down the effects of global warming as lusher vegetation with more leaves will have a greater capacity to remove carbon dioxide from the atmosphere.

Summary Questions

1. Draw a concept map linking the following terms. Don't forget to label your links.
   acid rain; global warming; carbon dioxide; sulphur dioxide; nitrogen oxides; fossil fuels; trees

2. a Name the salt formed when calcium carbonate reacts with a dilute solution of:
   i sulphuric acid
   ii nitric acid
   b What will be the effect of acid rain on a sandstone held together by a matrix of carbonate mineral?

3. This question is about the gas ozone. Find out the answers to the following questions:
   a What is the chemical formula of ozone?
   b Why has a hole appeared in the ozone layer?
   c Where is the hole in the ozone layer?
   d Why is ozone in the stratosphere important for life on Earth?
   e Ozone at ground level is considered a pollutant. Where does it come from?

End of unit Questions

1. The table shows the pH of five soil samples. Use letters from the table to answer questions **a**, **b** and **c**.

soil sample	pH of soil
A	6.0
B	7.5
C	7.0
D	4.5
E	8.0

   a Which soil sample is neutral? *1 mark*

   b i Most types of heather grow better in acidic soil. In which of the soil samples should heather grow well? *1 mark*

   ii Cabbage grows better in alkaline soil. In which of the soil samples should cabbage grow well? *1 mark*

   c Lime is an alkaline substance which is sometimes put onto acidic soils. What type of reaction takes place between the lime and the acid? *1 mark*

2. Copper can be obtained from its ore, copper sulfide, in two stages.

   First stage heating the ore in air
   Copper sulphide reacts with oxygen from the air to form copper oxide and sulphur dioxide gas.

   Second stage heating the copper oxide with carbon
   Copper oxide reacts with carbon to form copper and carbon dioxide gas.

   a Give the names of **three** elements mentioned above. *1 mark*

   b Give the name of **one** compound mentioned above. *1 mark*

   c Give the name of the compound, mentioned above, which causes 'acid rain'. *1 mark*

3. Copper can be extracted from an ore called copper pyrites. The formula of copper pyrites is $CuFeS_2$.

   a Give the names of the three elements present in copper pyrites. *1 mark*

   b Copper is obtained by heating the ore in a controlled supply of air with sand (SiO_2). Overall the reaction is:

   $2CuFeS_2 + 5O_2 + 2SiO_2 \rightarrow 2Cu + 4SO_2 + 2FeSiO_3$

   i The amount of oxygen in the reaction must be carefully controlled. If there is too much, the copper could react with the oxygen.
   What substance would be formed? *1 mark*

   ii In the industrial process, the waste gas sulphur dioxide (SO_2) is removed. It is bubbled through a solution that reacts with the sulphur dioxide and prevents it escaping.
   Explain why the sulphur dioxide should be removed from the waste gases. *2 marks*

   iii What **type** of solution is used to remove the sulphur dioxide? *1 mark*

4. Petrol contains a compound called octane. The chemical formula of octane is C_8H_{18}.

   a Write a word equation for the complete combustion of octane. *1 mark*

   b Other gases are produced when petrol burns in a car's engine. Compounds of nitrogen formed contribute to acid rain. Which compounds of nitrogen are given off? *1 mark*

   c A catalytic converter, once warm, can remove these compounds of nitrogen from the exhaust gases from a car. It can also convert toxic carbon monoxide to carbon dioxide. However carbon dioxide is associated with an environmental issue itself. Which problem is associated with carbon dioxide gas? *1 mark*

   d Give two ways in which we can reduce the amount of carbon dioxide gas in the atmosphere. *2 marks*

9H Using chemistry

Introduction

In this unit you can remind yourself of earlier work on chemical reactions. You will focus on the use of chemical reactions as the sources of energy and as the means to manufacture new materials, developing your understanding of chemical equations as you see the relevance of chemistry in everyday life.

You already know

- the test for carbon dioxide
- that burning involves a reaction with oxygen in which oxides are formed
- that new materials are formed when chemical reactions occur and can identify evidence for these reactions
- how to represent chemical reactions by word and symbol equations
- that metals are placed in order of their reactivity in the Reactivity Series

In this topic you will learn

- more about how we can use chemical reactions as a source of energy
- how chemical reactions are used to make new materials
- how to model chemical reactions as the rearrangement of atoms, and use the model to explain why no matter is lost in a reaction
- to show more chemical reactions by their word and symbol equations

1 What can you remember?

a Which gas from the air is used up as a match burns?
b How can you tell that a chemical reaction is taking place?
c Carbon dioxide gas is one of the products of the burning match. How can you test for the presence of carbon dioxide?

CHEMISTRY   Using chemistry

H1 Energy from burning fuels

YOU WILL LEARN!
- that fuels burn and release energy
- that when fuels containing hydrogen and carbon burn in plenty of oxygen we get water and carbon dioxide formed
- that when fuels burn in insufficient oxygen we can get carbon monoxide and carbon formed as well as other products of combustion
- to evaluate advantages and disadvantages of a fuel
- to apply knowledge and understanding of burning to an everyday context

In *Ascent! Book 1* you saw what happens when we burn natural gas containing methane, CH_4. Methane is called a **hydrocarbon** because it is a compound made up of only hydrogen and carbon. Hydrocarbons make up the majority of compounds in the fossil fuels oil and natural gas. When a hydrocarbon burns in a plentiful supply of air (so that they get sufficient oxygen to burn completely), carbon dioxide and water are the **products of combustion**.

For example, propane gas, C_3H_8, from crude oil is used in some household gas heaters:

$$\text{propane} + \text{oxygen} \rightarrow \text{carbon dioxide} + \text{water}$$
$$C_3H_8 + 5\,O_2 \rightarrow 3\,CO_2 + 4\,H_2O$$

Reactions that give out heat are called **exothermic** reactions.

So, the combustion of a fuel is an example of an exothermic reaction.

Another fuel is ethanol, C_2H_5OH. This is the compound found in all alcoholic drinks. (Why isn't ethanol a hydrocarbon?) In Brazil, cars run on ethanol (or a mixture of ethanol and petrol). They can grow plenty of sugar cane which they ferment with yeast to make ethanol. Unlike Britain, they don't have their own supplies of crude oil – from which we separate our petrol.

You can see what happens when we burn ethanol in the experiment below:

Did you know
The mixture of petrol and ethanol used in Brazilian cars is called 'gasohol'. Can you think where the name came from?

1 Burning ethanol

a Predict the word equation for the combustion of ethanol.
  Now watch the experiment:

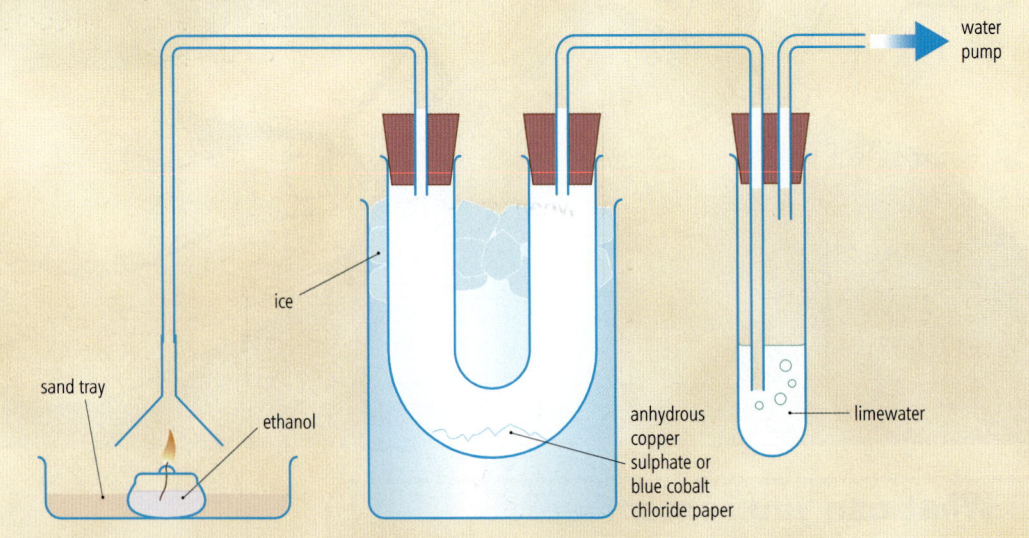

[Diagram labels: water pump, sand tray, ethanol, ice, anhydrous copper sulphate or blue cobalt chloride paper, limewater]

b Which product do we test for in the U tube? Why is the U tube surrounded by ice?
c Which product do we test for with limewater?
d Describe your observations.
e Construct a word and symbol equation for the combustion of ethanol.
f Why would it be a good idea to conduct a control experiment. How could you do this?

CHEMISTRY Using chemistry

Some of the energy released when fuels burn can be transferred into useful energy, such as the energy from burning ethanol used in Brazilian cars.

The ethanol burns with a 'clean' blue flame in the previous experiment. However, liquid hydrocarbon fuels tend to produce some black smoke as they burn with yellow flames. The smoke is made up of small particles of solid carbon from the fuel. Not all the carbon in the fuel is converted completely into carbon dioxide. We call this **incomplete combustion**. These fine particles are given off from diesel engines and are harmful when breathed into our lungs. They can cause cancer.

In a car engine, petrol or diesel is ignited in a limited space inside the pistons, so we get incomplete combustion of the fuel. As well as carbon dioxide and water vapour, we also get the toxic gas carbon monoxide, CO, released as a pollutant (along with unburnt hydrocarbon fuel and carbon particles). This gas is so dangerous because it is odourless and effectively starves your cells of oxygen. It bonds to haemoglobin, the molecule that carries oxygen around your bloodstream, just like oxygen does. However, the oxygen–haemoglobin bond breaks when the oxygen arrives at the point it is needed for respiration, whereas the carbon monoxide–haemoglobin bond is permanent. After breathing in the toxic gas for a while, the carbon monoxide takes up most of the haemoglobin molecules so you suffer from a lack of oxygen. Drowsiness is followed by unconsciousness and death.

We use the energy from fuels in transport

Cars release a variety of pollutants into the air. Catalytic converters (once they are warmed up) can turn carbon monoxide into carbon dioxide and nitrogen oxides into nitrogen. They also convert unburnt hydrocarbons to carbon dioxide and water vapour.

2 Hydrogen – fuel of the future?

Find out about the advantages and disadvantages of using hydrogen gas as a fuel.

Present your findings in a two-column table.

Burning matches

Have you ever wondered how matches ignite when you strike them?

Look at the match head below:

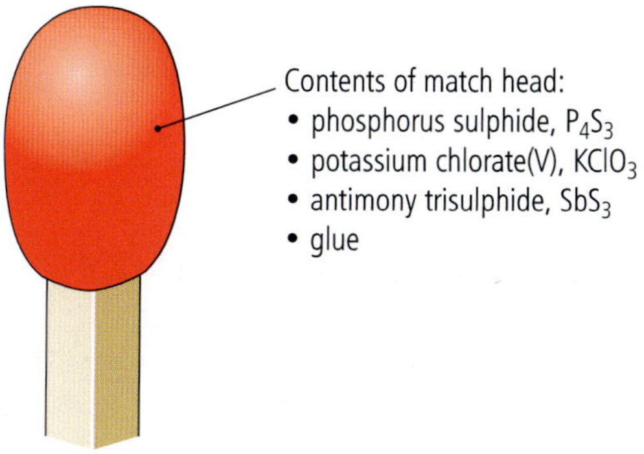

Contents of match head:
- phosphorus sulphide, P_4S_3
- potassium chlorate(V), $KClO_3$
- antimony trisulphide, SbS_3
- glue

127

CHEMISTRY   Using chemistry

When you strike the match on a rough surface (such as the sandpaper on the side of the box) the friction causes heat energy to start a chemical reaction in the head of the match. The phosphorus sulphide decomposes and burns at this relatively low temperature. This sets off the combustion reaction of antimony sulphide, which is made more vigorous by potassium chlorate(V). The potassium chlorate(V) is called an **oxidising agent** and provides oxygen for the combustion. The temperature is now hot enough to set fire to the wooden matchstick.

Did you know

The first friction match was invented in 1826 by a pharmacist called John Walker from Stockton-on-Tees. He made very little money from his invention as he refused to patent his idea.

3 Matches

a Summarise the information above in a flow diagram entitled 'Striking a match'.
b How many atoms are in a molecule of phosphorus sulphide?
c How many elements are there in antimony trisulphide?
d How can you tell from the name of potassium chlorate(V) that it contains the element oxygen?
e Potassium chlorate(V) decomposes on heating to form potassium chloride and oxygen. Write a word equation and a symbol equation for this thermal decomposition reaction.

Read the information below then answer the questions:

'Safety' matches work by separating some of the reactants in the match-making mixture between the match head and the striking board on the side of the box.

A mixture of red phosphorus and powdered glass is glued to the side of the box. The match head contains a mixture of sulphur, antimony trisulphide and potassium chlorate. The red phosphorus turns into the more reactive white phosphorus in the heat from the friction as the match is struck. This white phosphorus bursts into flame spontaneously as it reacts with oxygen in the air, setting off the combustion reaction in the match head.

f Why is powdered glass used in the manufacture of safety matches?
g Which two substances are used in the form of elements in safety matches?
h White phosorus, P_4, burns in air to form phosphorus pentoxide, P_2O_5.
   Write a word equation and a symbol equation for this reaction.

Did you know

Many matchmakers a hundred years ago suffered from a bone disease called 'phossy jaw' because the mixture contained toxic white phosphorus. The Diamond Matchmaking Company patented the use of non-toxic phosphorus sulphide in 1910, but was persuaded the next year to release the patent by the US president 'for the good of mankind'.

CHEMISTRY Using chemistry

H2 Energy from other chemical reactions

> **YOU WILL LEARN!**
> ► that displacement reactions involving metals and their compounds release energy
> ► that energy from these reactions can be used
> ► to link energy produced in displacement reactions to differences in the reactivity of metals

Chemical energy into heat energy

In Unit 9F we looked at the Reactivity Series of metals. On page 101 we saw how a more reactive metal can displace a less reactive metal from a solution of one of its salts. These displacement reactions, like combustion reactions, are exothermic. They release stored chemical energy as heat. For example:

zinc sulphate + magnesium → magnesium sulphate + zinc

$ZnSO_4$ + Mg → $MgSO_4$ + Zn

You can investigate the energy given out during these reactions in the following activity.

1 Heat energy from displacement reactions

Using the same metals and solutions as Activity 2 on page 102, plan an investigation to find out which reactions give out most energy.

Remember to make your tests as fair as possible. How will you do this?

What measuring equipment will you need?

Predict the outcome of your investigation by placing the various reactions in order of energy released. Explain your reasoning.

Design a table to record your results in.

Show your plan to your teacher before you start any practical work.

What conclusions can you draw?

Evaluate the quality of the data collected.

I SUPPOSE YOU THINK YOU'RE PRETTY HOT STUFF, EH MAGNESIUM!

CHEMISTRY   Using chemistry

Chemical energy into electrical energy

We can use the energy from displacement reactions to make electrical cells. The chemical energy stored can be transferred directly to electrical energy by connecting the metals in the following arrangement:

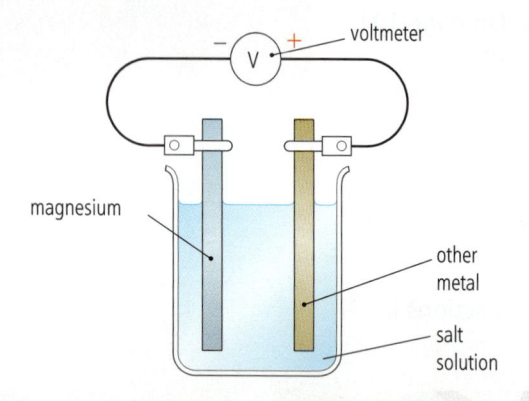

2 Measuring differences in reactivity

Using the apparatus above, measure the voltage between different pairs of metals used in the previous investigation.

Record your results in a table.

Were your results as expected?

You know the position of lead in the Reactivity Series.

Predict the voltage you will obtain by combining lead with each of the other 4 metals.

Evaluate your predictions experimentally.

We find that:

the greater the difference in reactivity between two metals, the larger the voltage produced.

You can find out more about making electrical cells in Unit 9I.

Endothermic reactions

Not all reactions are exothermic, giving out energy.

Some reactions take in energy from their surroundings and the temperature falls. These are called **endothermic** reactions.

3 Endothermic changes

Take the temperature of 25 cm³ of sodium hydrogencarbonate solution in a poly(styrene) beaker.

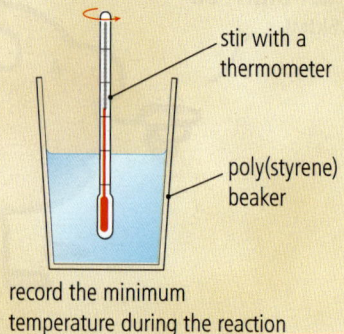

a Record this initial temperature.

Now add a spatula of citric acid crystals and stir with your thermometer.

b Record the minimum temperature.
c What do you observe in the reaction?
d Which have more energy – the reactants or the products? Explain your reasoning.

Watch your teacher dissolve ammonium nitrate in water. Touch the outside of the glass beaker.

e What do you feel?

CHEMISTRY Using chemistry

H3 More useful exothermic reactions

YOU WILL LEARN!
- that other reactions can be used as sources of energy
- about ways in which these reactions can be used
- about when to use different styles of writing

Do you watch any sporting events in winter? If you do, you will know that spectators can get painfully cold. And that's when chemical hand and body warmers can be very useful. These products use exothermic reactions to warm you up.

Read the information provided by one distributor about how hand warmers work:

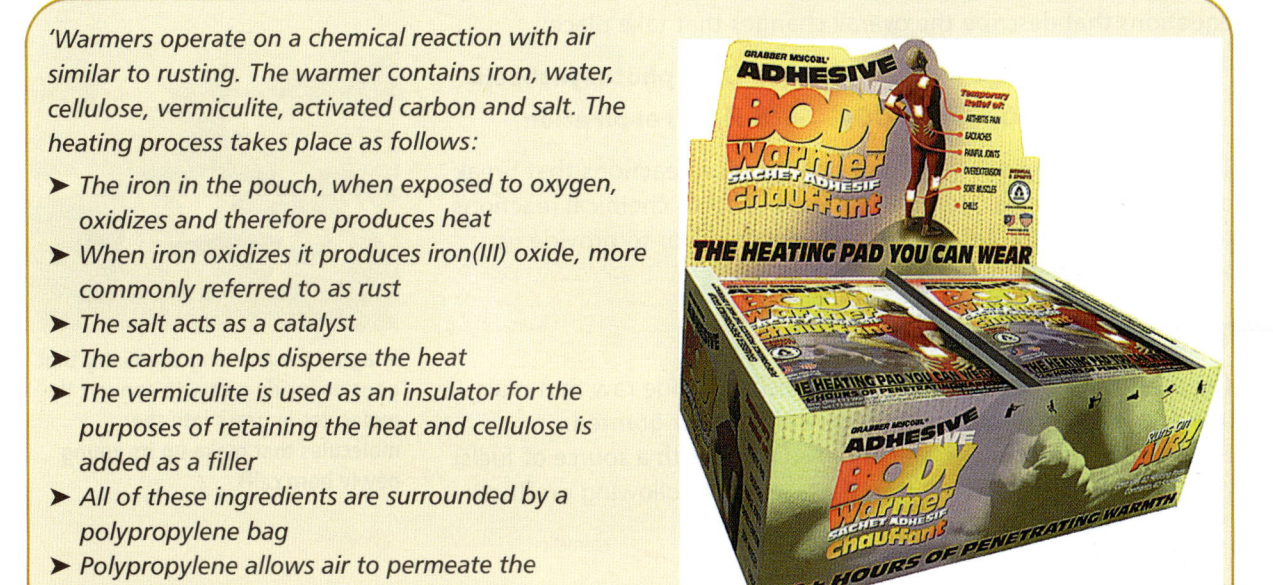

> 'Warmers operate on a chemical reaction with air similar to rusting. The warmer contains iron, water, cellulose, vermiculite, activated carbon and salt. The heating process takes place as follows:
> - The iron in the pouch, when exposed to oxygen, oxidizes and therefore produces heat
> - When iron oxidizes it produces iron(III) oxide, more commonly referred to as rust
> - The salt acts as a catalyst
> - The carbon helps disperse the heat
> - The vermiculite is used as an insulator for the purposes of retaining the heat and cellulose is added as a filler
> - All of these ingredients are surrounded by a polypropylene bag
> - Polypropylene allows air to permeate the ingredients while holding in moisture.'
>
> (from Grabber Performance Group)

1 Hand warmers

Using the information above and reference books answer the following questions:

a Write a word equation for the exothermic reaction that produces the heat.

b Common salt is used as a catalyst in the hand warmers. What does this mean?

c What is the chemical name and formula of common salt?

d How do you think that the exothermic reaction is started?

e How does the plastic bag allow the reactants to meet?

2 Hot food

Mountaineers and explorers can take 'self-heating' foods with them on their adventures. One sort uses the energy given out when calcium oxide reacts with water to heat the food.

a Design a self-heating, disposable food container for stew. Consider any safety issues involved in using your product.

b Write a technical specification describing how to manufacture your container.

c Write an advert for a mountaineering magazine to publicise your invention.

CHEMISTRY Using chemistry

H4 Making new materials

> **YOU WILL LEARN!**
> ▶ about the range of materials made through chemical reactions
> ▶ about the stages of development of a new product

Biochemistry

Living things are amazing chemical factories, making new large molecules from small ones, and breaking down others, by means of chemical reactions. The study of reactions in living things is called biochemistry. Our understanding of the reactions has made giant strides in the last hundred years. Biological processes, such as photosynthesis and respiration can be summarised by chemical equations that describe the overall changes that take place:

$$6\ CO_2 + 6\ H_2O \rightarrow C_6H_{12}O_6 + 6\ O_2 \quad \text{photosynthesis}$$
$$C_6H_{12}O_6 + 6\ O_2 \rightarrow 6\ CO_2 + 6\ H_2O \quad \text{respiration}$$

The process of digestion is a series of chemical reactions that break down food molecules, ready to be used in other chemical reactions to make new molecules (for example, proteins) or to provide us with the energy we need in respiration.

The chemical industry

The chemical industry relies on reactions to change raw materials into a vast range of products that we all take for granted. For example, crude oil (as well as providing us with a source of fuels) is also a raw material in the manufacture of the following products:

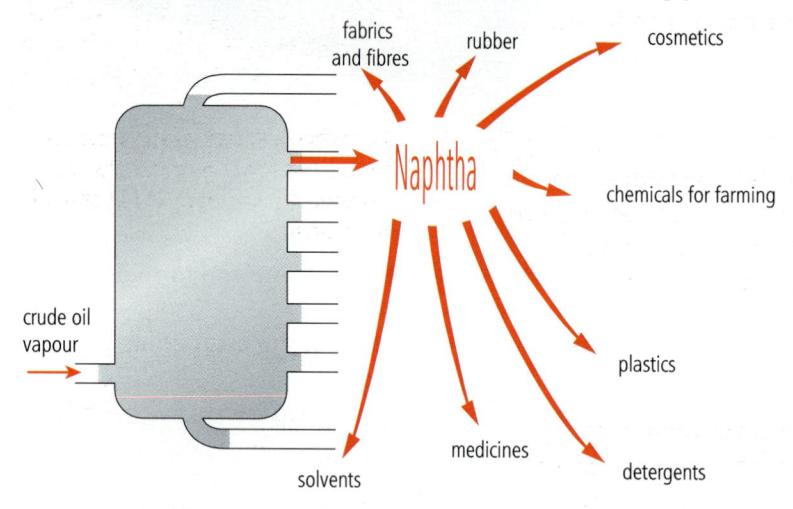

Imagine the amazing chemistry that goes on inside a cow to convert the molecules in grass into the molecules that make up its young newly born calf!

crude oil vapour → Naphtha → fabrics and fibres, rubber, cosmetics, chemicals for farming, plastics, detergents, medicines, solvents

Case study: Kevlar – a revolutionary fibre

Can you imagine the satisfaction you must get from inventing a new material that has literally saved thousands of lives? A new fibre was discovered by Stephanie Kwolek in 1965 that had properties that even she found hard to believe. Stephanie had been working as a research chemist for DuPont, a chemical company based in the USA, for almost 30 years. She worked with a team of chemists in DuPont's Pioneering Research Laboratory, looking for new polymers (very large molecules made of thousands of repeating units).

In the 1960s people started to worry about a shortage of crude oil and DuPont wanted to make a new material for lightweight, but

Stephanie Louise Kwolek was born in 1923

CHEMISTRY   Using chemistry

durable car tyres. Their theory was that the new lighter tyres would help save fuel. Stephanie and her team worked on the problem and one day the chemicals she mixed formed a milky liquid, unlike the clear liquid she was expecting. Instead of throwing the liquid away and starting again, her experience and intuition told her to test the liquid. This involved 'spinning' the liquid into fibres by forcing it through narrow jets in a machine called a spinneret.

She sent her discovery to the test lab, but they were reluctant to 'spin' it into a fibre, arguing that it would probably block up their spinneret. Eventually, they relented and sent the results of their tests on the fibre back to Stephanie. This stuff was incredible! It was 9 times stronger than a similar mass of steel, but was only half the density of fibreglass. Stephanie insisted on re-tests until she was absolutely sure no mistake had been made.

She and her team then had to work out how to scale up the reaction she had performed in her laboratory into a process that could manufacture tonnes of the new fibre. This included the necessary safety and environmental checks on their process and the new fibre. Finally in 1971, the new fibre was launched under the name of Kevlar. It was used to reinforce tyres but research continued and it is now used in hundreds of different applications. Some of these are called composites, in which Kevlar fibres are mixed with other materials to give new products with improved properties. For example, it is used extensively in commuter aircraft to reduce weight but maintain strength. But perhaps its most famous application is in bullet-proof vests – and that is why Stephanie Kwolek can be proud that she has helped to save thousands of lives.

Sheets of Kevlar fibre are compressed together to make body armour

The racing 'leathers' of this rider are in fact synthetic and contain Kevlar to protect against abrasion in case of an accident

Did you know

Following the Concorde air disaster in Paris, in which a fuel tank was pierced and caught fire on take-off, the supersonic planes were only allowed to fly again once their fuel tanks had been strengthened by lining them with a Kevlar composite.

1 Making nylon

In 1959, Stephanie Kwolek and a co-worker produced a paper in a chemistry journal, detailing the 'nylon rope trick'.

Watch your teacher demonstrate the reaction that makes the nylon polymer.

Safety: Do not touch the nylon formed. No naked flames.

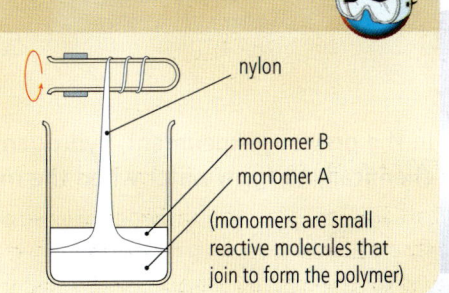

nylon
monomer B
monomer A
(monomers are small reactive molecules that join to form the polymer)

2 Developing new products

a Draw a flow diagram outlining the processes involved in developing a new polymer, such as Kevlar.
b Conduct some research to find out about the development of another product. It might be a pharmaceutical drug, plastic, or foodstuff. Present the stages in its development as a flow diagram.

CHEMISTRY Using chemistry

H5 A closer look at chemical reactions

YOU WILL LEARN!
- to use preliminary work to decide on appropriate apparatus
- that mass is conserved in chemical reactions
- that atoms combine in different ways as a result of chemical reactions
- that when gases are formed in reactions, mass may appear to decrease because gas escapes
- that mass is also conserved in dissolving and changing state

You have now seen and carried out many chemical reactions, and can appreciate their importance in all our lives.

Points to discuss

1. Consider which is your favourite chemical reaction and list the ways in which you can tell a reaction takes place. Discuss any differences in the choices made in your group.
2. Write a word equation and a symbol equation for the chosen reaction.

In Unit 9E we saw how atoms swap partners in chemical reactions and used this to balance symbol equations. Let's consider another example.

1 Exploding mixture

Watch your teacher collect hydrogen and oxygen together and trap the gases in soap bubbles.

We saw the decomposition of water with a little sulphuric acid added in *Ascent! Book 2*.

a Which gases are given off?
b What happens when a lighted splint is applied to the mixture of gases in the soap bubbles? Which gas do we use this reaction to test for?
c What is formed in the reaction?

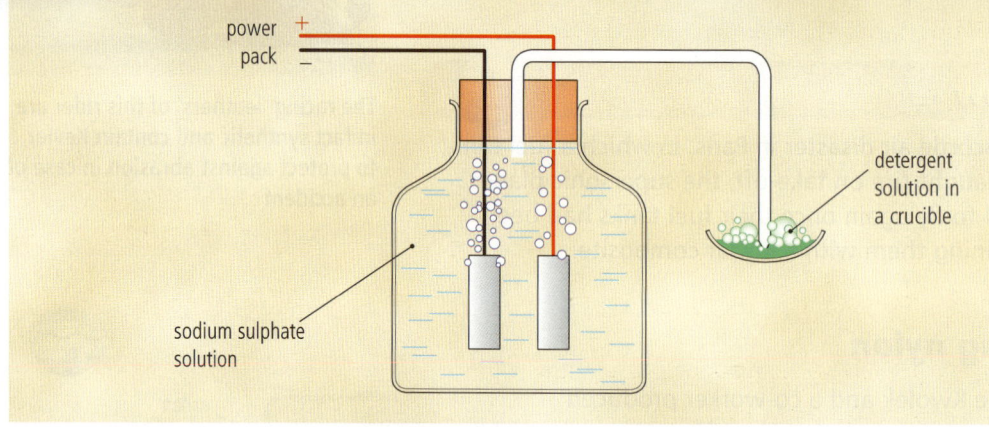

In the previous experiment, hydrogen and oxygen combined chemically to form water when the mixture was ignited.

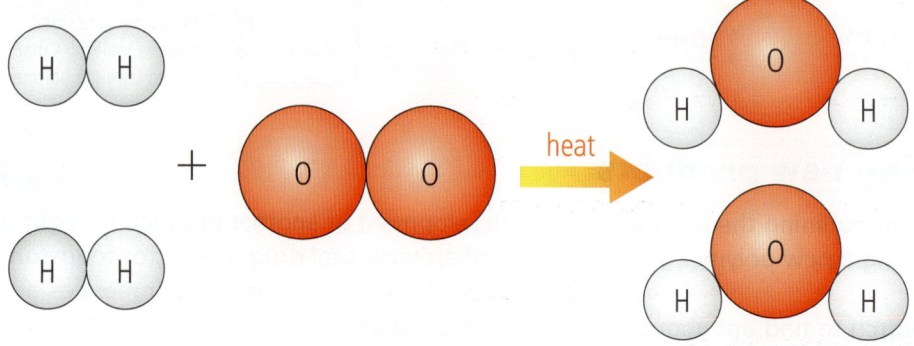

CHEMISTRY Using chemistry

Did you know

The space shuttle uses hydrogen and oxygen, stored as liquids in separate fuel tanks, to help it to blast off into orbit.

The word equation and symbol equation are:

hydrogen + oxygen → water

$2H_2 + O_2 \rightarrow 2H_2O$

Points to discuss

How do you think the mass of the H_2O formed in the reaction above compares with the total mass of hydrogen and oxygen we started with? Explain your reasoning.

You can check out your ideas in the following investigation. However, it is difficult to measure the mass of gases, so we will be investigating a **precipitation** reaction. In precipitation reactions, solutions react to form an insoluble solid.

2 Investigating the mass of reactants and products

You are given solutions of magnesium sulphate and barium chloride (toxic).

Investigate what happens when a small volume of each solution is added together in a test tube.

a What do you see happen?

The formula of magnesium sulphate is $MgSO_4$ and barium chloride is $BaCl_2$.

The precipitate formed in the reaction is barium sulphate, $BaSO_4$.

b Predict a word equation and a symbol equation for the reaction.
c Draw a diagram of the atoms involved in the reaction. (Remember that they 'swap partners'.)
d How do you think that the mass of reactants compares with the mass of the products?

Now plan an experiment to test your answer to question **d**.

Show your plan to your teacher before you do the experiment.

Alternatively, your teacher might use your ideas to demonstrate the experiment.

As no new atoms are ever created or destroyed in a chemical reaction:

the mass of reactants = the mass of products

This is called the **conservation of mass**.

CHEMISTRY   Using chemistry

Reactions involving gases

Look at the activity below to follow the mass as a reaction that produces a gas takes place.

3 What happens when gases are given off?

The apparatus opposite will be used to investigate the reaction between small pieces of limestone chips, containing calcium carbonate, and dilute hydrochloric acid.

a What is the word and symbol equation for the reaction above?

b Predict what will happen to the mass readings on the balance as the reaction proceeds. Explain your answer.

Check your prediction as you observe the experiment.

c What would happen to the mass if the gas could be contained within the apparatus?

d What piece of apparatus could we use to collect and contain a small volume of gas given off?

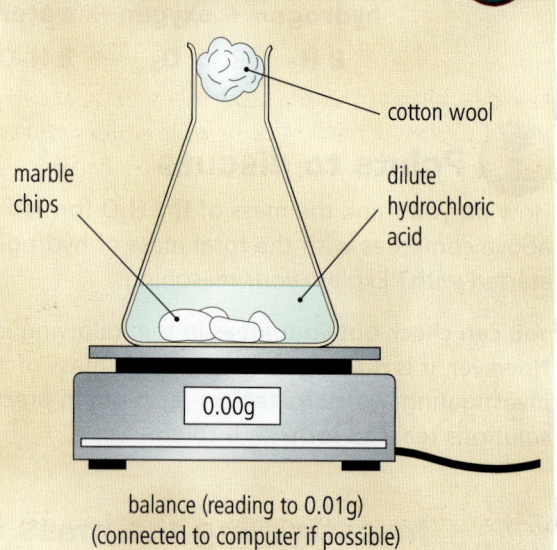

marble chips
cotton wool
dilute hydrochloric acid
0.00g
balance (reading to 0.01g) (connected to computer if possible)

Points to discuss

Discuss the following statements and correct them:

'When paper burns, lots of mass is lost in the reaction – the ashes are really light.'

'I've seen some gunpowder burn. It disappears to nothing.'

Conservation of mass in physical changes

So far we have seen how mass is conserved when atoms 'swap partners' in chemical changes (reactions). In *Ascent! Book 1* we also saw how mass does not change when solids dissolve in water. But what happens in other physical changes, such as changes of state, like melting?

4 Investigating melting

a Do you think that a substance changes mass when it melts? Why?

Plan an investigation to see if crushed ice changes mass as it melts.

Remember to prevent any water evaporating from your apparatus.

b Was your prediction in question a supported by your results?

c Evaluate the method you used.

CHEMISTRY   Using chemistry

H6 Making magnesium oxide

YOU WILL LEARN!
- that the oxide weighs more than the elements from which it was made
- to plot a graph and use it to obtain quantitative data
- that we can predict masses of the oxide formed from given masses of magnesium

In *Ascent! Book 2* we looked at making compounds from elements. One of the reactions we met was:

magnesium + oxygen → magnesium oxide

2 Mg + O_2 → 2 MgO

We can think of the particles reacting as shown below (although the Mg atoms and the particles in MgO would really be in giant structures similar to those in *Ascent! Book 2*).

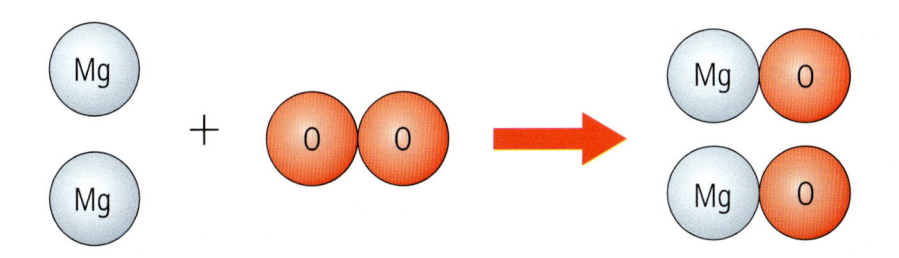

In the following experiment, you can find the mass before and after the reaction:

1 How much magnesium oxide forms?

You will need to weigh some magnesium ribbon before it is heated in a crucible. You also need to weigh the empty crucible and its lid.

a Enter your results in a table like the one below:

	Mass (g)
Mass of magnesium ribbon before heating	
Mass of empty crucible and its lid (a)	
Mass of crucible, lid and magnesium oxide after heating (b)	
Mass of magnesium oxide formed (b − a)	

Set up the apparatus as shown:

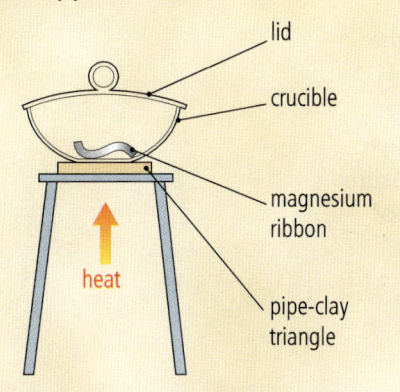

(lid, crucible, magnesium ribbon, pipe-clay triangle, heat)

Start heating the crucible.

Use a pair of tongs to occasionally lift the lid of the crucible slightly for a short length of time. This lets in some more oxygen for the magnesium to react with. Try not to let any white smoke (which is magnesium oxide) escape.

When the reaction has finished, let the crucible and its contents cool down.

Weigh the crucible, its lid and its contents after the reaction.

b Complete your table of results.
c Which weighed more – the magnesium or the magnesium oxide?
d Explain the results of your experiment.
e Now collect the results from other groups and enter them into a spreadsheet.

Plot a graph with the same axes as the graph on page 138.

f Explain your graph.
g In this experiment it is very difficult to get really reliable results. Why?

137

CHEMISTRY   Using chemistry

We know that the formula of magnesium oxide is MgO. The ratio of magnesium particles to oxygen particles is always 1 : 1. Therefore, we should get a straight line when we plot a series of points showing the mass of magnesium we started with and the mass of magnesium oxide it can form. Here are some sample data from a series of experiments:

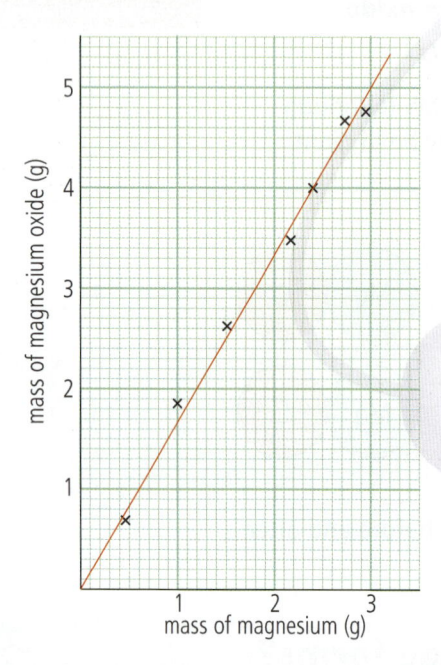

2 Data handling exercise

Use the graph above to help answer these questions.

a Why does the graph have a definite point at 0, 0?
b How much magnesium oxide can be made from 2.0 g of magnesium?
c How much magnesium is contained in 5.0 g of magnesium oxide?
d How much magnesium would we need if it was all converted into 100 g of magnesium oxide?
e A group did their own experiment to find how much magnesium oxide we get from a known mass of magnesium. However, they allowed quite a bit of white smoke to drift out of their crucible. If they started with 2.0 g of magnesium, would their point be above or below the line shown on the graph above? Explain your answer.
f Another group tried the same experiment but used copper turnings instead of magnesium ribbon. In theory, from their 6.4 g of copper, they should have formed 8 g of copper oxide. However, they only had 7.1 g of copper oxide at the end of their experiment. Explain their results.

CHEMISTRY Using chemistry
H7 A closer look at combustion

YOU WILL LEARN!
- that carbon dioxide and water are formed when a compound containing both carbon and hydrogen is burned
- that the carbon dioxide and water escape into the atmosphere
- that mass is conserved when materials burn
- to select relevant information and link it to other information
- that sometimes new evidence requires changes to theories

We know that when hydrocarbons (compounds containing hydrogen and carbon only) burn in plenty of oxygen, carbon dioxide and water are formed:

hydrocarbon + oxygen → carbon dioxide + water

Candle wax contains a mixture of long hydrocarbon molecules.

1 Candles
a How can we show that carbon dioxide and water are formed when a candle burns?
b Why does a candle *appear* to lose mass as it burns?
c One of the hydrocarbons in candle wax has the formula $C_{25}H_{52}$. See if you can write a symbol equation for its complete combustion.
d Name one other gas that is formed when you extinguish a candle under a beaker.
e Why is this gas dangerous?

Changing our ideas about burning

In *Ascent! Book 1* we saw briefly how scientists 300 years ago believed that combustible materials contained a substance called phlogiston. They also contained ash. Scientists in the late 18th century thought that when something burned, the phlogiston was given off and the true substance, the ash, was left behind. This was a good theory as it explained many of the observations about burning known at that time. For example:

- Hardly anything is left when charcoal (carbon) burns. ('That's because it contains so much phlogiston.')
- We can turn the ash from a metal back into the metal by heating it with charcoal. ('That's because the phlogiston from the charcoal is transferred to the ash – remember that a metal is its ash plus phlogiston!')
- Flames go out in a fixed volume of air. ('That's because the air gets saturated in phlogiston and can't hold any more.')

This phlogiston theory of burning persisted even after Joseph Priestley had discovered oxygen gas. Priestley heated mercury oxide and collected a gas in which candles burned more brightly. Mice could survive longer in an enclosed space in this new gas.

mercury oxide → mercury + oxygen
2 HgO → 2 Hg + O_2

Priestley called the gas dephlogisticated air. It could accept more phlogiston than normal air before it became saturated. He shared his discovery with a French scientist called Antoine Lavoisier.

Did you know?
Some people credit Carl Wilhelm Scheele, a Swedish chemist, with the discovery of oxygen. He was a great practical investigator who has had to 'share' the discovery of another six elements (nitrogen, chlorine, manganese, molybdenum, barium and tungsten) because he preferred experimenting to publishing his results! Do you know anyone like that?

CHEMISTRY   Using chemistry

With his newly constructed accurate balance, Lavoisier set about investigating burning and came up with a new theory that could explain the one big flaw in the existing phlogiston theory. The mass of a metal actually *increases* when it burns. This doesn't seem likely if it is *losing* phlogiston. Believers in phlogiston defended the theory stoutly – 'The phlogiston in metals must have negative mass!' or 'Metals get heavier when they burn because air rushes in to fill the gaps left by phlogiston'.

Joseph Priestley

Lavoisier's impressive apparatus for heating substances. (The Bunsen burner had not yet been invented!)

Lavoisier proposed that there was a reactive gas in the air, which he named oxygen. This gas added on to metals when they burned, explaining their increase in mass.

This theory could then explain more observations than the old one, and was eventually accepted.

2 Phlogiston v. oxidation

a How could Lavoisier explain that a mouse could survive longer in a closed container of oxygen than in air?
b Explain the bullet pointed observations in the passage on page 139 using Lavoisier's theory of oxidation.
c Why would the phlogiston theory fail to explain what happens when a metal 'ash', such as sodium oxide, is heated with charcoal?
d Write a letter from Antoine Lavoisier to Joseph Priestley trying to persuade him to change his views on the phlogiston theory. (He never succeeded, as Priestley died in 1804 still a firm believer in phlogiston despite his discovery of oxygen!)

CHEMISTRY   Using chemistry

Summary

Hydrocarbons (compounds containing hydrogen and carbon only) are used as fuels – substances that we burn to release their stored chemical energy.

When a hydrocarbon burns in a good supply of oxygen, carbon dioxide and water are the products of combustion.

hydrocarbon + oxygen → carbon dioxide + water

However, if there is an insufficient supply of oxygen we get **incomplete combustion**, and the pollutants carbon monoxide (a toxic gas) and tiny particles of carbon (smoke or soot) are formed.

Combustion is an example of an **exothermic** reaction – one that gives out energy and the temperature of the surroundings increases.

Some reactions are **endothermic** – taking in energy from the surroundings, causing a decrease in temperature.

We can use the differences in the reactivity between metals to make electrical cells. The greater the difference in reactivity, the higher the voltage the cell can produce.

Chemical reactions keep living things alive and functioning.

They also produce the vast range of products from the chemical industry.

In any chemical reaction, the mass of the reactants is the same as the mass of the products formed. This is because atoms just 'swap partners' in reactions – no new atoms are created or destroyed.

This is called the **conservation of matter**, and it also applies to physical changes, such as melting or dissolving.

Key words
conservation of mass
endothermic reaction
exothermic reaction
hydrocarbon
incomplete combustion
phlogiston
polymer
precipitation

Summary Questions

1 Match the following equations to the best word to describe the type of reaction, using words from this list:
displacement; combustion; photosynthesis; precipitation
   a $CH_4 + 2 O_2 \rightarrow CO_2 + 2 H_2O$
   b $Na_2SO_4 + BaCl_2 \rightarrow 2 NaCl + BaSO_4$
   c $2 AgNO_3 + Cu \rightarrow Cu(NO_3)_2 + 2 Ag$
   d $6 CO_2 + 6 H_2O \rightarrow C_6H_{12}O_6 + 6 O_2$

2 Balance the following equations:
   a $C_2H_6 + O_2 \rightarrow CO_2 + H_2O$
   b $Al + O_2 \rightarrow Al_2O_3$
   c $KNO_3 \rightarrow KNO_2 + O_2$
   d $Li + H_2O \rightarrow LiOH + H_2$
   e $W_2O_3 + H_2 \rightarrow H_2O + W$
   f $MgSO_4 + NaOH \rightarrow Mg(OH)_2 + Na_2SO_4$

3 Look at the experiment below:

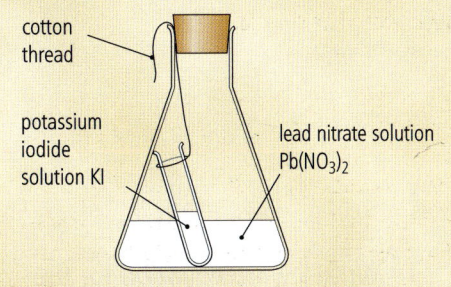

A yellow precipitate of lead iodide forms when the solutions come into contact with each other.
   a How could you use this reaction to demonstrate the conservation of matter?
   b Explain the conservation of matter using this reaction.

141

CHEMISTRY Using chemistry

End of unit Questions

1 a Two pupils heated some copper carbonate in a crucible. They recorded the mass of the crucible and contents before and after heating.

empty crucible   crucible and copper carbonate   crucible and copper oxide

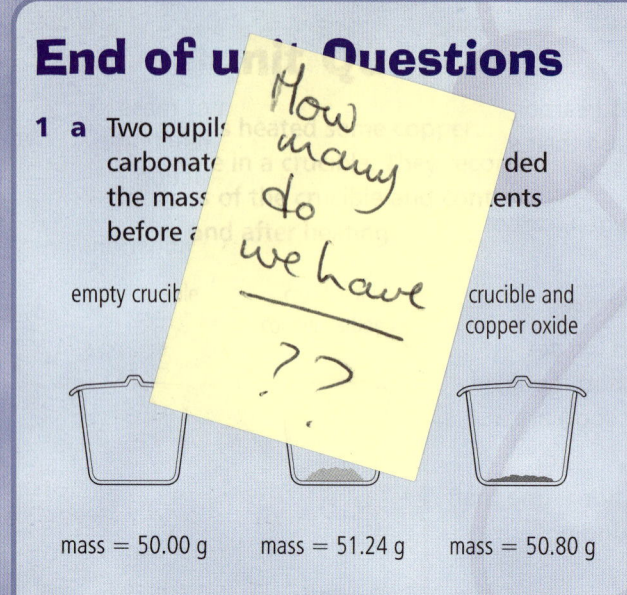

mass = 50.00 g   mass = 51.24 g   mass = 50.80 g

The word equation for this reaction is:

copper carbonate → copper oxide + carbon dioxide

  i What mass of carbon dioxide is given off in this reaction?
  Give the unit.   *1 mark*
  ii What is the name of this type of chemical reaction?
  Choose from the list.   *1 mark*

combustion   oxidation   reduction   thermal decomposition

b The pupils then heated some magnesium in another crucible. They worked carefully and did not lose any of the magnesium oxide which formed. They recorded the mass of the crucible and contents before and after heating.

empty crucible   crucible and magnesium   crucible and magnesium oxide

mass = 50.00 g   mass = 50.12 g   mass = 50.20 g

  i Write a word equation for the reaction.   *1 mark*
  ii Why does the mass of the contents of the crucible increase in this reaction?   *1 mark*
  iii What is this type of chemical reaction called?   *1 mark*

2 Ammonium nitrate is used as a garden fertiliser. It is manufactured by the reaction between ammonia gas and nitric acid. The diagram below represents stages in the process for making ammonium nitrate.

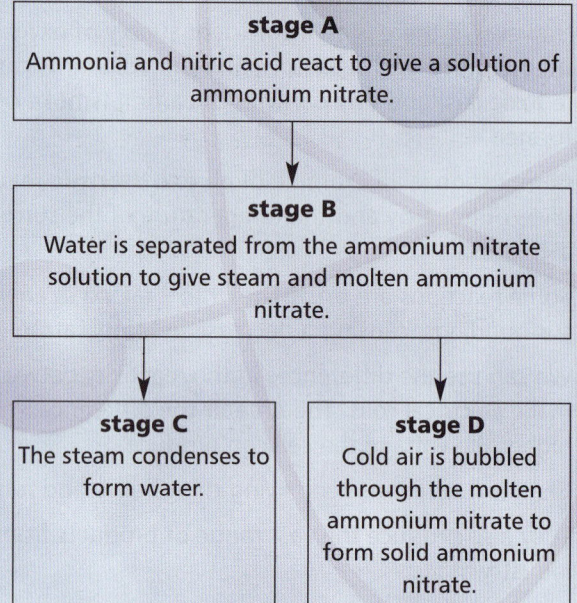

| **stage A** |
| Ammonia and nitric acid react to give a solution of ammonium nitrate. |

| **stage B** |
| Water is separated from the ammonium nitrate solution to give steam and molten ammonium nitrate. |

| **stage C** | **stage D** |
| The steam condenses to form water. | Cold air is bubbled through the molten ammonium nitrate to form solid ammonium nitrate. |

a Ammonia is an alkaline gas. In stage A, an alkali reacts with an acid.
What effect does an alkali have on an acid?   *1 mark*

b The formula for ammonium nitrate is NH_4NO_3.
  i How many different elements are there in ammonium nitrate?   *1 mark*
  ii How many atoms are represented in the formula for ammonium nitrate?   *1 mark*

c Potassium nitrate is also a fertiliser. It can be made from the reaction between potassium hydroxide and an acid. Complete the word equation for the reaction, naming the acid used.

potassium hydroxide + ... → potassium nitrate + ...

2 marks

[sticky note: How many do we have ??]

142

9I Energy and electricity

Introduction

We all use electricity almost every day of our lives. It is a convenient and easy to use form of energy that can be changed into many other useful forms of energy. In this unit you will learn about some of the wide range of energy transfers and transformations involving electricity and how to calculate the cost of the energy used by different electrical appliances. You will find out about the environmental impact of generating and using electricity, applying this knowledge to decide whether or not the typical view of electricity as a clean and safe energy source is true.

You already know

- how to follow circuit diagrams to build series and parallel circuits
- a wide range of different energy resources, including fossil fuels, the Sun, wind and wave power

In this topic you will learn

- about a range of useful energy transfers and energy transformations
- about the use of electricity to transfer energy
- about the voltage of cells and how voltage is associated with the transfer of energy in a circuit
- how electricity is generated and the environmental impact of different methods
- how to use the principle of conservation of energy to identify how energy is dissipated in different energy transfers

1 What can you remember?

a Identify as many different forms of energy as you can.
b i How many different appliances can you find that use electricity?
  ii What types of energy do they transform the electrical energy into?

PHYSICS — Energy and electricity

11 How is energy involved in doing useful things?

YOU WILL LEARN!
- that useful changes involve energy transfers and transformations
- how to use the terms 'kinetic', 'potential', 'chemical' and 'radiation' correctly when describing energy
- that electrical energy is transferred around electrical circuits and can be transformed in components to perform a variety of useful tasks
- examples of devices and situations that act as energy stores

You are already familiar with the idea that fuels provide energy. Hopefully, you also remember that fuels are substances you burn to provide energy, and there are many other types of energy resources as well. When we use energy resources, the energy is often transformed from one form to another, more useful, form. Sometimes some of the energy is transformed into types that are not useful. We call this **wasted energy**.

Different forms of energy

Scientists often define energy as the 'ability to do something'. So whenever you see a change happening, such as movement, heating or cooling, light or sound, energy is involved. Because energy can be seen in so many different situations, scientists use a range of words to describe the different forms energy takes. The table shows the most common forms of energy you are likely to come across.

Type of energy	What is this type of energy associated with?
Kinetic	Movement
Potential	An object's position or shape
• Elastic potential energy	• an object's shape. Stretched elastic is able to return to its original length when released; a tightly wound spring is able to unwind when released – so they both have elastic potential energy.
• Gravitational potential energy	• an object's position above the Earth's surface. An object that is high up moves to the lowest position possible when released, so it has gravitational potential energy
Chemical	Chemicals. Fuels contain chemicals that give out energy when burned, so fuels store chemical energy.
Heat	The movement or vibration of particles. Temperature is a measure of the average kinetic energy of particles. It tells us how concentrated the heat energy is.
Light	Radiation that is detected by our eyes.
Sound	Vibration of objects, giving off longitudinal waves detected by our ears.
Electrical	Energy transferred by the movement of electrically charged particles, called electrons, through electrical conductors.

Energy transfers and energy transformations

If energy is transferred (moved) from one place to another, like heat energy travelling along a metal rod, it is described as an **energy transfer**.

If energy is transformed (changed) from one form to another, like electrical energy changing to light energy in a light bulb, it is described as an **energy transformation**.

Points to discuss

Can you think of real devices that carry out the following energy transformations?
1. Electrical energy to sound energy.
2. Kinetic energy to potential energy.
3. Kinetic energy to electrical energy.

Elastic potential energy

Kinetic energy and sound energy

PHYSICS   Energy and electricity

The photograph shows a working, steam-powered model. The model burns methylated spirits to heat water to make the vehicle move along.

1 Identifying energy transformations

Your teacher may demonstrate a model similar to that in the photograph.

a Think carefully about how the model works and describe all the energy transformations or transfers that take place in the model.
b For each transformation, state whether the new type of energy is useful or wasted.

A working model steam engine

Points to discuss

Can you work out the energy transformations that take place in these situations?

1 Eating food.
2 A clockwork alarm clock.
3 An electric guitar.

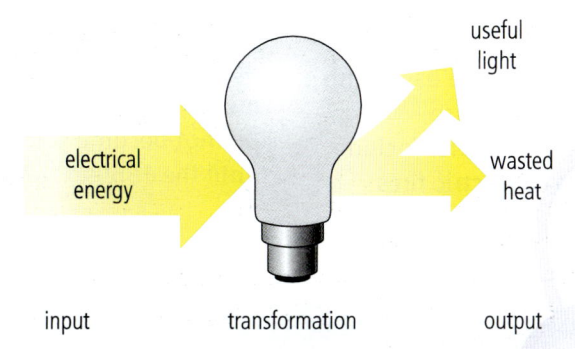

Energy flow diagram for a light bulb
input — transformation — output
electrical energy → useful light / wasted heat

Did you know

Model steam engines work in the same way as the steam engines first used in 1804 to pull trains in mines. Similar steam engines were used throughout the nineteenth and early twentieth centuries to power trains, ships, agricultural machinery, lorries and even cars and motor bikes.

Did you know

It is not possible to make energy. It is only possible to change it from one form to another, or to move it from one place to another. No device for transforming energy is ever 100% efficient – no device ever transforms 100% of the input energy into useful forms of energy. Some energy always changes into forms we don't want, so we never get as much useful energy out as we put in.

2 Energy flow diagrams

Look at the range of devices you have been given.

For each device draw an energy flow diagram to show the energy transfers or transformations taking place.

Storing energy

Often we need to store energy so that it can be moved from place to place, or so that it can be saved until we are ready to use it. Most fuels are substances that are natural stores of energy, but many energy stores are made by humans.

145

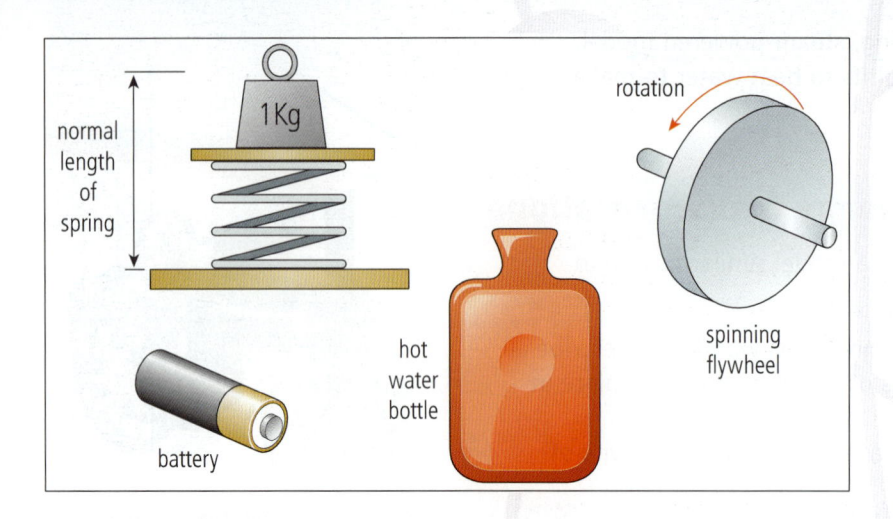

PHYSICS — Energy and electricity

Points to discuss

Look at the energy storage devices in the picture.

1. How are they used to store energy?
2. In what form is the energy stored?
3. Can you think of any other ways to store energy?
4. Can you think of any forms of energy that cannot be stored?

Electrical energy

Electrical energy is one of the most common forms of energy in our everyday lives. It is a form of energy that can be changed easily into many other forms. There are many occasions when we use electricity in preference to other forms of energy. Examples include electric train sets instead of clockwork train sets or electric fires instead of coal fires.

Did you know

Although the first electrically powered lawn mowers were invented in the 1920s they did not become common until the 1960s.

3 Advantages and disadvantages of electricity as an energy source

Look at these examples of things that can use electricity or other sources of energy.

Use these devices, and any others you can think of, to help you make a two-column table showing the advantages and disadvantages of electricity compared with other energy sources.

Include examples of different devices to illustrate the advantages and disadvantages you mention.

Electric lawn mower

Clockwork radio

Mains radio

146

PHYSICS — Energy and electricity

12 How does electricity transfer energy?

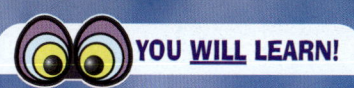

YOU WILL LEARN!

- how current and voltage vary in electrical circuits
- simple models to show current flow and energy transfer around a circuit
- that the chemical energy in a cell is transformed into electrical energy in a circuit
- how to carry out and evaluate an investigation into voltage
- where high voltages are used, and what are the advantages and hazards

You already know that circuits only work when there is a complete loop so that an electric current can flow from the cell, or battery, round the circuit through the electrical components and back to the cell. You have probably used an ammeter to measure the size of electric currents and you may know that an electric current is a flow of electrically charged particles called **electrons**.

Points to discuss

All of these circuit diagrams have something wrong with them. Can you find the mistake in each?

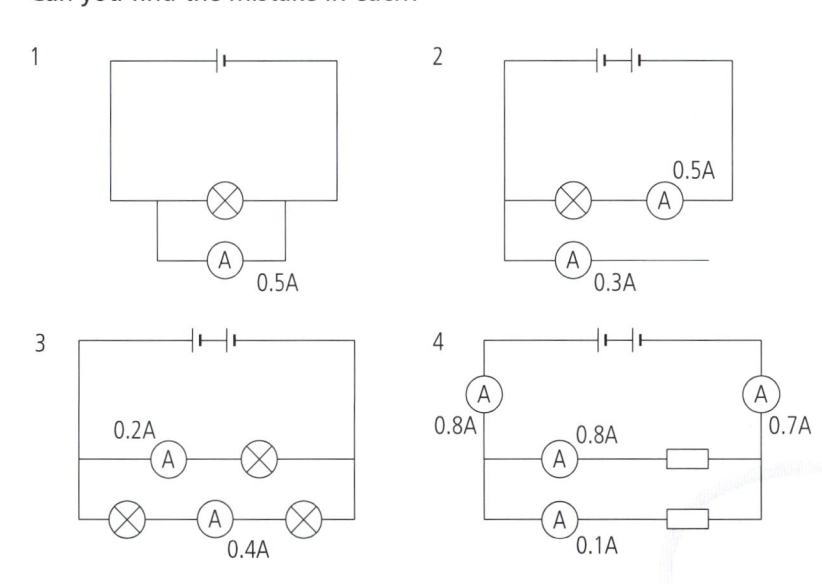

1. (circuit with ammeter reading 0.5A)
2. (circuit with ammeters reading 0.5A and 0.3A)
3. (circuit with ammeters reading 0.2A and 0.4A)
4. (circuit with ammeters reading 0.8A, 0.8A, 0.7A, and 0.1A)

Points to discuss

Can you design a simple ammeter? You will need to use knowledge about electromagnets. Hints are given below if you need them.

- What 'device' is made when current flows through a coil of wire?
- What happens to this 'device' when the size of the current in the coil of wire changes?
- What would you make a pointer from and where could you attach it so that it moved when the current increased?

Voltage

You may have used batteries with different voltages, and you may have been told that mains electricity is dangerous because it has a high voltage, but do you know what voltage is? One of the most important things you need to remember is that voltage is **NOT** just another name for electricity or electric current.

147

PHYSICS — Energy and electricity

1 Measuring voltage

Voltage is measured using a voltmeter. The units for voltage are volts (V).

A voltmeter is always connected **in parallel across a component**.

a Set up the series circuit shown in the diagram.

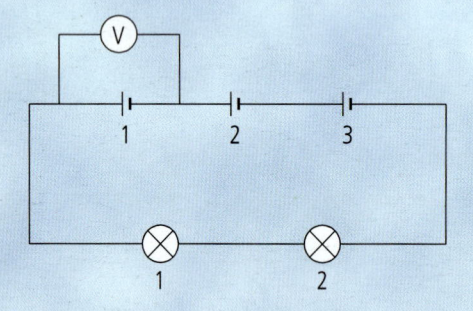

b Connect a voltmeter across each of the cells and each of the bulbs in turn, as shown in the diagram. Record the voltage across each component.

c Record the total voltage across all the components that produce electrical energy, and the total voltage across all the components that transform electrical energy into some other form.

d What do you notice?

Adjust the number of cells and bulbs to give a very brightly lit bulb. Measure the voltage across the bulb. Measure the voltage across a very dim bulb.

e Describe how voltage and the brightness of the bulb are related.

Voltage and energy

The voltage across a component tells us how much electrical energy is being transformed by that component. For a cell, it tells us how much chemical energy is being transformed into electrical energy by the cell. For components like bulbs or buzzers it tells us how much electrical energy is being transformed into other types of energy, such as light, heat or sound.

In Activity 1, the total voltage across the cells was the same as the total voltage across the bulbs because all the electrical energy being produced by the cells is transformed into light and heat by the bulbs. Bulbs with a high voltage across them look bright because they are transforming a large amount of electrical energy into light energy.

Points to discuss

Even though the voltmeter is connected across an electrical component, not in series, a very small amount of current still flows through the voltmeter. It is very important to make this current very small, so that measuring the voltage changes the circuit as little as possible. What component can be put inside the voltmeter to ensure the current flowing through it is tiny?

Did you know

Voltage is sometimes called electromotive force (from 'electrons' and 'motion'). This is a good name because it tells us that a voltage is a force that makes electrons move. A big voltage has a big force, so it makes a big current flow in the circuit. The big current supplies lots of energy to bulbs in the circuit, making them shine brightly.

The high voltage of the lightning supplied so much energy that the sap in this tree turned to steam and blew the tree apart

PHYSICS   Energy and electricity

2 Why are high voltages dangerous?

You have seen that the voltage across a cell is a measure of the energy the cell is able to put into a circuit. The high voltage of the mains, or lightning, or overhead power cables, means these are able to transfer large amounts of energy.

a Use secondary sources to find out about the hazards of high voltages.
b Write a safety leaflet for teenagers, explaining the dangers of high voltages.

Models of electricity

People often invent models of electrical circuits to make it easier to imagine what is happening around the circuit. You might remember the model we used in *Ascent! Book 1* in which marbles on a marble track were used to represent the electric current. The picture shows a 'money model' of an electrical circuit. Students are collecting money from a bank, then travelling round a market spending the money before returning to the bank.

3 The 'money model' of electricity

In the 'money model' of an electrical circuit decide:
a what type of circuit is being modelled, series or parallel
b which bits represent the cell, the wires, the electrical current, energy
c if this a good analogy. Are there any ways in which this is not a good 'picture' of an electrical circuit and, if so, what are they?
d are there any types of circuit it would be hard to use this 'money model' for?
e can you use a better analogy to describe what happens in an electrical circuit?

4 Making a simple electrical cell

Connect zinc and copper electrodes to a sensitive voltmeter, as the diagram shows.

Place the zinc and copper electrodes in saturated salt solution. Make sure they do not touch each other. Observe the solution, the electrodes and the voltmeter carefully.

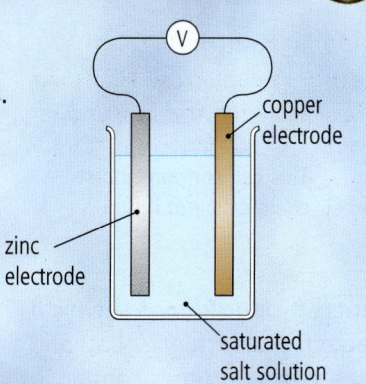

a Note all the things you observe.
b Use your observations to explain the energy transfers and transformations taking place in the cell.
c Use secondary sources to find out about some of the earliest cells made. What did they contain? How did they work?

Did you know

Voltage is named after Count Alessandro Volta, an Italian physicist. In 1800, Volta also invented the very first electric cell, called a voltaic pile.

The voltaic pile

PHYSICS   Energy and electricity

Points to discuss
Cells are able to give out an electrical current because they transform stored chemical energy into electrical energy.

Which cell would 'go flat' sooner, a cell which supplied a low current, or an identical cell with the same amount of stored chemical energy which supplied a high current? Explain why.

A wide range of solutions or moist chemicals, including those in fruit and vegetables, can be used to make electrical cells. Zinc and copper are not the only metals that we can use to make electrodes.

5 Grow your own electricity
Make an electrical cell from a fruit or vegetable. Carry out a fair test to produce the highest possible voltage from your cell. You should attempt to produce results that are accurate and reliable. Things you could vary include:
- the type of fruit or vegetable
- the types of metal used for electrodes
- the size of the electrodes
- the distance between electrodes

If you have already completed Unit 9F on reactivity, use this to explain your results.

These potatoes supply enough energy to run a clock

What is inside a dry cell?
Early cells contained liquids, like the simple cell you made using salt solution. So when cells were invented that contained moist chemicals instead of solutions they were called 'dry cells'. All modern batteries, except car batteries, are dry cells.

The electrodes are the powdered chemicals (powdered zinc in the centre and powdered manganese(IV) oxide and graphite around the outside). There is a thin layer of material between the electrodes to stop them mixing. This material has been soaked in the electrolyte solution (the equivalent of your salt solution or your fruit).

This cell contains moist chemicals, not liquid

Did you know
The first dry cell was called a Leclanché cell, after its inventor the French chemist Georges Leclanché. When it was invented in the 1860s it was very popular because all earlier batteries had given off poisonous fumes. Many of the dry cells we use today are almost identical to Leclanché's original dry cell.

Rechargeable batteries
In 'ordinary' batteries, the electric current is produced by a chemical change. Once all the chemicals have reacted, the battery is 'flat' and cannot produce any more current. Rechargeable batteries contain chemicals such as nickel–cadmium (Ni–Cd) or nickel–metal hydride (Ni–MH). As the battery produces an electric current these chemicals are changed into other chemicals, but passing a current through the 'flat' cell reverses the chemical reaction and regenerates the original Ni–Cd or Ni–MH, so the battery is able to give a current again.

PHYSICS   Energy and electricity

13 What are we paying for when we use electricity?

When we plug any electrical appliance into the mains supply in our homes, an electric current flows from the mains, through the appliance and back to the mains. In any home there may be dozens of complete circuits carrying current from the mains.

Points to discuss

Current is not used up when it flows through electrical appliances. The current leaving our house is the same size as the current entering our house. So when an electricity bill charges us for the 'electricity we have used', what exactly is it charging us for?

Although electrical appliances don't 'use current' they do transform electrical energy carried by the current into other forms of energy such as heat or light. So when we pay an electricity bill we are really paying for the electrical energy our appliances have transformed.

YOU WILL LEARN!

- that electric current is conducted from 'the mains' to components in electrical circuits
- that the electric current transmits energy to an appliance, where it is converted to another form of energy
- that some appliances transform more energy in a given time than others
- how to identify the power rating of common household electrical devices
- to present advice based on scientific understanding

1 Which appliances transform most energy?

Look at the range of electrical appliances you have been given.

a Predict which appliances will use most and least energy.

Use a joulemeter and a datalogger to record the energy used by each appliance.

Safety: Take care when using mains electricity

b Write down how you make sure your comparison is fair.

c Record your results in the first two columns of a table like this:

| Appliance | Amount of electrical energy used (J) | Power rating (W) |

Somewhere on each appliance you will find a power rating, in watts (symbol W).

d Fill in the 'Power rating' column of your results table (1 kW = 1000 W).

e What do you think the power rating of an appliance tells you?

Belling   MICROWAVE APPLIANCE MW820T
POWER SOURCE : 240V~A.C. 50Hz
POWER CONSUMPTION : 1200WATTS
RATED INPUT CURRENT : 5.5A
RATED OUTPUT FREQUENCY : 2450MHz
MANUFACTURED   NOVEMBER 1998
SERIAL NUMBER   31100588
COUNTRY OF ORIGIN-KOREA   P/NO. 4B75726A

151

PHYSICS — Energy and electricity

Power rating

The power rating of an electrical appliance tells us the rate at which electrical energy is transformed by an appliance. It is measured in joules of energy transformed per second (J/s). Joules per second are usually called watts, symbol W. So a light bulb with a power rating of 60 W transforms 60 J of energy for every 1 second that it is turned on.

Finding out how much it costs

There are three things that affect how much an appliance costs to run.

- The power rating of the appliance (usually measured in kW).
- How long it is turned on for (usually measured in hours).
- How much the electricity company charges for each unit of energy used (usually measured in pence per unit, p/unit).

Cost is calculated from the equation

cost (p) = power rating (kW) × time (hr) × cost per unit (p/unit)

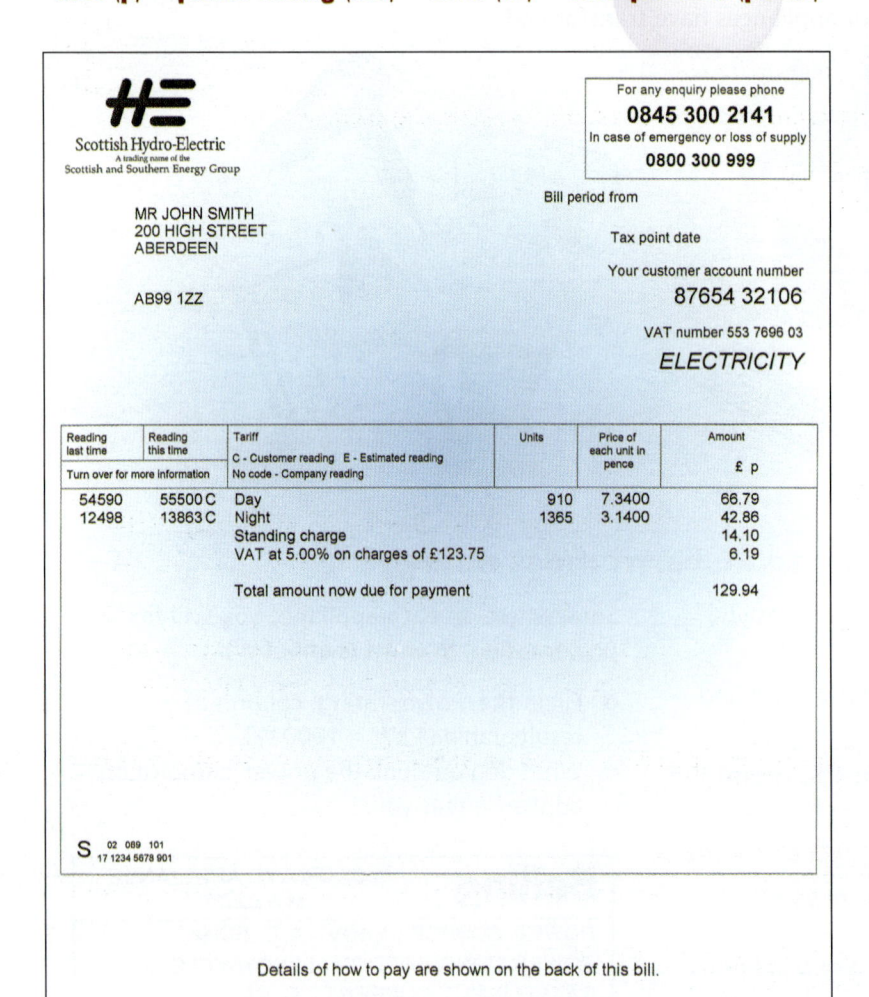

Did you know?

Another name for a 'unit' of electricity is a 'kilowatt hour'. So if an appliance with a power rating of 1 kW is left on for 1 hour it will use 1 unit of electricity (1 × 1 = 1). An appliance with a power rating of 2 kW left on for $\frac{1}{2}$ hour will also use 1 unit of electricity (2 × $\frac{1}{2}$ = 1).

Did you know?

You could use a laptop computer for about one hour for the same cost as using an electric kettle to boil the water to make one mug of coffee.

A typical electricity bill

Scottish Hydro-Electric
A trading name of the Scottish and Southern Energy Group

MR JOHN SMITH
200 HIGH STREET
ABERDEEN
AB99 1ZZ

For any enquiry please phone **0845 300 2141**
In case of emergency or loss of supply **0800 300 999**

Bill period from
Tax point date
Your customer account number
87654 32106
VAT number 553 7696 03

ELECTRICITY

Reading last time	Reading this time	Tariff C - Customer reading E - Estimated reading No code - Company reading	Units	Price of each unit in pence	Amount £ p
54590	55500 C	Day	910	7.3400	66.79
12498	13863 C	Night	1365	3.1400	42.86
		Standing charge			14.10
		VAT at 5.00% on charges of £123.75			6.19
		Total amount now due for payment			129.94

S 02 089 101
17 1234 5678 901

Details of how to pay are shown on the back of this bill.
Please use these details to complete the enclosed payment slip.

Account Number	Total Due
87654 32106	£129.94

PHYSICS — Energy and electricity

Example 1:
Find the cost of leaving a 60 W light bulb on for 10 hours. Electricity costs 6p per unit.

cost (p) = power rating (kW) × time (hr) × cost per unit (p/unit)

$$\text{cost} = \frac{60}{1000} \times 10 \times 6$$

cost = 3.6p

Example 2:
A microwave 'ready-meal' says '800 W oven: heat on full power for 12 minutes'. How much will the meal cost to heat? Assume electricity costs 6p per unit.

cost (p) = power rating (kW) × time (hr) × cost per unit (p/unit)

$$\text{cost} = \frac{800}{1000} \times \frac{12}{60} \times 6$$

cost = 0.96p

Did you know
Sometimes leaflets encouraging us to save energy tell us that we can save pounds by turning our televisions off overnight instead of leaving them on standby. Most televisions use about 3 W when they are on standby. So if you left a television on standby for 10 hours every night instead of turning it off it would cost you about 66p a year. However, televisions left on standby for long periods of time can occasionally overheat, so it is safer to turn them off.

2 How much does it cost?

Look at the table of typical power ratings for some common electrical appliances.

Appliance	Power rating
Toaster	1300 W
Computer + monitor	300 W
Kettle	2 kW
Stereo system	150 W
Electric fire	3 kW
Television	50 W
Radio	4 W
Video recorder	20 W
Microwave oven	800 W
Bright bulb	60 W
Night light	15 W
Fluorescent tube light	36 W
Hair dryer	1500 W
Electronic keyboard	8 W

a Make a table like the one below listing all the appliances you use in a day and working out the cost of each appliance.

b Work out the total cost of the electricity you use each day. Assume a cost of 6p per unit.

Appliance	Power rating (kW)	Hours used for (hr)	Units used (kW × hr)	Cost (p)

3 Make an information leaflet

Tom says 'My parents say it costs them a fortune when I keep playing on the computer'. Write an information leaflet for Tom and his parents, to help them decide on the best ways to save money on their electricity bill.

PHYSICS — Energy and electricity

14 Where do we get electricity from?

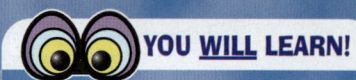

YOU WILL LEARN!
- that an electric current can be generated by movement in an electrical generator
- that electrical energy cannot be stored
- that fossil fuels, nuclear fuels and renewable energy sources can be used to drive electrical generators
- how to follow instructions to construct and/or test a generator
- how to examine evidence about the environmental impact of electricity generation and arrive at a considered viewpoint

You know that electrical energy from a battery comes from chemical changes within the battery. You are probably aware that our mains electricity supply comes along cables from a power station. Have you ever wondered how the electricity is made at the power station?

1 Investigating an electric motor

Assemble a small electric motor from a kit. (Your teacher may do this as a demonstration.)

The motor uses an electric current to make a coil of wire rotate between the poles of a magnet. A magnetic field goes from the north pole of the magnet to the south pole of the magnet.

a What happens to the motor if the magnets are turned round, reversing the magnetic field?
b What happens to the motor if the magnets are removed, so there is no magnetic field?
c What two things are essential to create movement of the motor?

Electric current, magnetic fields and movement are always linked to each other. Whenever two of them are present, the third will be created.

2 Using an electric motor

The diagram shows an electric motor connected to a windmill.

a Predict what would happen if you turned the windmill by hand.
b Connect a sensitive ammeter to the electric motor instead of a power supply.
Turn the windmill.
Was your prediction correct?
c Find out some of the things that affect the output from your 'motor in reverse'.

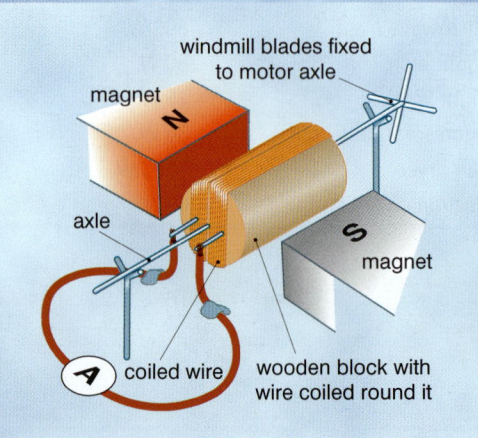

Electric generators

An electric generator is any device that changes movement energy into electrical energy. Small electric generators are often called **dynamos** or **alternators**. In 1831, Michael Faraday discovered how electricity and magnetism were linked to each other, and built

PHYSICS — Energy and electricity

a small dynamo to show how electricity could be generated. The first practical dynamo was used in 1858 to provide electricity for the light in a lighthouse. In 1882, Thomas Edison developed a much more efficient dynamo that made electricity cheaper than coal gas and made electric lights in homes possible for the first time.

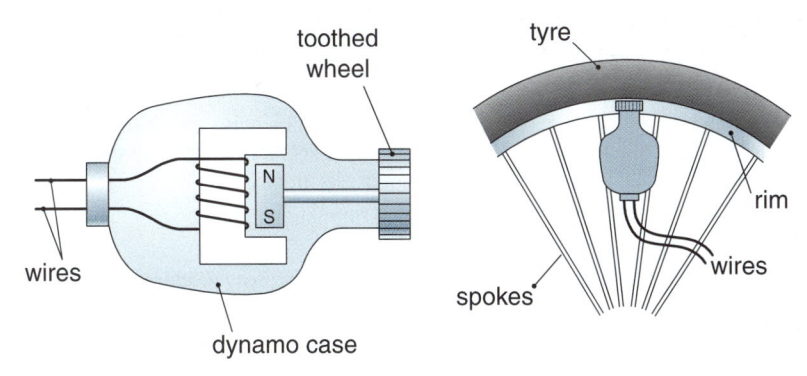

A bicycle dynamo, or electric generator

Points to discuss

The diagram shows a typical bicycle dynamo, used to power bicycle lights.

1 How will the output of the dynamo be affected by the speed of the cyclist?
2 What problems might this cause for the cyclist?

Power stations

The electric generators in power stations are like enormous bicycle dynamos, and they work in the same way. Steam power is used to drive huge fan-like machines called turbines, connected to generators. The generators are huge electromagnets free to rotate inside stationary coils of wire. As the turbines rotate, they turn the electromagnets in the generators, creating a current in the coils of wire.

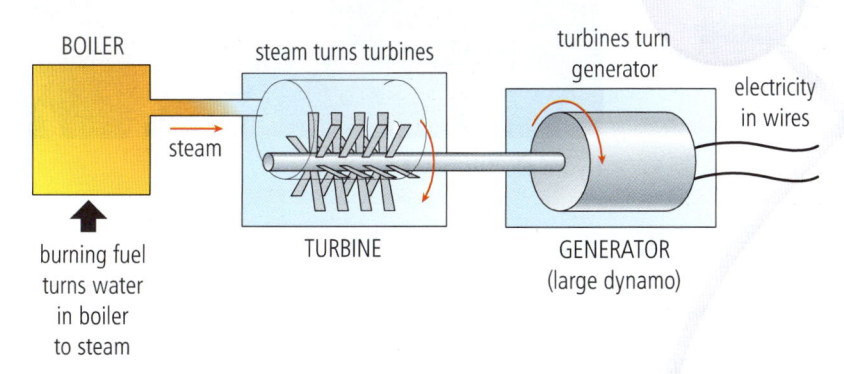

Power stations use a wide variety of different energy resources to turn the turbines that drive the generators. All the different energy resources have some impact on the environment. The table on page 156 shows a few of the effects of different types of power stations.

Did you know

Because electrical energy cannot be stored, power stations adjust the amount of electricity they produce to meet the demand, by switching turbines on or off. So at times when people use less electricity, such as overnight, the power stations produce less. They even have to plan ahead for events such as major football matches on television. In a major game, demand for electricity can go up suddenly at half time because millions of households all switch on a kettle at the same time!

PHYSICS Energy and electricity

Type of power station	How it works	Environmental effect
Gas turbine	Burning fossil fuels, such as coal, oil or gas, heat steam to drive turbines.	Polluting gases are released, contributing to global warming and acid rain.
Nuclear	A nuclear reactor heats steam to drive turbines.	Nuclear waste (spent nuclear fuel) can remain radioactive for hundreds of years.
Hydro-electric	Turbines are driven by water falling through a dam.	No pollution. Large volumes of water from a river or reservoir are needed.
Tidal flow	Tidal water flows through a tidal barrage, driving turbines.	Tidal barrages can affect shipping, natural water flow and wildlife habitats.
Wind	Wind power drives turbines.	'Wind farms' can be noisy and unsightly. Each turbine generates a relatively small amount of electricity.
Biofuel	Gas turbines are driven by burning traditional fuels such as wood or other plant material.	Pollution from burning fuels.
Solar	Semiconductor materials in solar cells convert the energy in sunlight directly into electrical energy.	The amount of electricity produced is small, so many solar cells are needed.
Geothermal	Water is pumped down to hot regions deep within the Earth. The returning hot water or steam drives turbines.	Expensive to operate, but becoming cheaper as technology improves.

Nuclear power station

Geothermal power station

Hydro-electric power station

3 Electricity generation

Find out more about one type of electricity generation.

a Prepare a report or a short talk explaining how your chosen method of electricity generation affects people and the environment.
b Listen to what other groups have found out about other methods of electricity generation. Which types of electricity generation do you think should become most common in the future and why?

PHYSICS   Energy and electricity

15   How can we reduce the waste of energy?

YOU WILL LEARN!
- that in energy transfers, energy is wasted
- that when energy is transferred the total amount of energy remains constant
- how to use flow diagrams to show how energy is transferred and/or transformed in devices

Although electricity, in our homes and in industry, is a safe and clean energy resource, using electricity often has a large, hidden, environmental impact. Many power stations produce pollution and environmental damage that we don't usually see and use up non-renewable energy resources.

Wasted energy

Whenever energy is transformed, some energy changes into unwanted forms. This is wasted energy. An efficient power station is one that gives out a lot of electrical energy for a given energy input.

As our awareness of wasted energy issues increases and our technology improves we are building power stations that are more efficient, and use less non-renewable energy resources.

A typical fossil fuel power station

Points to discuss

Identify where there are forms of wasted energy in a power station burning fossil fuel. Can you think of any ways to reduce this wasted energy, or to use the wasted energy for anything useful?

Much of the wasted energy in power stations is an unavoidable result of changing the chemical energy in fuel into heat energy, then into electricity energy. Power stations changing movement energy, such as wind or wave energy, directly into electrical energy are usually more efficient.

Did you know

Typical fossil fuel power stations are usually less than 40% efficient. Over 60% of the energy input is wasted, mostly as heat. Modern gas-fired power stations are nearly 55% efficient. They are more efficient because they use the hot exhaust gas to heat steam to generate more electricity.

1 How efficient are different cars?

Battery cars and fuel cell-powered cars are often described as being much more 'environmentally friendly' than petrol or diesel cars, but is this really so? Use information below to decide what you think. Write a short report.

- Petrol cars: energy in petrol transformed into movement energy with an efficiency of 20 to 25%.
- Diesel cars: energy in diesel transformed into movement energy with an efficiency of slightly over 40%.
- Battery cars: electricity generated in power station with an efficiency of approximately 30%. Electrical energy transformed into movement energy with an efficiency of about 80%.
- Fuel cell cars: energy in methanol transformed into energy in hydrogen then into electrical energy with an overall efficiency of about 30 to 40%. (Hydrogen is generally considered too dangerous to store in large quantities in a car.) Electrical energy transformed into movement energy with an efficiency of about 80%.

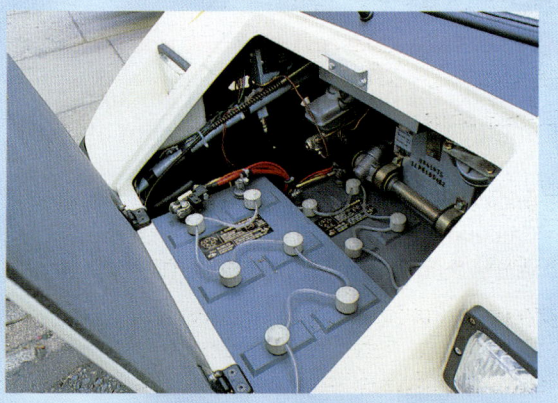

This car uses electricity very efficiently, but the electricity has to be generated in a power station first.

PHYSICS — Energy and electricity

Energy conservation

In the first half of the nineteenth century, scientists were discovering that energy could exist in many forms, such as heat, light, electricity and movement. In 1847, the German scientist Hermann Helmholtz summed up many of their findings in the now famous principle of conservation of energy, which states that:

The total energy of any system remains unchanged when energy is transferred or transformed.

We can use this principle to draw energy flow diagrams for energy transfers. Sankey energy flow diagrams show the proportion of the energy that ends up in different forms. The width of the 'arrow' shows how much energy is in that form.

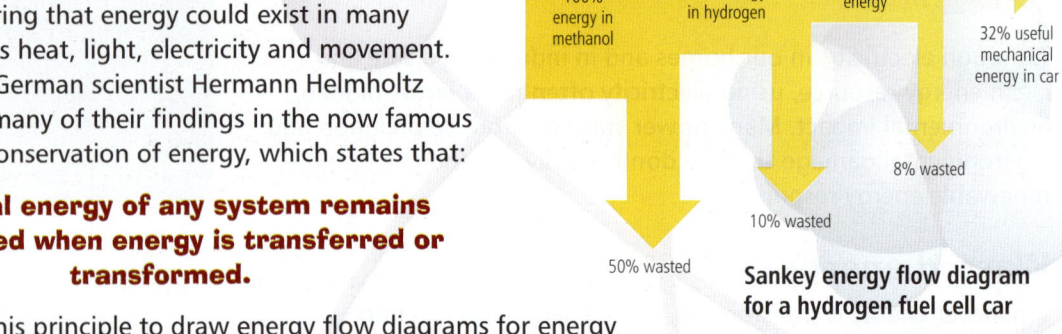

Sankey energy flow diagram for a hydrogen fuel cell car
- 100% energy in methanol
- 50% energy in hydrogen
- 40% as electrical energy
- 32% useful mechanical energy in car
- 8% wasted
- 10% wasted
- 50% wasted

2 Sankey energy flow diagrams

Draw energy flow diagrams to show where the energy goes for

a a petrol engine car (assume 25% efficiency)
b a diesel engine car (assume 40% efficiency)
c a battery car (start with the energy input to the power station).

Did you know?

If every household in the UK replaced one 100 W light bulb with a 20 W energy saver bulb it would save the output from 2 medium sized power stations. The reduction in electricity consumption would reduce greenhouse gases by 2 million tonnes a year.

3 Investigating energy saver light bulbs

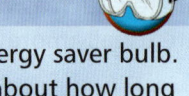

'A 20 W energy saver bulb gives the same light as an ordinary (incandescent) 100 W bulb and lasts up to 15 times longer.'

Advertising like this is common, but can it be true? If the ordinary bulb uses 100 W to give the same light as a 20 W energy saver bulb, what happens to the other 80 W of energy?

Hold your hand near a 100 W ordinary bulb and a 20 W energy saver bulb.

SAFETY: Take care not to burn yourself.

a Why do the bulbs use different amounts of energy to produce the same amount of light?
b Draw a Sankey energy flow diagram for an ordinary 100 W light bulb.
c Calculate approximately how much money you would save by replacing a 100 W ordinary bulb with a 20 W energy saver bulb. Make a sensible assumption about how long the bulb is on for. Assume electricity costs 6p per unit.

Is this a daft idea? You could stay fit and save money on the electricity bill at the same time!

PHYSICS — Energy and electricity

Summary

Energy is the ability to do something.

Energy exists in many forms, such as kinetic, potential, chemical, electrical, heat, light and sound.

An **energy transfer** is when energy moves from one place to another.

An **energy transformation** is when energy changes from one form to another.

Whenever an energy transformation takes place, some energy changes to wasted forms of energy.

Electric current transfers energy around a circuit.

The **voltage** across an electrical component is a measure of how much energy that component transforms.

A voltmeter is always connected across an electrical component.

High voltages are hazardous because they transfer large amounts of energy.

An **electrical cell** is a device for transforming chemical energy into electrical energy.

An electric current transfers electrical energy to an appliance, where it is transformed into another form of energy.

When we 'pay for electricity' we are really paying for the energy we have used.

The **power rating** of an appliance tells us how much electrical energy the appliance transforms.

The cost of using an electrical appliance is calculated from the equation

cost (p) = power rating (kW) × time (hr) × cost per unit (p/unit)

An **electric generator** is a device that transforms movement energy into electrical energy.

Power stations generate electricity from a range of other renewable and non-renewable energy resources.

All methods of generating electricity have some environmental impact.

The **principle of conservation** of energy tells us that:

the total energy of any system remains unchanged when energy is transferred or transformed.

Key words

efficient
electric generator
electrical appliance
electrical cell
energy
energy flow diagram
energy transfer
energy transformation
power rating
Sankey diagram
unit of electricity
voltage

Summary Questions

1. Make your own glossary (list of meanings) for the Key words. Keep your definitions short.

2. A funicular railway is used to carry passengers up short stretches of hill that are too steep for normal train wheels to grip the rails. Two carriages are attached to a cable that passes over a pulley at the top of the hill. The weight of one carriage going down helps pull the other carriage up the hill. The weight of the carriage going up stops the other carriage rushing down too quickly.
   a Why is an engine needed to drive the pulley round?
   b Describe the energy transfers and transformations taking place as one carriage goes up and the other comes down.
   c Draw an energy flow diagram for a carriage going down.

3. Electrical energy is a common and useful form of energy in our homes and in industry.
   a Give two examples of devices that transform electrical energy into kinetic energy.
   b Give two examples of devices that transform kinetic energy into electrical energy.
   c Give one advantage and one disadvantage of electricity as an energy source.

PHYSICS   Energy and electricity

End of unit Questions

1 A flywheel is a rotating wheel which is used to store energy.

   a Energy must be transferred to a flywheel to make it rotate. How is the energy in the rotating flywheel classified? Choose from the list.
as chemical energy; as kinetic energy; as potential energy; as thermal energy
1 mark

   b A flywheel is rotating at a high speed. No energy is being supplied to it. The flywheel is used to turn a dynamo, and the energy from the dynamo is used to light a bulb.
      i The bulb is left connected until the flywheel stops rotating.
Not all the energy stored in the flywheel is transferred to the bulb. Some of it is lost. Give **two** places from which it is lost, and explain how it is lost. *2 marks*
      ii The experiment is repeated using a different bulb which gives out more energy each second.
Compared to the first light bulb, describe how the second light bulb will affect the motion of the flywheel, and explain your answer. *2 marks*

2 The flow of water through tubes can be used as a model to explain some of the rules about electrical circuits.

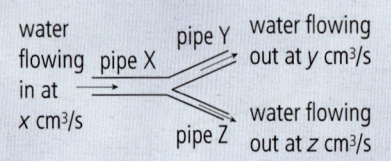

The diagram shows a junction in a water pipe. The rate of flow in the pipes is measured in cm^3/s.

   a What is the relationship between the rate of flow in the three pipes, X, Y and Z?
1 mark

   b The diagram below shows a 'water circuit', in which water is forced round by a pump. The rates of flow at two places are written on the diagram.

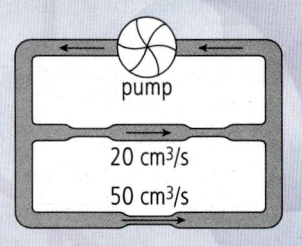

      i At what rate is water flowing:
into the pump?
out of the pump? *1 mark*
      ii The 'water circuit' can be used as a model of an electrical circuit. Each part of the 'water circuit' is equivalent to a part of an electrical circuit.
What is the electrical equivalent of the water? *1 mark*

A family, who did not understand electricity very well, always made sure there was a bulb in each of the light fittings in their house. They were afraid that electricity would escape from an empty light socket when the switch was turned on.

   c Explain why electricity does **not** escape from an empty light socket. *1 mark*

3 The drawings below show what happens to the energy supplied to four appliances.

98% heat, 2% wasted   50% sound, 50% wasted   – light, 95% wasted   40% movement, – wasted

   a i What are the missing percentages? *2 marks*
     ii Copy and complete the sentence below. *1 mark*
Parts of the mixer become hot because some of the electrical energy is changed into .... energy which is wasted.

   b Energy is wasted as sound in many appliances.
Which appliance in the drawings produces sound which is **not** wasted? *1 mark*

9J Gravity and space

Introduction

We grow up being affected by Earth's gravity. We learn to take account of gravity in many things we do, such as deciding how hard to jump to clear a high jump bar, or what angle to throw a ball at so it goes as far as possible. In this unit you will find out about the factors that affect the strength of the force of gravity, and about places where the force of gravity is much larger or much smaller than it is on Earth. You will learn some of the scientific discoveries connected with gravity and how important gravity is to modern scientists working in areas such as space exploration or satellite communications.

You already know

- that the gravitational pull of the Earth on a mass is called weight
- that the solar system has planets orbiting about the Sun, and satellites such as moons orbiting about some of the planets
- that forces acting on a moving body make it change speed and/or direction

In this topic you will learn

- how the gravitational pull between bodies is affected by their mass and the distance between them
- how gravity affects the movement of planets around the Sun and satellites around Earth
- how artificial satellites orbit the Earth and what they are used for
- how gravity affects space exploration

1 What can you remember?

a Which of the riders on the roller coaster ride above will feel the greatest force due to gravity? Why?
b How will the speed of the riders change as they go round the ride? Explain why.
c Will there be any other forces affecting their motion? How do you know?

PHYSICS — Gravity and space

J1 What is gravity?

YOU WILL LEARN!
- that gravity on Earth acts towards the centre of the planet
- that gravity is an attractive force that acts between objects with mass
- how scientists used observations to develop ideas about gravity

Mass, weight and gravity

The mass of an object is a measure of how much matter it contains. Mass is measured in kilograms. Weight is the name given to the force of gravity acting on an object. We sometimes talk incorrectly about our weight in kilograms when we mean our mass in kilograms. Our weight is actually a force and should be measured in newtons, N.

Points to discuss

1. Decide which of the things below are connected with the mass of the object and which are connected with its weight.
   - The density of an object.
   - An object rolling or sliding down a hill.
   - A cricket ball thrown horizontally would hurt if it hit you, a tennis ball would hurt less.
   - An object hung on an elastic band makes the band stretch.
2. Can you explain how it is possible for a single person to pull a canal boat along a canal, but impossible for them to lift it? Use forces in your answer.

Did you know

You can still see a descendent of the apple tree Newton is supposed to have watched an apple fall from, in the garden of Newton's house, Woolsthorpe Manor in Lincolnshire.

Newton

Forces, including weight, are measured in newtons because of the important work that Isaac Newton did on gravity. Legend says that Newton thought out his ideas about gravity after watching an apple fall from a tree in his garden. By coincidence, the weight of an average sized apple is about 1 newton. On Earth, a mass of 1 kg has a weight of 9.8 N, (rounded to 10 N for most calculations).

1 Isaac Newton

Find out more about Isaac Newton's work on gravity. Find out how he thought planets were affected by gravity. Write a short report.

162

Gravity and mass

Gravity is a force of attraction between masses. All masses exert a gravitational force on objects around them. The larger the mass of an object, the larger the force of gravity the object exerts but the force of gravity is such a weak force that we only notice the force of gravity due to really large masses, like the Earth.

Finding the mass of the Earth

In 1798, the British scientist Henry Cavendish used gravity to find the mass of the Earth. He placed a large lead sphere near a torsional balance and measured how much the wire twisted. This told him the force of attraction pulling the small spheres of the balance towards the large lead sphere. He compared this with the force of attraction pulling the small spheres towards the Earth and found the mass of the Earth was 6.0×10^{24} kg, very close to the most accurate value measured by modern scientists.

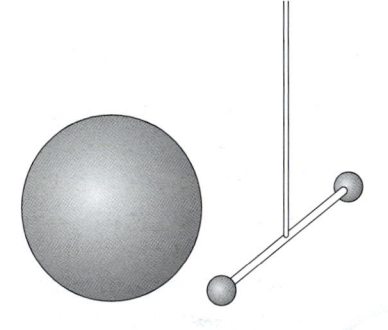

Which way does gravity act?

Things fall downwards, so gravity acts downwards. You probably think that's obvious, but which way is 'down'? For someone on the opposite side of the Earth, things fall in the opposite direction, so 'down' is in the opposite direction. For both of you, 'down' is actually towards the centre of mass of the Earth (the 'middle point' of the Earth's mass).

Eros is a tiny asteroid, so it exerts only a very small force due to gravity. If you stood on Eros you would just be able to detect which way was 'down'. However, because Eros is an elongated shape instead of a sphere, its centre of mass might be off to one side instead of exactly under your feet. So you would lean over and feel as if you were walking 'uphill' when you moved.

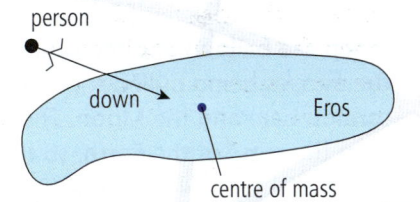

A torsional balance like the one Henry Cavendish used to weigh the Earth

Points to discuss

It is possible to create simulated gravity. Imagine the following situations.

1. A lift is moving downwards faster than gravity would make it fall. What will happen to a coin dropped from the pocket of someone in the lift? Which way will the people in the lift think is 'down'?

2. Some people are inside a huge cylinder that is spinning round like a playground roundabout. Which way will things fall? Which way will the people think is 'down'?

Did you know

All large heavenly bodies such as stars and planets are spheres. This is because their force due to gravity is strong enough to make all the bits move as far 'downwards' towards the centre of mass as they can. For a model of the Earth the size of a football even Mount Everest would 'stick up' less than the width of a human hair.

PHYSICS — Gravity and space

J2 How does gravity change?

YOU WILL LEARN!
- that the mass of an object always stays the same, but the weight can change
- how to use the gravitational force of a planet to calculate weights of objects of given mass on that planet
- that gravitational attraction between objects decreases as the distance between them increases
- how gravity affects space exploration

In his work on gravity, Newton explained that gravity is a two-way force. The Earth pulls on the falling apple, but the apple pulls on the Earth as well! We see the apple moving because it is much easier for the tiny mass of the apple to move than it is for the huge mass of the Earth to move. (Also an apple falling on the opposite side of the Earth at the same time would pull the Earth the other way!)

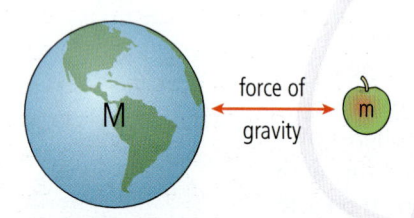

Gravity is a two-way force

How big is the gravitational force?

The size of gravity, the attractive gravitational force between two masses, depends on how big the two masses are.

When the balloon is dropped, the masses being pulled together by gravity are the mass of the Earth and the mass of the balloon. The balloon has a very small mass so the force of gravity between it and Earth is very small. The cannon ball has a much larger mass, so the force of gravity between it and Earth is much larger. We say that the cannon ball is heavier.

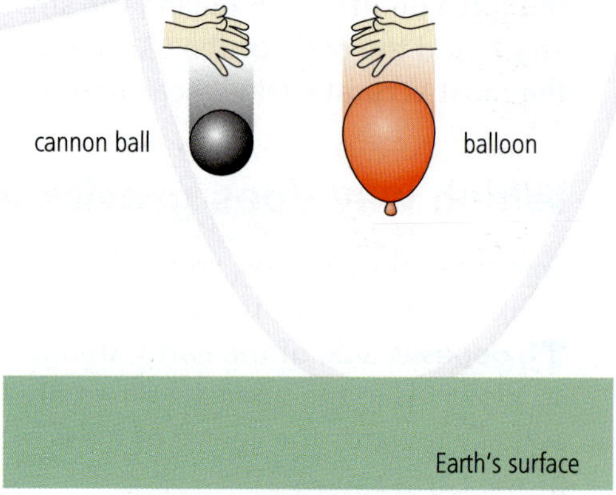

When the balloon and the cannon ball are dropped on the Moon the masses being pulled together by gravity are the balloon (or cannon ball) and the Moon. The mass of the Moon is much less than the mass of the Earth, so the force of gravity between the Moon and the balloon (or cannon ball) is much smaller than on Earth. We say that on the Moon the balloon and the cannon ball both weigh less than they do on Earth.

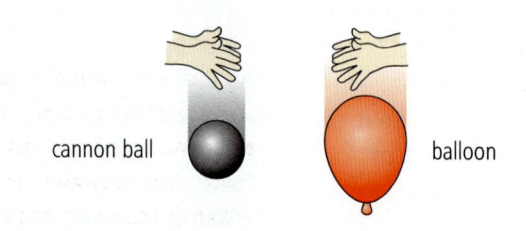

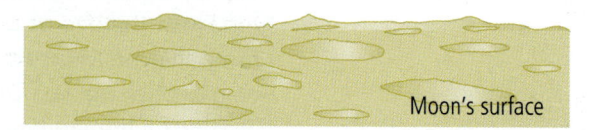

Which is heavier on Earth?

These are both much lighter than they were on Earth

Did you know ?

The force of gravity between the moon rock and the Moon is less than the force of gravity between the moon rock and Earth, so the rock weighs less on the Moon. The mass of the moon rock stays the same wherever it is, so it is just as hard to make the moon rock move by kicking it on the Moon as it would be on Earth.

PHYSICS   Gravity and space

Points to discuss

The force of gravity between an object and the Moon is about $\frac{1}{6}$ the force of gravity between the same object and the Earth. Imagine you are an astronaut on the surface of the Moon

1. What things will the smaller force of gravity make easier to do?
2. What things will the smaller force of gravity make harder to do?
3. What things will be unchanged by the smaller force of gravity?

1 Weights in different places

The table shows the force due to gravity on a 1 kg mass in different places.

Place	Force due to gravity on a 1 kg mass (N)	My approximate weight on this planet
Earth	10.0	
Moon	1.7	
Jupiter	25.0	
Mars	4.0	
Sun	280.0	
Saturn	10.0	
Pluto	0.6	

a. Copy out the table and use the information in it to calculate and record approximately how much you would weigh in each place.
b. Look at the range of objects you have been given, each labelled with its weight on Earth and its weight in a different place. Work out where each object would weigh the labelled weight.
c. Which place would you feel most at home in – if gravity were the only consideration? Why?

Thought model of gravity

The force of gravity between two objects also depends on how far apart they are. Increasing the distance between them decreases the gravitational attraction between them.

The force of gravity around a planet is a bit like the magnetic field around a magnet. The strength of the gravitational force gets weaker as the distance from the planet increases. The dotted gravitational field lines show which way an object would fall if it were dropped near the planet.

Rockets and space travel

If rockets are to travel into space, they have to escape the Earth's pull of gravity on them. If the forward thrust of the rocket is greater than the attractive force of gravity between the Earth and the rocket, then the rocket can escape the gravitational force holding it to Earth.

The large dog can escape because it can pull harder than the person. The rocket can escape if the forward thrust of the rocket is greater than the attractive force of gravity between the Earth and the rocket.

Did you know

We need gravity to keep our bones and muscles healthy. When astronauts are in weightless conditions they have to do special exercises to prevent their muscles weakening and their bones gradually wasting away.

PHYSICS — Gravity and space

Points to discuss

The force of gravity between the Earth and the rocket is called the weight of the rocket.

1. As the distance between the rocket and the Earth increases, the force of gravity between them gets less. How does the rocket's weight change? How would its speed change if the forward thrust stayed the same?
2. The forward thrust of the rocket comes from burning fuel. As fuel is burned the mass of the rocket decreases. How does this affect its weight? How would this affect its speed even if the gravity stayed the same?

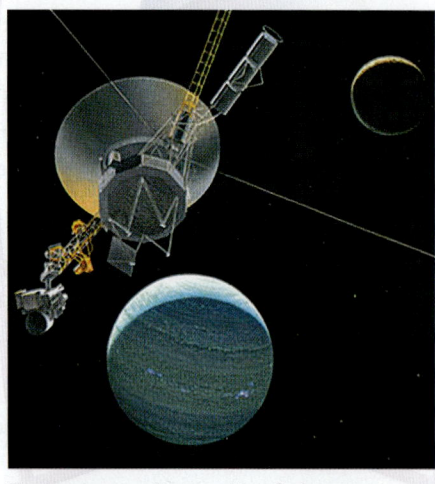

Using gravity to steer

Scientists can steer a spacecraft using the gravity of different planets. If a spacecraft goes close enough to a planet, the gravitational attraction of the planet will pull on the spacecraft and make it change direction. It is important to plan the path of the spacecraft very carefully. If the spacecraft goes too near the planet or goes too slowly it will be trapped by the force of gravity and crash into the surface of the planet.

Voyager uses the gravity of planets to change direction

2 Space exploration

Find out more about some aspect of space exploration. Write a short report. Possible topics to find out about could include:
- a particular space mission or spacecraft
- an individual astronaut
- a timeline of the major developments in space exploration.

Manned space travel

You have probably heard the expression 'There's no gravity in space'. Far enough away from any stars or planets that is true, but no manned spacecraft have ever gone that far out into space. The astronauts in the photo are still being affected by gravity from the Sun and planets. So how are they able to float around?

The astronauts are in free fall. They are falling freely under gravity, so to them no way seems to be 'downwards'. Imagine yourself inside a lift that was falling freely 'downwards'. If you let go of a coin, it would fall 'downwards' at the same speed as the lift. It would not move towards any of the walls, floor or ceiling. It would seem to just float in front of you.

Astronauts on a 'space walk'

3 Life in free fall

Imagine yourself in a space capsule in free fall.
a. How will you move around? How will you stop or change direction? What things will be easy or hard to do?
b. Draw a cartoon strip to illustrate some aspect of living in free fall.

Did you know

Astronauts doing 'space walks' have to be tied to the spacecraft. Even though both astronauts and spacecraft are in free fall, astronauts would find it very hard to get back to the spacecraft if they accidentally pushed themselves away. They cannot 'swim' back because there is no air to push against.

PHYSICS   Gravity and space

J3 How have our ideas about the solar system changed?

YOU WILL LEARN!
- that our ideas about the solar system have changed over time
- how to consider and evaluate evidence

People have been fascinated by the sky above them, and the objects in it, for thousands of years, since before written records began. The first attempts to explain the Sun, Moon and stars were probably in the form of legends.

1 Legends

Find out about a legend connected with either the Sun or the Moon. How old is the legend? Where does it come from? Does it attempt to explain the motion of the Sun or Moon?

The science of astronomy began with efforts to measure and explain aspects of the solar system. One of the earliest examples of astronomy was when the ancient Egyptians used their observations of the Sun to invent a calendar with 365 days in a year.

Is this an early calendar?

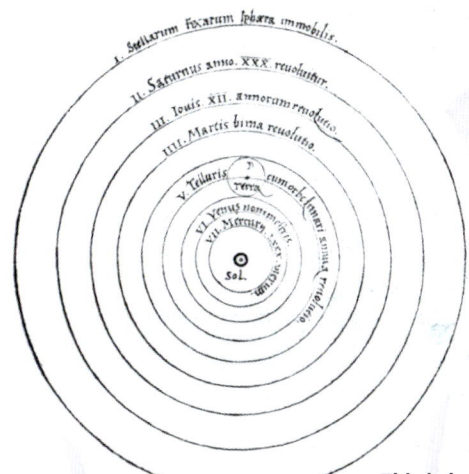

One of the major developments in our understanding of the solar system was the idea that the Earth and other planets circle the Sun, rather than all the 'heavenly bodies' circling the Earth. People sometimes think this is a relatively new idea, developed by Copernicus or Galileo, but 'heliocentric' models (from the Greek words for Sun and centre) of the solar system have been found dating from the 5th century AD in India, and the 3rd century BC in Greece. Chinese, Arab and African scientists were all centuries ahead of Europeans in their understanding of the movement of the Sun and planets.

This is how Copernicus pictured the solar system

2 History of astronomy

Find out more about one aspect of the history of astronomy. Possible ideas to research are given below:

- the history of astronomy in a country of your choice,
- the work of one astronomer,
- the discoveries about one planet, such as the Earth.

Make a poster to illustrate what you have found out.

Points to discuss

Scientists were generally slow to accept the idea that the Earth moved round the Sun because they had no understanding of gravity. Discuss some of the evidence that might have led them to accept this idea and reject earlier ideas about the Earth being the centre of the universe.

167

PHYSICS — Gravity and space

J4 What keeps the planets and satellites in orbit?

YOU WILL LEARN!
- that the Sun is massive and exerts a very large gravitational force which keeps planets in orbit
- how to relate the model of circular motion to data on the orbits of planets and satellites
- that the Moon is a natural satellite of the Earth, and its orbit is maintained by the Earth's gravitational pull

Scientists believe that all of our solar system formed over 4.5 billion years ago from a cloud of swirling dust and gas. If you look at a cloud of dust or smoke you will see that it has patches where the dust is thick and patches where it is more spread out. The early solar system would have been the same. Gravity tells us why this cloud became lots of individual objects instead of just one large lump of matter. Each tiny piece of matter felt a force of attraction from lots of directions, and moved in the direction of the resultant force.

Points to discuss
Imagine the dust cloud that became the solar system.
1. Which particles would exert the largest gravitational force on their neighbours, large particles or small particles?
2. Which particles would attract neighbouring particles from furthest away, large particles or small particles? Use gravity to explain why.

Why don't all the planets fall into the Sun?
The simple answer is because they are moving. You know from earlier work on forces that a moving object only changes speed or direction if a force acts on it. The force of gravity from the Sun is strong enough to make the planets change direction but not strong enough to pull them into the Sun.

Did you know
Nearly 99.9% of all the matter in our solar system is found in the Sun.

Did you know
The proportion of heavy elements like iron in our solar system tells scientists that our solar system actually formed from the remains of an earlier star that exploded in a supernova explosion.

1 Investigating circular motion

SAFETY: This investigation must be done outside, well away from other groups, so that any flying rubber bungs hit the ground before they reach any people.

Use the apparatus shown to whirl a rubber bung around at a steady speed on the end of a piece of string.

a. Predict what will happen to the motion of the whirling rubber bung if the string is cut. Use scissors to cut the string next to the metre rule.
b. Was your prediction correct? Use forces to explain what happened.

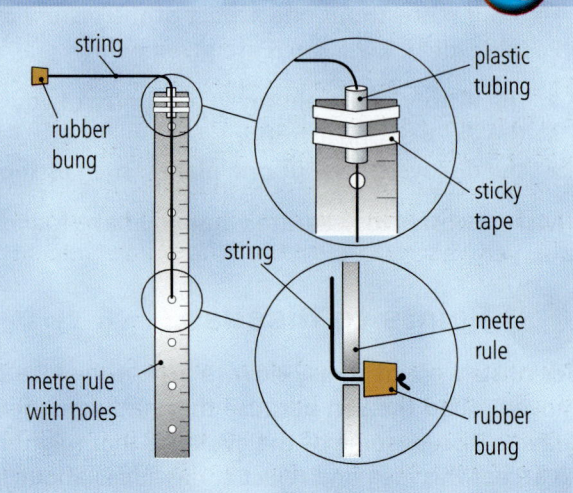

PHYSICS — Gravity and space

2 Circular motion, force and speed

SAFETY: This investigation must be done outside, well away from other groups, so that any flying rubber bungs hit the ground before they reach any people.

Use a force meter to show the force being exerted by a whirling rubber bung.

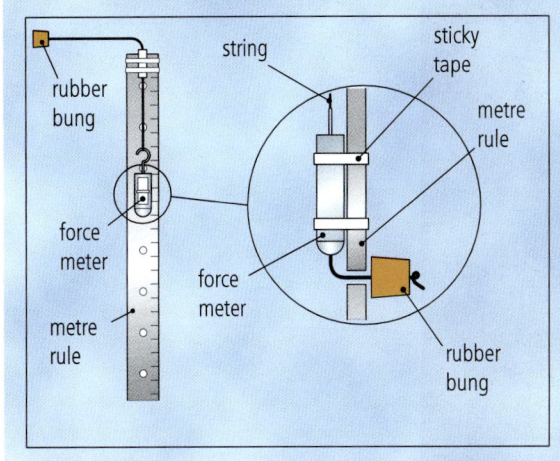

a   Whirl the rubber bung as slowly as you can. Count how many revolutions it does in 30 seconds. Record the force it exerts on the force meter.
b   Increase the speed of the bung. Again, record how many revolutions it does in 30 seconds, and the force it exerts on the force meter.
c   Try to take readings at 5 or 6 different speeds for the rubber bung.
d   Write a short conclusion stating how the force needed to keep the bung from flying off in a straight line is related to the speed the bung moves at.
e   Use forces to explain your conclusion.
f   Do you think any other factors affect the force needed to keep the bung moving in a circle? What could you do to find out?

Points to discuss

1   Assuming the mass of the Sun does not change, what 2 factors affect the size of the gravitational force between a planet and the Sun?

Imagine you could move the Earth around, but could not change the speed it moves at.

2   What would happen to the Earth if you moved it out to Pluto's orbit? (Hint: think about the force needed to make the Earth change direction).
3   What would happen to the Earth if you moved it inwards to Mercury's orbit?
(Hint: think about the force that would act on the Earth here).

Why doesn't the Moon orbit the Sun?

The gravitational force between the Moon and the Earth is approximately twice as strong as the gravitational force between the Moon and the Sun. This is because although the mass of the Earth is very much smaller than the mass of the Sun, the Earth is also very much closer to the Moon than the Sun is.

Where did the Moon come from?

Most scientists believe that the Moon formed early in the life of the solar system when an asteroid about the same size as Mars crashed into Earth. Large amounts of debris were thrown off into space. Gravity kept the debris orbiting about Earth, and pulled it together to form the Moon.

The surface of the Moon

3 Origins of the Moon

Two earlier theories about the origin of the Moon were:
- The Moon and the Earth formed together from the same cloud of dust.
- An asteroid came close to Earth and was captured by Earth's gravity.

Find out more about the theories of how the Moon formed in its orbit, and why scientists decided the earlier theories were incorrect.

169

PHYSICS   Gravity and space

J5   Artificial satellites

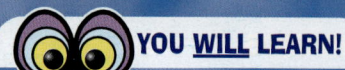

YOU WILL LEARN!
- about some uses of artificial satellites
- about information that can be gained using satellites
- how scientists work together to collect information and make predictions

Artificial satellites are man-made objects put into orbit around the Earth. They are used for many different purposes, such as scientific research, weather forecasting, communications and various observations of the Earth's surface.

The Vanguard satellite is used for scientific research

1 Uses of artificial satellites

Find out more about one of the uses of artificial satellites. Write a report or give a short talk.

How are satellites put into orbit?

Isaac Newton was the first person to ask himself this question, long before artificial satellites had been invented.

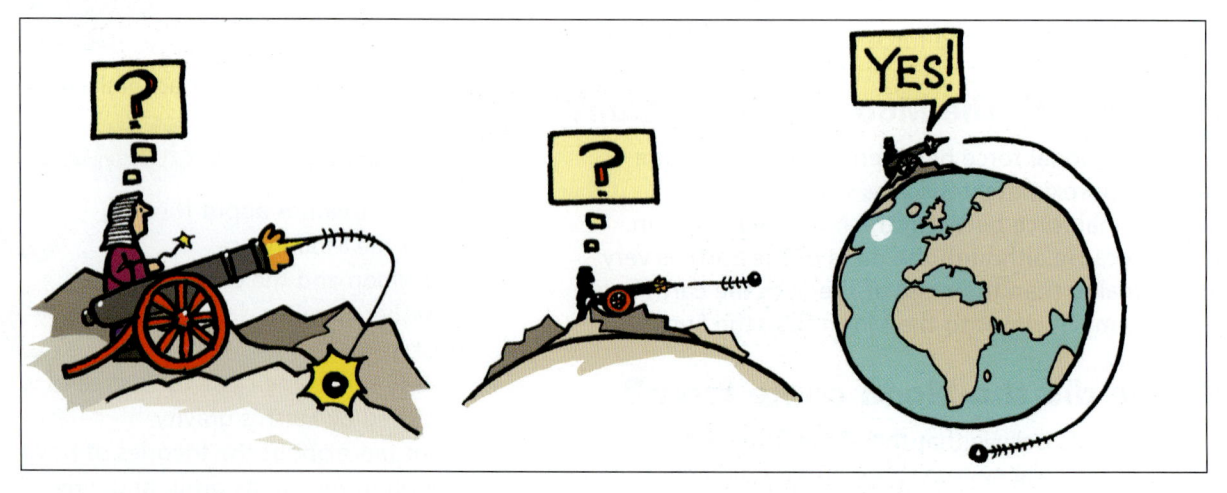

Newton imagined a cannon ball being fired from a cannon on top of a very tall mountain. If the cannon ball moved slowly, the gravitational force between it and Earth would quickly pull it down to the Earth's surface. If the cannon ball moved too quickly, the gravitational force would not make it change direction enough and it would hurtle out into space, never to be seen again. If it travelled at exactly the right speed it would fall downwards towards the Earth but never hit it – it would go into orbit around the Earth.

Launching real satellites

Real satellites could be launched into orbit in the same way as Newton's imaginary cannon ball. However, they are actually launched by firing them straight up from the Earth's surface. Smaller rockets on board the satellite itself are fired to adjust its speed and direction when it gets to the right height. The small rockets are used occasionally while the satellite is in orbit, to adjust its height and direction to keep it on the right track.

Points to discuss

1. How will the Earth's atmosphere affect a satellite travelling through it?
2. What thickness of atmosphere does a rocket launched straight up travel through, compared with a rocket launched horizontally?
3. Suggest a reason why satellites are launched vertically from the Earth's surface.

Geostationary orbits and polar orbits

There are two main types of satellite orbits.

- In a **geostationary orbit**, a satellite moves around the Earth in the same direction as the Earth itself is rotating in. It also takes 24 hours to complete one orbit. This means the satellite always stays above the same point on the Earth's surface.
- In a **polar orbit**, a satellite orbits the Earth much more quickly than in a geostationary orbit. The satellite travels in an orbit that takes it above the North Pole and the South Pole. As the Earth rotates beneath the satellite, instruments on board the satellite are able to view every part of the Earth's surface three or four times each day.

Did you know

The first artificial satellite was called Sputnik. It was launched by the Russians on October 4th 1957. In 1962 the 'Mariner 1' space probe was launched to find out about the planet Venus. Four minutes later it crashed into the Atlantic Ocean. A minus sign had been accidentally left out of the computer program!

There are two main types of satellite orbit

PHYSICS   Gravity and space

2 Which orbit is better?

a List as many uses as you can for each main type of satellite orbit.

b A satellite in a polar orbit travels much faster than a satellite in a geostationary orbit. What does this tell you about the height above the Earth's surface of each type of orbit?

c Use forces to explain your answer to part **b**.

Global Positioning System

The Global Positioning System (GPS) is a system of satellites sending out continual signals to say where they are above the Earth's surface.

The GPS tells this walker exactly where he is on the map

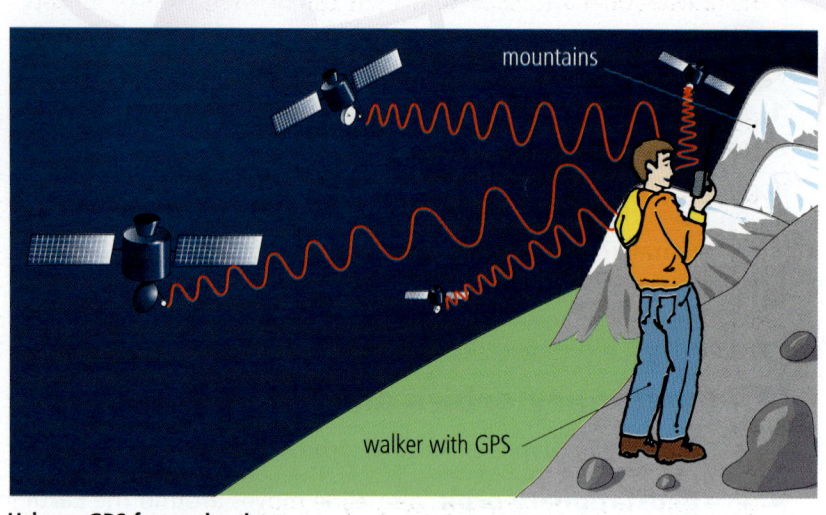

Using a GPS for navigation

Each satellite has an accurate atomic clock, so each signal carries a record of when the signal was sent. The hand-held GPS receiver receives signals from 4 different satellites at once. Because the signals have all come different distances they all carry different times. The receiver uses the different times to work out how far it is to each satellite and therefore the position of the receiver on the Earth's surface. The sort of GPS receivers used by walkers and leisure sailors give a position accurate to 100 m.

Did you know ?

The Global Positioning System was first developed by the United States Department of Defense in 1973.

Did you know ?

Mobile phone manufacturers can now put GPS receivers into mobile phones. So one day, when mobile phones are used to call the emergency services, they will also be able to send them a record of the phone's exact position.

PHYSICS — Gravity and space

Summary

Weight is the name given to the force of gravity acting on an object.

Weight is measured in newtons.

Gravity is a two-way force of attraction between masses.

All masses exert a **gravitational force** on objects around them.

Increasing the mass of an object increases the gravitational force it exerts.

Increasing the distance between objects decreases the gravitational force between them.

'**Downwards**' is the direction something falls under gravity.

Rockets can only leave Earth if the forward thrust of the rocket is greater than the gravitational force between Earth and the rocket.

The gravitational attraction of planets can be used to steer rockets.

When astronauts are '**weightless**' they are falling freely under the effect of gravity.

The planets are held in their orbits by the gravitational force between the Sun and the planets.

The Moon orbits the Earth because there is a larger gravitational force between Earth and Moon than between Moon and Sun.

Artificial satellites are man-made objects orbiting Earth.

Artificial satellites can be used for scientific research, observation, weather forecasting and communications.

Satellites in **geostationary orbit** remain above the same place on the Earth's surface.

Satellites in **polar orbit** move in orbits over the poles. They can view all of the Earth's surface every few hours.

Key words
artificial satellite
centre of mass
circular motion
downwards
free fall
geostationary orbit
GPS
gravitational force
gravity
polar orbit
weight
weightlessness

Summary Questions

1. Make your own glossary (list of meanings) for the Key words. Keep your definitions short.

2. On Earth a mass of 1 kg has a weight of 10 N.
   a. Explain the difference between mass and weight.
   b. Give two ways in which the weight of an object could be decreased without changing its mass.

3. On the surface of the Earth, objects fall 'downwards' under gravity.
   a. Give an example where objects would not fall in the same direction as gravity is acting.
   b. How could you create 'artificial gravity' for astronauts in free fall in a space station?

4. Two satellites of the same mass, S1 and S2, are in stable orbits about Earth, above the Equator. S1 is closer to Earth than S2.
   a. Which satellite will have the greater gravitational force between it and Earth? Why?
   b. Which satellite will be travelling faster? Why?
   c. What could you do to satellite S1 so that it experienced the same gravitational force as satellite S2?

173

PHYSICS Gravity and space

End of unit Questions

1 In our solar system, Pluto is usually the furthest planet from the Sun.
The shape of its orbit is not quite a circle. The diagram shows the shape of Pluto's orbit and the position of the Sun.

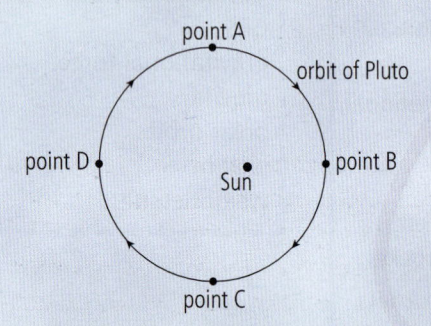

a Describe how the gravitational force of the Sun, acting on Pluto, alters as Pluto moves round its orbit through points A, B, C and D.
Give reasons for your answers. **3 marks**

b At which point, A, B, C or D, will Pluto have:
  i the most potential energy?
     Explain your answer. **1 mark**
  ii the most kinetic energy?
     Explain your answer. **1 mark**

2 The picture shows a man called Aristotle. He lived in Greece over 2000 years ago.

Aristotle said that the heavier an object is, the faster it will fall to the ground.

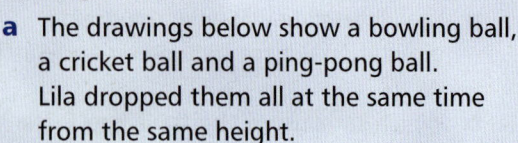

a The drawings below show a bowling ball, a cricket ball and a ping-pong ball. Lila dropped them all at the same time from the same height.

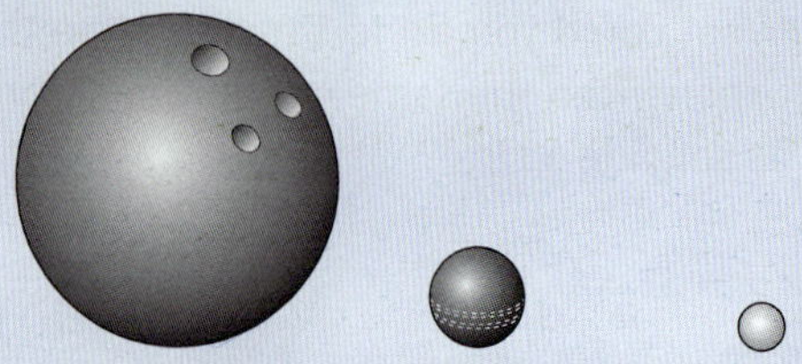

bowling ball mass = 5000g
cricket ball mass = 160g
ping-pong ball mass = 2.5g

If Aristotle was correct, which of the three balls would you expect to reach the ground first? Give the reason for your answer. **1 mark**

b Joe said that it would be a fairer test if Lila had only used a cricket ball and a hollow plastic ball as shown below.

cricket ball mass = 160g
hollow plastic ball mass = 56g

Why was Joe correct? **1 mark**

c About 400 years ago in Italy, a man called Galileo had a different idea. He said that all objects dropped from the same height would reach the ground at the same time.

  i Lila dropped a hammer and a feather at the same time from the same height.

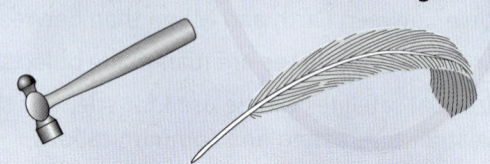

If Galileo was correct, which, if either, would reach the ground first? **1 mark**

  ii Gravity acts on both the hammer and the feather as they fall. Give the name of one other force which acts on them as they fall. **1 mark**

  iii An astronaut on the Moon dropped a hammer and a feather at the same time from the same height.

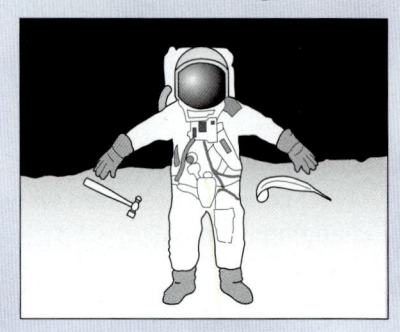

How would the results of the astronaut's experiment on the Moon be different from Lila's experiment on the Earth?
Explain your answer. **2 marks**

9K Speeding up

Introduction

Many people find travelling at high speed exciting. You probably have treasured memories of racing downhill on a bike or being scared by the speed of the latest theme park ride. From about 11 years old, a child's ability to judge speed and distance accurately improves very quickly. However, thousands of people still die in car accidents each year, often caused because they went at the wrong speed or misjudged someone else's speed.
In this unit you will find out about ways different sportsmen and women use forces to change the speed of themselves or objects, how to design objects that need to travel quickly or slowly, some safety features to cope with the dangers of travelling at high speed, and much, much more.

You already know

- what speed is and how to describe changes in speed
- that forces can cause an object to change speed or direction

In this topic you will learn

- the relationship between the balanced or unbalanced forces on an object and the way the object moves
- the effects of water resistance or air resistance on the speed of an object
- how streamlining reduces the effects of water or air resistance
- how balanced and unbalanced forces can be used to explain the movement of falling objects.

1 What can you remember?

Speed is important in many ways in the picture above. How many ways can you find? What effects do high or low speeds have in the situations you have found?

PHYSICS   Speeding up

K1   How fast is it moving?

YOU WILL LEARN!
- that speed can be calculated from the distance travelled and the time taken
- the units of speed
- how to use ICT to determine speed
- how to describe changes in a speed–time graph
- how to compare and evaluate different methods of measuring speed

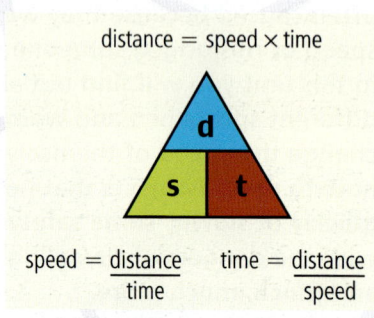

The speed of something tells us how far it travels in a certain time. At 20 miles per hour (20 mph) a cyclist travels 20 miles in one hour. At a speed of 20 metres per second (20 m/s or 20 ms^{-1}) a car travels 20 metres in one second. So to find out the speed of an object we need to know

- how far it travels
- how long it takes

The Speed Distance Time triangle

If we know values for any two of distance or speed or time, we can use the Speed Distance Time triangle to work out the other one.

The Speed Distance Time triangle does not tell us exactly what speed an object is travelling at for every moment in its journey. It tells us an average speed for the whole journey.

1 Calculating speed

Use the Speed Distance Time triangle to work out the answers to all the questions below. Remember to put the correct units in all your answers.

a A cyclist travels 30 km in 2 hours. What is her average speed?
b A duck swims at 1.5 m/s. How long will it take to complete 1 length of a standard (25 m) swimming pool?
c Class 9J's swimming robot can swim at 75 cm/s. How far will it be able to swim in the 5 minute time limit allowed in the 'Swimming Robot Finals'?

distance = speed × time

$$\text{speed} = \frac{\text{distance}}{\text{time}} \qquad \text{time} = \frac{\text{distance}}{\text{speed}}$$

Remember the Speed Distance Time triangle and you will always get the correct equation

What are the 'correct' units of speed?

The units of speed are always (a distance) per (a time), though these can be written in different ways, such as

    Kilometres per hour – kph (*not* kmph)
    Metres per second – m/s or ms^{-1}

The most common unit used in science is metres per second, m/s, but you should always choose a unit that is suitable for the object you are considering. A unit of m/s would not be sensible to measure the speed of a snail, or a glacier. A unit of kph or mph might be easier to visualise for a vehicle. A car travelling at a speed of 40 mph has a speed of 64 kph and 17.8 m/s, or 17.8 m s^{-1}.

Choose sensible units for the speed you want to measure

176

PHYSICS — Speeding up

Points to discuss

What would be sensible units of speed for each of the following?

A snail	A boat	The wind	A bullet	Light
A glacier	A sprinter	Continental drift	A car	Sound

2 Comparing speeds

We can only compare the speeds of two objects if their speeds are given in the same units. For each pair of objects given below, convert their speeds to the same units then decide which object is faster.

a A runner running at 15 mph, a cyclist cycling at 19 kph.
b A dolphin swimming at 3 m/s, a boat sailing at 8 kph.
c A car driving at 60 mph, a train travelling at 25 m/s.

Where necessary use the conversion factor: 5 miles = 8 kilometres.

Did you know

We can work out how fast the Earth moves through space. Earth completes one circle round the Sun, radius = 150 million km, in one year. Using the Speed Distance Time triangle gives us:

$$\text{Speed} = \frac{2 \times \pi \times 150\,000\,000}{365 \times 24}$$

speed = 107 589 kph

This speed can be converted to m/s by changing kilometres into metres and hours into seconds. This gives:

$$\text{speed} = \frac{107\,589 \times 1000}{60 \times 60}$$

speed = 29 886 m/s

Did you know

Scientists once said the Earth couldn't possibly move through space because if it did the high winds would blow us all off. We now know we don't feel the movement because the Earth's atmosphere moves as well.

3 Speeds that change

Let a car roll down a steep slope. Don't push it; just let it move down under gravity.

a What do you observe about the car's speed as it travels down the track?

Use a pair of light gates connected to a datalogger and computer to measure the speed of the car at different points down the track. The light gates work by measuring how long it takes the car to pass from one light gate to the next. The faster the car is travelling the shorter the time it takes to pass through the gates.

b Plot a graph of the car's speed against its distance down the slope.
c Describe how the speed of the car is changing as it goes down the slope.

Predict how the speed of the car down the slope would be affected by changing the mass of the car or the steepness of the slope.

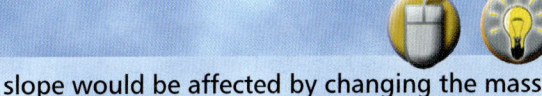

d Take whatever readings are necessary to test your prediction.
e Write a conclusion. Was your prediction correct?

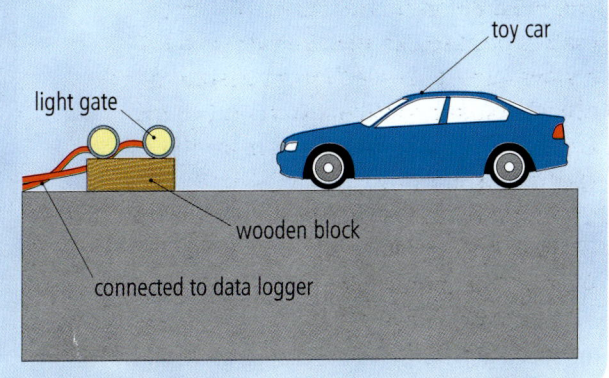

177

PHYSICS — Speeding up

Points to discuss

It is easier and more accurate to measure the speed of a car on a track using light gates than using hand-held timers. Discuss:

1. What measurements you would have to make and what calculations you would have to do, to complete Activity 3 using hand-held timers.
2. Why the light gates give more accurate values of speed than hand-held timers would.
3. Your school sports events almost certainly use hand-held stopwatches for measuring times. Suggest why these timers would be unsuitable at world-class athletics events.
4. What methods of timing, and methods of deciding the winner when runners cross the line 'together', are used at major athletics events?

Very accurate timing is needed to decide which of these is faster

Did you know

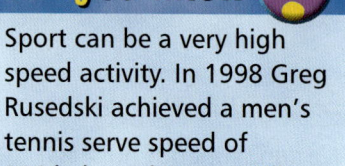

Sport can be a very high speed activity. In 1998 Greg Rusedski achieved a men's tennis serve speed of 238 kph, and Venus Williams achieved a women's tennis serve speed of 203 kph. In 2002 Shoaib Akhtar broke the '100 mph barrier' with a cricket bowling speed of 161 kph (100.04 mph).

Measuring very high speeds

There are many occasions when people want to measure high speeds. Weapons designers need to know how fast bullets and other missiles travel. Police officers need to measure how fast speeding cars are going. Cricket fast bowlers want to know if they have broken the 100 mph barrier yet, tennis players want to know how fast their serve is, and so on. There are two main ways to measure very fast speeds; high speed photography and speed guns.

High-speed photography takes lots of photos of the moving object, with a tiny fraction of a second between each picture. By measuring how far the object has moved between photos, its speed can be calculated.

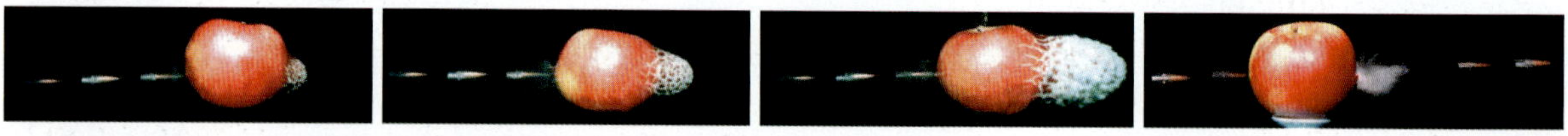

A time lapse photo of a moving bullet

A speed gun sends out radar or laser signals that bounce off the moving target and back to the speed gun. The moving object changes the wavelength of the radar or laser signal. The speed can be calculated from how much the wavelength has changed. Faster objects make the wavelength change more.

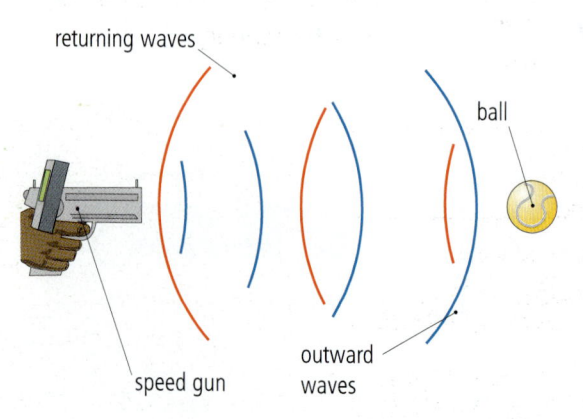

The speed gun measures the change between waves going out and waves returning

'Service speed' is important. Fast serves are harder to return correctly than slow ones.

PHYSICS   Speeding up

K2 How do forces affect speed?

YOU WILL LEARN!
- that a force on an object can produce a change in speed, called an acceleration
- that if no forces act, objects remain stationary or moving at a steady speed
- that the speed of an object is not changed if a force acts at right angles to the direction of movement

1 Forces on a moving object

Push an object so that it slides, first on a rough surface, then on a smooth surface.

a Describe carefully all the changes you observe in the speed of the object, on both surfaces.
b Draw a diagram to show the forces that act on the moving object.
c State any differences in the size of these forces between the rough and smooth surface.

When you first push the object there is a forward force from you, making the object speed up. As soon as you stop pushing there is no forward force. Two forces act to make the object slow down, friction and air resistance. We often ignore air resistance because it is usually very small compared with the friction.

An ice skater will slide a very long way without slowing down much because the ice in an ice rink is very smooth. The friction force slowing down the skater is very small. Imagine what would happen if you could make the ice friction-free, so there was no friction force.

The friction slowing down this skater is very small

Points to discuss

1 Are there any forces, other than friction, which would make the ice skater slow down or speed up?
2 In which direction do forces have to act to change the speed of the skater?
3 What effect might forces acting in a different direction have? (Imagine pulling sideways on a rope around the skater's waist – but not hard enough to make the skater fall over!)

Acceleration and deceleration

In everyday language, acceleration means speeding up. When something gets slower we say it is decelerating. Scientists often define acceleration as 'the rate of change of speed'. So a scientist would call slowing down 'negative acceleration', because the speed is changing, but getting smaller instead of larger. Something with a high positive acceleration gets faster very quickly, like a racing car leaving the starting line. Something with a low positive acceleration gets faster very gradually, like a bus. A car hitting a wall would have high negative acceleration.

slow positive acceleration

high positive acceleration

high negative acceleration

Did you know?
Ice is only slippery because the pressure of your weight on the ice makes some of the ice melt. You slide on the thin layer of water on top of the ice, just as you might slide on water on a smooth floor. Ducks can walk easily on the ice because they don't cause enough pressure for the ice to melt. For them, ice isn't slippery!

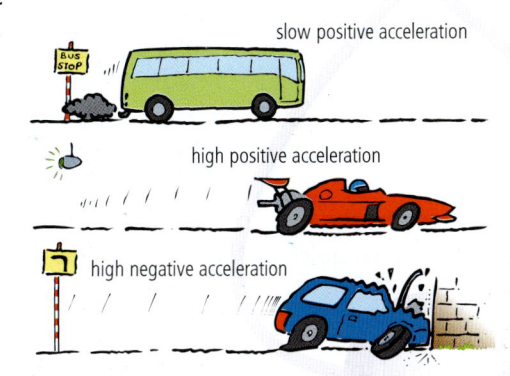

Ice isn't slippery for ducks!

179

PHYSICS   Speeding up

Points to discuss

Can you work out a relationship between the direction of the forces acting on an object, the direction of movement of the object and whether the acceleration is positive or negative?

2 Investigating acceleration and mass

Set up a long slope that a trolley can roll down. Use a pair of light gates to measure the speed of the trolley, as in K1 Activity 3.

Adjust the slope to compensate for friction. Make the slope just steep enough so that a trolley will rest on it without moving but will roll down the slope at a constant speed if given a gentle push. Because the speed is constant, the force of gravity pulling the trolley down the slope is just balanced by the friction force slowing it down.

Use a force meter to pull the trolley down the slope with a constant force. (Practise a few times until you can keep the force meter reading constant while you are pulling.)

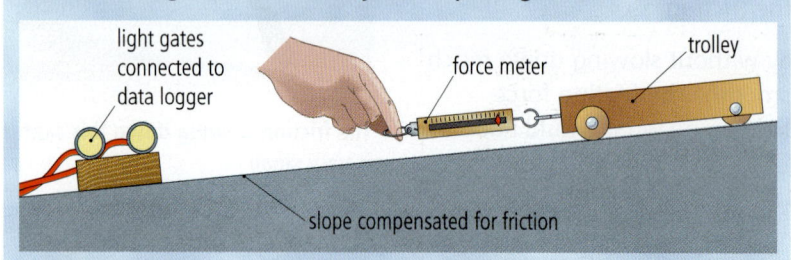

a Record the speed of the trolley at different points down the slope.
b Plot a graph of speed against distance down the slope.
c Increase the mass of the trolley. Repeat **a** and **b** for the new mass. Plot the graph of speed against distance on the same axes as before. Label the new line with the new mass of the trolley.
d Increase the mass of the trolley again. Repeat readings of speed again and draw a third line on your graph.
e Write a conclusion to explain how the acceleration (how quickly the speed changes – that is the gradient of your graph) changes as the mass increases.
f Predict the effect of changing the force used to pull a trolley of constant mass.
g Test your prediction using a trolley of constant mass and large and small forces. Were you correct?
h Write a statement explaining the connection between force and acceleration (how quickly the speed changes).

You found in Activity 2 that increasing the mass of a trolley made its acceleration less; it did not speed up so quickly. We can write this as

$$\text{acceleration} \propto \frac{1}{\text{mass}}$$

The symbol $\propto$ means 'is proportional to'.

Did you know

The acceleration of fighter planes is measured in 'g-force', where an acceleration of 1 'g-force' (1G) is the same as the acceleration due to gravity. If a fighter plane accelerates too quickly, the large 'g-force' could kill the pilot. An acceleration of 5G will make a pilot pass out and 9G for more than a few seconds is fatal.

PHYSICS — Speeding up

Increasing the mass decreases the acceleration.

Also, increasing the force on the trolley increases its acceleration. We can write this as

$$\text{Force} \propto \text{acceleration}$$

We can use these relationships to explain many of the everyday effects we see.

Making objects start to move

Imagine you have to throw two objects of similar size but very different mass, such as a shot and a plastic ball. Which is harder to throw? To make an object begin to move you have to use force to change its speed, to give it acceleration. The mass of the shot is much bigger, so the same amount of force from you makes it accelerate much less. You have to use much more force to make it move forward fast enough so that it does not land on your toes.

Racing cars

Racing cars need a very high acceleration, so they get up to maximum speed as quickly as possible. They achieve this in two ways:

- Powerful engines capable of exerting large forces. For any given mass of car, a bigger force means higher acceleration.
- Very small, light structure. For any given force from the engine, the less mass the car has, the higher its acceleration.

Points to discuss

Use your knowledge of force, mass and acceleration to explain these things.

1. Runners and shot-putters are both muscular, but runners tend to be light and shot-putters tend to be massive.
2. Buses have larger engines than cars, producing more force, but buses still have a smaller acceleration than cars.
3. It is much harder to stop a shopping trolley full of heavy shopping than to stop an empty trolley.

Did you know?

In 1966, a jammed engine caused a Royal Navy ship to reverse slowly into a stone jetty. The negative acceleration was small, as the change in speed was small, but because the mass of the ship was so large, the force was enough to shorten the ship by more than 2 metres. The impact compressed the air in the ship. One sailor, who was halfway through a hatch at the time of impact, was shot nearly 5 metres into the air by the compressed air escaping.

PHYSICS — Speeding up

K3 How can we increase speed?

You know that in everyday situations, forces do not make objects accelerate continually. For example, if you were to pedal a bike as hard as you could you would speed up. But however hard you pedalled and whatever gear you used, you would eventually reach a speed where you couldn't go any faster.

When the forces on a moving object are balanced, the object will move at a constant speed. So when the forward force from you is equal to the friction and the air resistance you cannot accelerate any more, you cannot go any faster.

Points to discuss

Look at the forces acting on the cyclist.

1. What three changes to the forces would make the cyclist go faster?
2. How could you change any of the three forces shown?
3. Is there anything else you could change to make the cyclist faster?

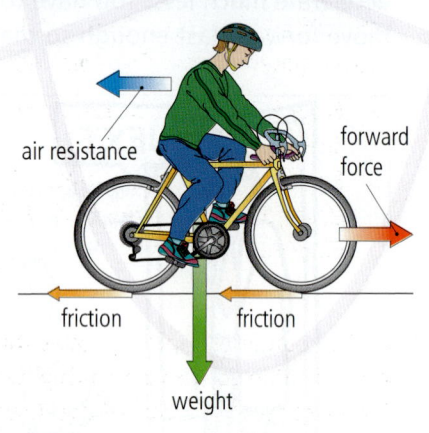

What is air resistance?

Whenever an object moves through air, it has to push the air out of the way. The air resists being moved – it pushes back. We can use the particle model to explain why air resistance exists. A force has to be used to accelerate each tiny particle of air, to make it move out of the way. Each particle only needs a tiny force to move it, but all the tiny forces add up to make the air resistance we notice.

YOU WILL LEARN!

- that air resistance and water resistance are forces that oppose motion
- how the effects of air resistance and water resistance can be reduced
- that air and water resistance change as the speed changes
- that the energy needed to keep an object moving depends on the resistance to movement
- how to use the particle model to explain some effects of air resistance

The size of some of these forces changes as the speed changes

The cyclist on the right has to push many more particles of air out of the way as he moves along, so he has a much greater air resistance

Points to discuss

If you have ever tried to wade across a swimming pool you will know that it is much harder to move through water than through air.

1. Use the particle model to explain why water resistance is much greater than air resistance.
2. Why is it easier to move through water by swimming than by wading?

182

PHYSICS Speeding up

Reducing resistance to motion

If air or water resistance is decreased, less forward force is needed to balance the force slowing the object down. Less energy is needed to make the object move forward at a constant speed, so a fish or a cyclist needs less food and a vehicle uses less fuel. If the air resistance of a vehicle can be reduced, more of the forward force of the engine can be used to make the vehicle accelerate, so the vehicle will have a better acceleration and a higher top speed than a similar vehicle with more air resistance. We reduce the air or water resistance of an object by making it more streamlined.

1 What shapes are streamlined?

Use a fixed mass of plasticine to make a range of different shapes. Drop them through a viscous liquid and record the time the different shapes take to fall a fixed distance. Find the most streamlined shape. Consider how to gather reliable data.

a How is the 'time of fall' used to tell how streamlined a shape is?
b Does it matter if the mass of plasticine is the same each time?
c Was your most streamlined shape the shape you expected? Give your reasons.

As a streamlined object moves through air or water, the air or water is able to flow smoothly round the edges of the object. A non-streamlined object produces vortices (swirls or whirlpools) of air or water around it, and areas where air or water are trying to rush back into the vacuum left by the moving object.

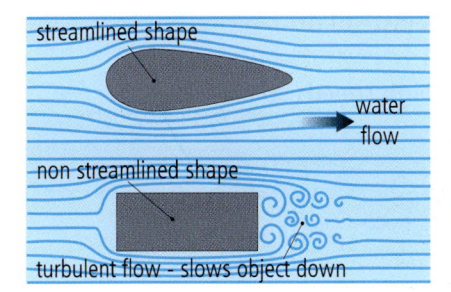

Points to discuss

Use your knowledge of water flow, air flow and streamlining to suggest why:

1 marine mammals usually have smooth skin instead of fur
2 fish scales all point 'backwards'
3 professional cyclists wear skin tight cycling shorts made from smooth 'Lycra' material, 'tear-drop' shaped helmets, and often shave their legs
4 boat owners regularly clean off barnacles that attach themselves to the underside of boats.

Did you know

Lorries, racing cars, motorbikes and cyclists can reduce the energy they use by over 25% by slipstreaming – following very close behind the vehicle in front. It is not only the vehicle behind that benefits, by not having to push air out the way. The vehicle in front saves energy as well. Any moving vehicle leaves a slight vacuum behind it, which pulls it backwards. If two vehicles are very close together, the air flows round both, and there is no vacuum behind the front vehicle. Slipstreaming is VERY, VERY DANGEROUS. The vehicle behind has NO chance of stopping safely if the vehicle in front brakes suddenly.

PHYSICS Speeding up

2 Speed and air resistance

Set up a pair of light gates to measure the speed at different points for a trolley rolling down a long slope, compensated for friction. (See K2 Activity 2 for details on how to compensate for friction.)

Attach a large sheet of card to the trolley to give it a large cross section. This makes the effect of air resistance easier to measure.

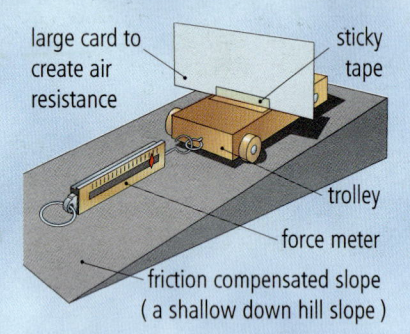

a Use a force meter to pull the trolley down the slope at a slow, constant speed. Record the value of the force on the force meter.

b Use a force meter to pull the trolley down the slope at a higher, constant speed. Again record the force needed to pull the trolley.

c Increase the speed again, and again record the force needed.

d What connection can you see between the force needed to pull the trolley and the speed it travels at?

e When the trolley travels at constant speed, what is the force from you being used for? (Remember you have already compensated for friction.)

f What is the relationship between air resistance and speed?

Points to discuss

Use your knowledge of speed and resistance to movement to explain the following things.

1 It is possible to walk holding an open umbrella in front of you, but much harder to run with it.
2 It is possible to walk through the water in a swimming pool, but impossible to run.
3 High-speed catamarans have two very narrow hulls instead of one much wider hull.
4 Speed boats and jet skis are designed to lift up at high speeds so much less of their hull is in contact with the water.

How do these boats reduce their water resistance?

PHYSICS   Speeding up

Some cars have a more streamlined shape than others

3 Fuel consumption of cars

The fuel consumption of a car is related to how much forward force the engine is producing. Look at the range of cars shown and answer these questions.

a When a car is travelling at constant speed on a horizontal road, what is the forward force of the engine being used for?
b For a car travelling at constant speed, how will the fuel consumption be related to the shape? Why?
c Which of the cars pictured would you expect to have the highest fuel consumption at any given speed? Which car would have the lowest fuel consumption? Why?
d For a car travelling at constant speed, how will the mass of the car affect the fuel consumption? Why?

Air resistance and heat

Our solar system contains many meteoroids (lumps of rock orbiting the Sun). If one enters the Earth's atmosphere it glows white-hot and burns up. We see it as a shooting star and call it a meteor. If part of it reaches the ground we call it a meteorite. The meteor glows white-hot in the Earth's atmosphere because it is falling at very high speed towards the Earth. As it pushes particles of air out of the way, the friction between the meteor and the air particles causes the meteor to get very hot, just as your hands get warm if you rub them firmly and quickly together.

Space craft returning to Earth's atmosphere also get very hot. Scientists prevent them from burning up in four ways:

- by making them as streamlined a shape as possible
- by building them from materials with very high melting points
- by coating them in tiles that are very smooth and non-stick, to reduce the friction as much as possible
- by using graphite in the tiles to conduct heat away from the nose of the spacecraft, the part that gets hottest when the spacecraft re-enters Earth's atmosphere.

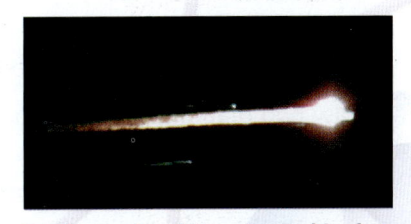

Friction makes this meteor white-hot as it enters the Earth's atmosphere

Did you know ?

The Teflon material that is now a common non-stick coating on saucepans was developed as a 'super-smooth' coating for spacecraft, to reduce the risk of them burning up on re-entry into the Earth's atmosphere.

PHYSICS   Speeding up

K4 Using graphs to show changes in speed

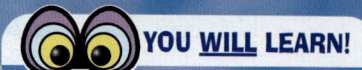

YOU WILL LEARN!
- how the upward force of air resistance and the downward force of weight affect the speed of a parachute
- how to interpret distance–time graphs and relate them to real situations
- how to draw and interpret speed–time graphs

These sky divers are in free fall

Sky divers are able to experience several minutes of free fall before they have to open their parachutes and slow down before landing. While they are in free fall and travelling at constant speed, they appear to be weightless. If they stood on bathroom scales as they fell, there would be no force between them and the scales, and the scales would read zero.

Even when they appear weightless, sky divers still have the force due to gravity (their weight) acting downwards on them and air resistance acting upwards. Friction acts upwards too, as the sky diver rubs against the air particles they pass, but it is usually just included as part of the air resistance force.

1 Forces on a sky diver

Draw two diagrams to show the forces acting on a sky diver
- before she opens her parachute
- after she opens her parachute.

a How do the forces change when the parachute is opened?
b How will the changing forces affect her speed?

The speed of the sky diver goes through several stages during their fall.

- When they leave the aeroplane their speed increases rapidly due to the effect of gravity.
- They reach a constant speed, called **terminal velocity**, when they are in free fall.
- They slow down very quickly as soon as they open their parachute.
- They reach a second, slower constant speed with their parachute open.

Did you know?
The record for the longest free fall was set in 1960 by Col. Joseph Kittinger, who fell over 25 km from a hot air balloon.

PHYSICS — Speeding up

We can show all these changes on a distance–time graph.

Points to discuss

1. Identify each of the different speed stages on the distance–time graph.
2. For each stage, decide the relative sizes of the weight and the air resistance.

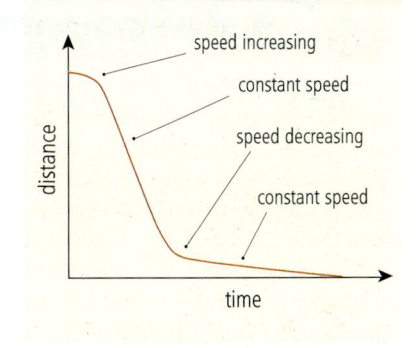

Speed–time graphs

Speed–time graphs show how speed changes much more easily than distance–time graphs do. Look at the speed–time graph for the sky diver falling.

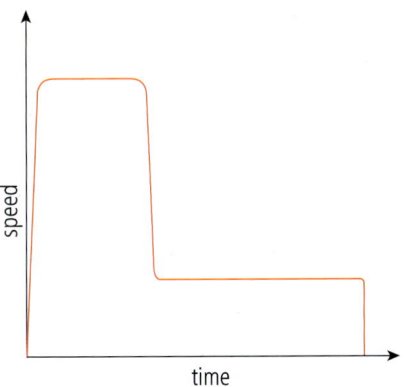

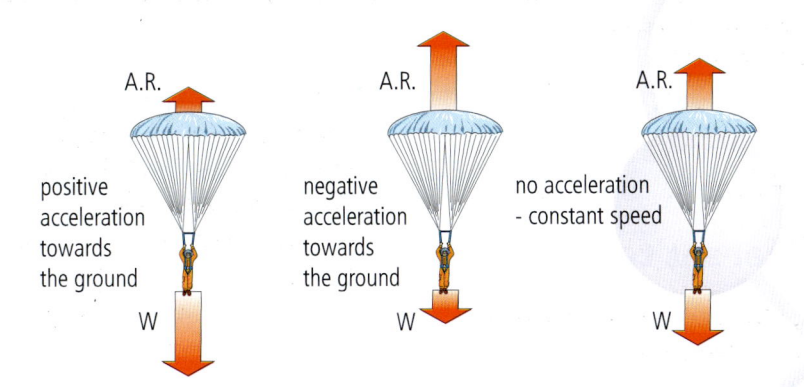

Did you know

The official record for the largest number of people to make up a free fall formation (sky divers in contact with each other) was 200. Parachutists from 10 nations stayed in the formation for over 6 seconds.

The diagram shows how the acceleration varies with the size of the upward and downward forces.

- positive acceleration towards the ground
- negative acceleration towards the ground
- no acceleration - constant speed

2 Interpreting a speed–time graph

a. Copy out the speed–time graph and put the following labels in the correct places.
   - Sky diver has landed.
   - High positive acceleration towards ground.
   - Low constant speed.
   - Negative acceleration towards ground.

PHYSICS Speeding up

3 More speed–time graphs

Each of the speed–time graphs below is for a ball.

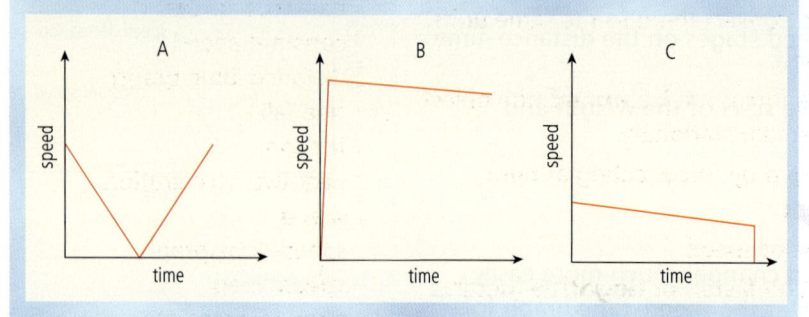

[Graph A: speed vs time — speed decreases to zero then increases]
[Graph B: speed vs time — speed rises sharply then decreases slightly]
[Graph C: speed vs time — speed stays roughly constant then drops]

For each graph:

a describe how the speed of the ball changes
b suggest a situation where the speed of the ball might change like this.

Terminal velocity

You have seen that sky divers do not accelerate continually, even without parachutes. You already know that cars reach a top speed where they cannot accelerate any more. So what causes moving objects to reach this terminal velocity where they cannot get any faster?

The answer is usually air resistance. As an object gets faster the air resistance gets larger. Eventually, the air resistance gets as large as the force making the object move. The forces on the object are balanced and the object can't speed up.

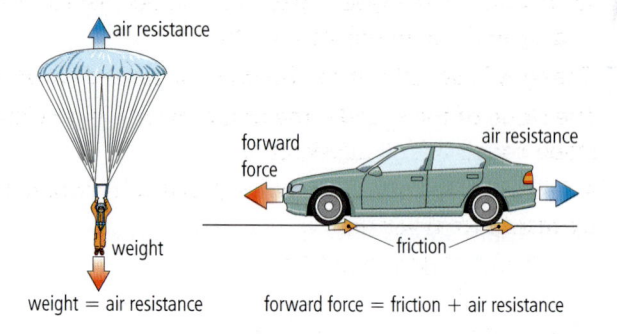

weight = air resistance

forward force = friction + air resistance

Why do objects have different terminal velocities?

If a sky diver's parachute failed to open, they would reach a terminal velocity of about 200 kph, which would certainly be fatal when they hit the ground. Yet, if a mouse jumped from the same aeroplane it would float slowly and gently to the ground and walk away unharmed. The secret is in the weight and the air resistance of the falling creature. The smaller an animal is, the larger its air resistance compared with its weight.

A falling mouse has a very small weight, compared with its air resistance, so it only accelerates for a short while under gravity before its weight and its air resistance balance and it reaches terminal velocity. It has a low terminal velocity because it only accelerated for a short while.

188

PHYSICS — Speeding up

Summary

The **speed** of something tells us how far it travels in a certain time.

The **Speed Distance Time triangle** can be used to calculate speeds.

To compare two speeds we have to convert them to the same units.

Forces can produce changes in speed.

If no forces act on an object, or the forces are **balanced**, the object will move at a constant speed or remain stationary.

The speed of an object is not changed by forces acting at right angles to the direction of movement.

Acceleration is the rate of change of speed.

Acceleration can be **positive** (getting faster) or **negative** (getting slower).

The acceleration can be increased by increasing the force on a constant mass, or by decreasing the mass for a constant force.

Air resistance and **water resistance** are forces that oppose movement.

Air resistance exists because an object moving through air has to push the particles of air out of its way.

Increasing the speed of an object increases its air resistance.

Air resistance at a given speed can be decreased by **streamlining** and by making an object smooth.

Changes in speed can be shown on a **speed–time graph**.

The slope of the speed–time graph gives the acceleration. A steep slope equals a high acceleration.

A falling object reaches **terminal velocity** when its weight and its air resistance balance.

Key words

- acceleration
- air resistance
- balanced forces
- constant speed
- distance–time graph
- free fall
- friction
- negative acceleration
- speed
- speed–time graph
- streamlined
- terminal velocity

Summary Questions

1. Make your own glossary (list of meanings) for the Key words. Keep your definitions short.

2. Use the Speed Distance Time triangle to calculate the following things.
   a. The speed in kph of a runner who completes 20 km in 1 hour 20 minutes.
   b. How far a car will travel in 5 minutes if it travels at an average speed of 12 m/s.
   c. The time it takes a person to walk 5 km if they walk at a speed of 1.5 m/s.

3. Find out which is travelling faster, a car driving at 35 m/s or a train travelling at 90 mph.

4. A car is allowed to roll down a hill, with its engine turned off. State, with reasons, how each of the things listed below would affect the speed of a car at the bottom of the hill.
   a. Steepness of the hill
   b. Friction between car and road
   c. Shape of the car
   d. The length of the hill
   e. Mass of the car

5. a. Use the particle model to explain why the terminal velocity of an object dropped through water is much less than the terminal velocity of the same object dropped in air.
   b. Suggest two ways in which the terminal velocity through water could be increased.

6. Draw speed–time graphs to show the vertical (downwards) speed for the following objects.
   a. A cannon ball fired from the top of a castle.
   b. A feather dropped from the same castle.

End of unit Questions

1 When a car is being driven along, two horizontal forces affect its motion. One is air resistance and the other is the forward force.

   a i Explain how molecules in the air cause air resistance. *1 mark*
      ii Explain why air resistance is larger when the car is travelling faster. *1 mark*
   b i Compare the sizes of the forward force and the air resistance when the car is speeding up. *1 mark*
      ii Compare the sizes of the two forces while the car is moving at a steady 30 miles per hour. *1 mark*
   c The forward force has to be larger when the car is travelling at a steady 60 mph than when it is travelling at a steady 30 mph. Why is this? *1 mark*
   d The forward force is the result of the tyres **not** being able to spin on the road surface.
      What is the name of the force that stops the tyres spinning? *1 mark*

2 Speed cameras are used to detect motorists who break the speed limit. A number of lines 2 m apart are painted on the road. As a speeding car crosses the painted lines, the camera takes two photographs, 0.5 s apart.

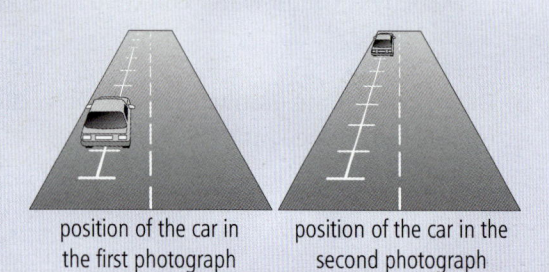

   a i How far did the car move between the two photographs?
         Give the correct unit. *1 mark*
      ii How fast is the car in the photographs moving in m/s? *1 mark*
   b It takes 0.0002 s to take each photograph. How far does the car move while the speed camera is taking **one** photograph? *1 mark*
   c The speed camera gives out bright flashes to provide enough light for the photographs.
      How does the light from the flash get back to the camera to produce the photographs? *1 mark*

3 A sky diver jumped out of an aeroplane. After falling for some time she opened her parachute. The graph below shows how the speed of the sky diver changed from the moment she jumped out of the aeroplane until she landed on the ground.

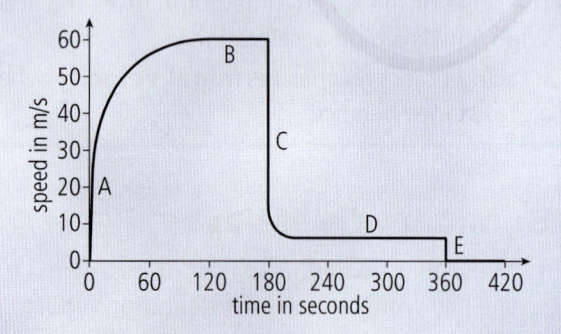

   a What happened at 180 seconds and at 360 seconds after the sky diver jumped out of the aeroplane? *2 marks*
   b There was an increase in air resistance on the sky diver as her speed increased. Explain how the graph shows this. *1 mark*
   c Two sections of the graph show where the air resistance was equal and opposite to the sky diver's weight. Which sections are they?
      Give the letters. *1 mark*
   d i Use the graph to estimate how far the sky diver fell between 180 s and 360 s. *1 mark*
      ii Why can this only be an approximate figure? *1 mark*

9L Pressure and moments

Introduction

Pressure is a familiar and important part of our everyday lives. You all know that it will hurt if you tread on a drawing pin, that a bench is more comfortable to sit on than a fence, that a sharp knife cuts better than a blunt one. This unit explains these and many more everyday examples of pressure. It moves on to look at pressure in liquids and gases and some of the many ways we use this, such as car brakes and spray cans. The final part of the unit looks at different types of levers, leading on to how moments of forces can be used to explain many familiar situations, including why 'top heavy' objects fall over and why door handles are not positioned in the middle of the door!

You already know

- how to identify the directions in which forces act
- how to represent forces using arrows
- how to calculate surface areas of shapes
- how muscles in the human body work in pairs to produce movement

In this topic you will learn

- what pressure is and its effect in a range of everyday situations
- about pressure in water and other liquids, and how it can be used
- about different types of levers, including levers in the human body
- the conditions that are necessary for objects to balance
- the principle of moments

1 What can you remember?

Forces do not always make an object move. What other effects can forces have? Identify places in the picture where a force is affecting an object. What effect is the force having?

PHYSICS   Pressure and moments

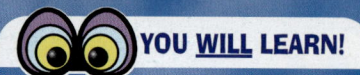

L1 What is pressure?

YOU WILL LEARN!
- ▶ how the effect of a force depends on the area it acts on
- ▶ how to calculate the pressure caused by a force
- ▶ how to use pressure to explain a range of everyday situations

People often speak of pressure 'pushing down' on something, perhaps using phrases like, 'a barometer measures air pressure pushing down on Earth' or 'the weight I lifted was my personal best but I could really feel the pressure pushing down on me'. This makes it sound as though pressure is just another word for force, but it isn't. Pressure is a measure of how concentrated the force is. The higher the pressure, the more you notice the effect the force is having. Our sense of touch is a good way to begin to compare pressures. High pressures hurt, low pressures don't.

Points to discuss

Look at the pairs of people.

1. Decide which picture in each pair represents high pressure and which low pressure. (Remember: high pressure hurts.)
2. Decide one factor that affects the size of the pressure. What effect does it have?

Points to discuss

Now find the second factor that affects how large the pressure is. Look at these pictures.

1. Again, decide which picture in each pair represents high pressure and which low pressure. (Remember: high pressure hurts.)
2. What is the second factor that affects the size of the pressure? What effect does it have?

PHYSICS   Pressure and moments

Calculating pressure

The factors affecting pressure can be summarised in two statements:

Pressure is directly proportional to force (doubling the force doubles the pressure)

$$P \propto F$$

Pressure is inversely proportional to area (halving the area doubles the pressure)

$$P \propto \frac{1}{A}$$

These relationships can be combined to give an equation that can be used to work out the exact size of the pressure.

$$\text{Pressure} = \frac{\text{Force}}{\text{Area}}$$

The normal units for pressure are N/m^2 (can be written as Nm^{-2}) or N/cm^2 (can be written as Ncm^{-2}), because force is measured in N and area is measured in m^2 or cm^2.

Did you know

Pressure is sometimes measured in pascals or bars. Pascals is just another name for N/m^2 and is named after Blaise Pascal, a seventeenth-century scientist who made early discoveries about pressure. Bars are used to measure the pressure of gases. 1 bar is 'normal' atmospheric pressure.
1 bar = 101 325 Pa
1 bar = 101 325 N/m^2

1 Calculating pressure

The diagram shows some of the different ways you could exert pressure on the floor.

a Calculate how much pressure you normally exert on the floor. (What will you need to measure?)
b Calculate the maximum and minimum pressure you could exert on the floor. Take care not to hurt yourself.

Who is exerting the most pressure on the floor?

To exert pressure on a surface, a force has to push directly onto the surface, at right angles to the surface. If the force acts parallel to the surface it will not exert any pressure on the surface at all. If the force is at an angle to the surface then some of the force, but not all of it, will exert a pressure on the surface. We can 'see' this happening if we imagine a heavy ball on a piece of rubber.

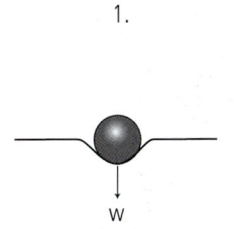

1.

W

2.

W

3.

W

The force acting downwards is the weight of the ball. All this force acts at right angles to the rubber sheet so the rubber sheet has a large pressure on it and is distorted a lot.

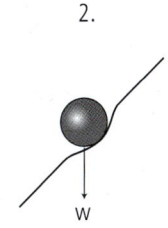

Now only some of the weight acts at right angles to the rubber sheet, so the pressure is less and the rubber sheet is distorted less.

The weight acts straight downwards, parallel to the surface of the rubber sheet. There is no pressure at all on the rubber sheet and it is not distorted.

PHYSICS — Pressure and moments

Using pressure

There are many situations where we want either high pressure or low pressure. Ice skaters use very narrow blades on their ice skates because the small area makes the pressure on the ice large. This melts a layer of the ice so that the ice skate can slide easily. Snowshoes are made with as large an area as possible. This is to make the pressure as low as possible so the snowshoe does not sink into soft snow.

Points to discuss

Use your knowledge of pressure to explain the following.

1 Sharp knives cut more easily than blunt knives.
2 Nails have a sharp point but a blunt head.
3 Firemen rescuing people who have fallen through ice put ladders out over the ice to crawl across.
4 Historic houses often have signs saying 'No stiletto heels to be worn'.
5 Camels have large, flat feet.
6 When we want to squash something we instinctively push straight down on it.

Did you know

The Dental Science Handbook (1970) published by the American Dental Association says that humans can bite with a pressure of up to 15 tons per square inch. That is roughly the same pressure that would be exerted by two African elephants standing on a postage stamp!

Did you know

Rounded shapes can stand more pressure than shapes with corners. That is partly why eggs are rounded, so they don't break when the adult bird sits on them. Also, rounded eggs are much easier to lay than cubic eggs! A dozen chicken eggs are supposed to be able to stand the pressure of an adult human. If you try this out, take care, and ask permission first.

2 High pressure advertising

Write a 'spoof advert' for a new product connected with pressure, such as a drawing pin with 'a new, thicker, pin'.

194

PHYSICS   Pressure and moments

L2 Pressure in gases and liquids

YOU WILL LEARN!
- that gases can be put under pressure, and some uses of pressurised gases
- that liquids can be put under pressure, and some uses of this
- how to use the particle model to explain the transmission of pressure
- that the internal pressure at any point within a liquid or gas depends on the weight of liquid or gas above that point

The most common gas around us is air, which is actually a mixture of several gases, but you are probably aware of many other gases.

Points to discuss

1. What gases are present in air?
2. Can you think of any uses of these gases on their own?
3. What other gases can you name?
4. Do you know any uses of these gases?

Many of the gases we use are pressurised – they have been compressed into a smaller volume than they would normally occupy. A gas contains many particles, all moving around and hitting the walls of the container they are in. The force of these particles pushing outwards on the walls of the container, causes the gas pressure in the container.

Because the gas particles move randomly in all directions, they push outwards in all directions on the walls of their containers.

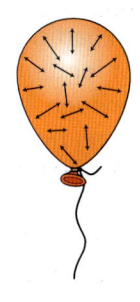

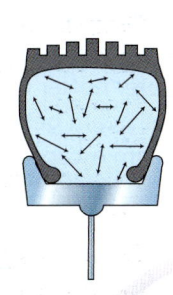

The particles in a balloon or a tyre push outwards in all directions

Points to discuss

Use the particle model to explain:

1. Why balloons and pumped up tyres are round in shape.
2. Why pumping more air into bicycle tyres makes them feel harder.
3. How increasing the temperature would affect the pressure inside a bicycle tyre or a balloon.

1 How strong is air pressure?

Your teacher will probably do this activity as a demonstration.

SAFETY: Use safety screens in case the can splits.

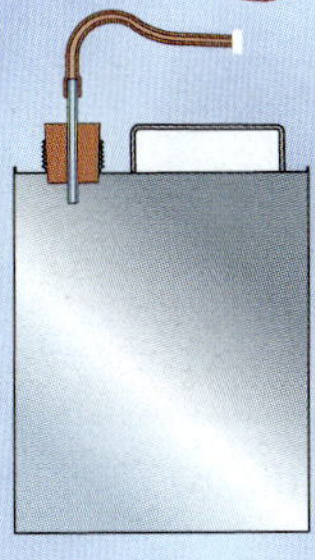

Connect a vacuum pump to a metal container, such as an 'empty' fuel can. Pump out the air from the container and watch what happens (if you hear a hissing noise, the can is not air-tight and the activity won't work).

a Draw a diagram to show the forces that act on the walls of the can initially – remember there is originally air in the can.
b Use the particle model to explain how the pressure inside the can changes.
c Use the idea of pressure to explain the result you saw.
d Air pressure exerts a force of approximately 100 000 N/m². Calculate the approximate force on one side of your can, due to air pressure.

Did you know?

The study of pressure in gases is called pneumatics. The word 'pneu' means 'tyre' in French and comes from the Latin and Greek words for 'air' or 'wind'.

Did you know?

It is reported that two weeks after the death of King Henry VIII, his lead coffin burst open and 'all the pavement of the church was with the fat and the corrupt and putrefied blood foully imbued'. Gases had formed inside the body as it decayed, increasing the pressure inside the body until it burst, forcing the lid off the coffin!

PHYSICS Pressure and moments

Using gas pressure

Pressurised gas is useful in many situations. An aerosol can uses pressurised gas to spray out the liquid contents. When the nozzle is pushed down, the high-pressure gas is able to push liquid up the tube and out of the spray can.

A pressure cooker uses pressurised steam to make food cook at higher temperatures than normal, making the food cook more quickly. The pressure cooker has an air-tight seal around the lid, and a valve with a weight on it. Normally, the water would reach 100 °C and stay at that temperature, while it turned to steam. In a pressure cooker, the steam cannot escape, so builds up in the top of the pan. The pressure of the steam pushing down on the surface of the water makes it harder for liquid water particles to leave the water and become gaseous steam particles. Heat energy is used to make the water hotter instead of for turning it to steam. When the pressure of the steam gets great enough, it is able to lift the weight and some steam escapes, preventing the pressure increasing any further.

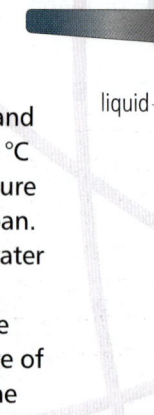

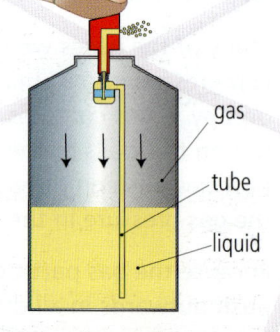

Pressure cookers and spray cans both use pressurised gas

Points to discuss

1. Why do you think aerosol cans always have a warning 'Do not expose to temperatures above 50 °C'?
2. Why do pressure cookers have a warning 'Allow to cool before opening lid'?
3. What is the safety valve on a pressure cooker for and how does it work?
4. How could you adjust the temperature at which food cooks in a pressure cooker?

How do you think gas pressure is used in these?

Did you know

When the Bombardier Beetle is threatened it uses a chemical reaction inside its abdomen to produce high-pressure oxygen and a hot, corrosive liquid. The high-pressure gas is used to squirt the near-boiling liquid at its attacker.

2 Pressurised gas

The photographs show two uses of pressurised gas, to make soft drinks fizzy and to make model rockets that can fly over 100 m into the air.

a. The soft drink has carbon dioxide gas dissolved in the liquid, but at normal atmospheric pressure carbon dioxide does not dissolve very well in water. Use this information and your knowledge of pressure to explain why the can 'fizzes' when it is opened.

b. Explain how pressure is used to make the model rocket fly into the air, and how you could attempt to adjust the height it reached.

PHYSICS   Pressure and moments

3 Pressure in liquids

The liquid inside a container would flow out if it could, so it exerts a pressure on the walls of the container. Fill a plastic bag with water and use it to find out about the pressure in a liquid.

SAFETY: Keep water away from electrical sockets and appliances.

a Make several pin holes all over the plastic bag. Watch the water coming out. What does the direction of the water tell you about the direction of the pressure acting in the liquid?

b Rest the bag on a surface and increase the pressure of the liquid by pushing on one part of the bag. What happens to the speed of the water coming out of the holes? What does this tell you about the effect of increasing the pressure at one point in a liquid?

How will the water come out?

Liquids cannot be compressed. (If you have not met this before, fill a syringe with water, cover the end, then try to depress the plunger.) The fact that liquids cannot be compressed means that pressure is transmitted easily from one part of a liquid to all other parts, just as a solid rubber bicycle tyre transmits all the bumps of the road to you. This is used in car brakes. The driver pushes on the brake pedal and the pressure is transmitted through the brake fluid to the brakes to stop the car.

Did you know?

The study of pressure in liquids is called hydraulics, from the Greek words for water (hudor) and pipe (aulos).

Points to discuss

When the brake fluid in cars is changed, it is very important to 'bleed' the brake system to get out all the bubbles of air. Explain why.

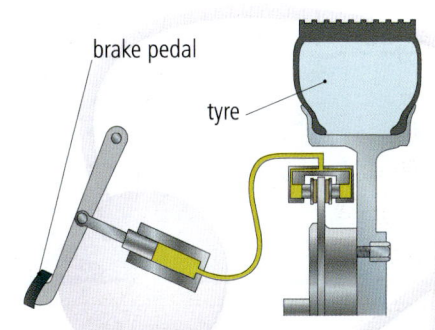

Simple car braking system

4 Force in a liquid

Your teacher may demonstrate this activity.

SAFETY: Use a board or box to protect feet from falling weights.

a When a force of a known size, such as a known weight, pushes down on cylinder 1, predict the size of the force pushing up on cylinder 2.

b Use a force on cylinder 1 to lift a weight on cylinder 2. Did the result surprise you?

c Can you find a relationship between the size of the forces at cylinder 1 and cylinder 2? (Hint: remember that the pressure stays the same at all points in the liquid and think about the formula for finding pressure.)

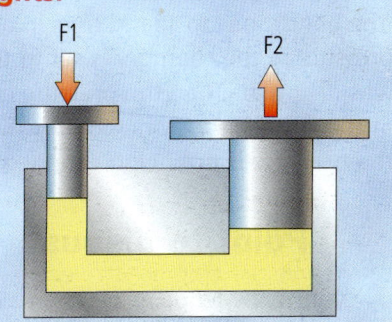

197

PHYSICS   Pressure and moments

Points to discuss

Sometimes people think the hydraulic jack is making energy, because it uses a small amount of force to lift a very heavy weight. You probably remember from Unit 7K that the amount of energy used depends on the force used to move an object and the distance it moves. Use your knowledge to explain why the jack isn't making energy.

5 Pressure and depth

Fill a tall can with water. (Your teacher may use a specially designed can, or you could use a 2 litre plastic drinks bottle.) Watch how water comes out of holes at the top, the middle and the bottom of the can.

SAFETY: Keep water away from electrical sockets and appliances.

a Use the idea of pressure to explain what you see.
b What happens as the level of the water in the can falls? Again, use pressure to explain what happens.

It is the force due to gravity that causes pressure to change with depth. All the air and all the water on the surface of the Earth is being pulled towards the centre of mass of the Earth. Imagine what a fish feels like at different depths. On the surface it only has the weight of a column of air 'pushing down on it'. Deeper down it has the weight of a column of air and a column of water 'pushing down on it'. On the sea floor the pressure is greater still, because the weight of water 'pushing down on it' is even greater.

Divers who have been deep underwater have to surface very slowly. As they go deeper and spend longer underwater more nitrogen gas dissolves into their blood and tissues. If they surface suddenly, the dissolved nitrogen gas turns back into bubbles, causing 'the bends' which can occasionally be fatal. Surfacing slowly allows the nitrogen to come out of the blood and tissues safely. A diver with 'the bends' has to spend time in a decompression chamber. The pressure in the chamber is set to the pressure at the depth the diver was diving at. Then the pressure is slowly reduced to the pressure at the surface. Doctors monitor the diver's condition to make sure the pressure is not being changed too rapidly.

Point to discuss

Use your knowledge of pressure and depth to explain why the hollow part of deep sea submersibles is spherical.

This jack uses force on the tiny cylinder to lift a weight on the big cylinder

Did you know

Weather forecasters measure air pressure to help predict how the weather is going to change. When the air pressure is high the weather is fine; low air pressure brings poorer weather. That is why 'lows' or 'depressions' – areas of low air pressure – bring poorer weather.

Did you know

10 m of water exerts the same pressure as the whole depth of the atmosphere. So if you go to a depth of 10 m the pressure will be twice what it is on the surface. At 20 m the pressure will be 3 times what it is on the surface and so on.

Deep sea submersibles are always spherical

PHYSICS   Pressure and moments

L3 How do levers work?

We all use forces to solve simple, everyday problems.

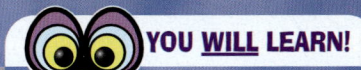

USE FORCE   USE PRESSURE   USE A LEVER

YOU WILL LEARN!
- that a lever is a simple machine which uses a pivot
- examples of situations where levers are used
- that the turning effect of a lever depends on the force and its distance from the pivot
- about examples of levers in the human body
- how pairs of antagonistic muscles produce turning effects at skeleton joints

Points to discuss

You already know which person is going to get the lid off their paint can first.

1. Suggest a way they could improve their lever to make it work better.
2. How many places can you think of where we use levers in the home?

A lever is simply a rigid bar able to rotate about a pivot. Many of the tools we use are single or double levers (two levers working together). Applying an effort (a force) to one end of the lever causes a turning effect. If the turning effect is large enough, the lever will rotate about the pivot and lift the load.

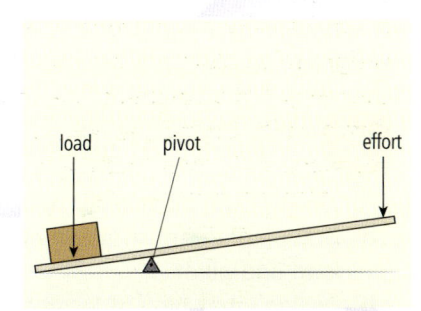

load   pivot   effort

Levers can be used to lift heavy loads

Points to discuss

Which of these will make it easier to lift the load?
- Making the effort larger.
- Making the effort smaller.
- Moving the effort nearer to the pivot.
- Moving the effort further from the pivot.
- Moving the load nearer to the pivot.
- Moving the load further from the pivot.

It is possible to calculate the turning effect of any force from the equation

turning effect = force × distance to pivot

The crowbar is easiest to use when the turning effect of the effort is as large as possible and the turning effect of the load is as small as possible. So the crowbar works best when:
- The effort is as far as possible from the pivot.
- The load is as close as possible to the pivot.

Did you know?
Levers are among the earliest machines invented. Levers were used by the ancient Egyptians to move large blocks of stone. The Romans made catapults, essentially just large levers used to throw large rocks. The ancient Greek, Archimedes, first explained how levers work, supposedly using the famous quotation 'Give me a place to stand and I will move the Earth'.

199

PHYSICS   Pressure and moments

Types of levers

There are three different types of levers.

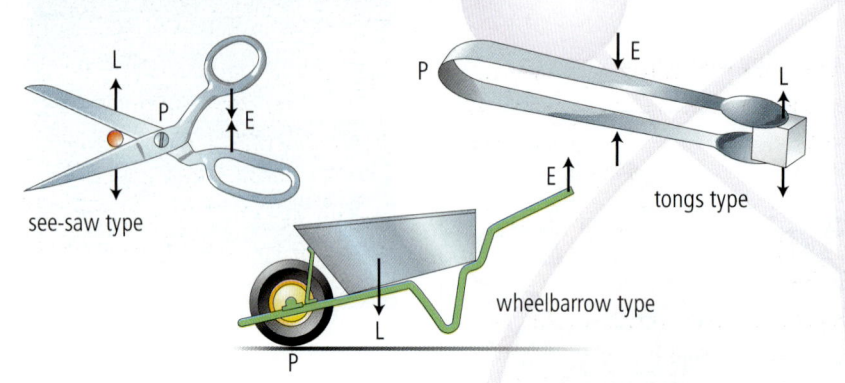

see-saw type

tongs type

wheelbarrow type

1. **See-saw type levers:** the pivot is in the middle. The crowbar is a see-saw type lever. Scissors are an example of a double see-saw type lever. Where would you put the card (the load) if you wanted to use scissors to cut thick card?
2. **Wheelbarrow type levers:** the load is in the middle. The wheelbarrow is a single wheelbarrow type lever. How long should the wheelbarrow handles be to make it very easy to carry heavy loads in the barrow?
3. **Tongs type levers:** the effort is in the middle. Sugar tongs are an example of a double tongs type lever. For this type of lever, which always has to be bigger, the load or the effort? Why?

Did you know
Modern cross blade scissors were invented in Rome in about 100AD but they did not become common in Britain until the sixteenth century.

1 Types of levers

For each of the objects shown:
a Draw a diagram showing effort, load and pivot.
b Decide what type of lever it is and whether it is a single or double lever.
c Explain how you could make it as easy as possible to use (small effort needed).

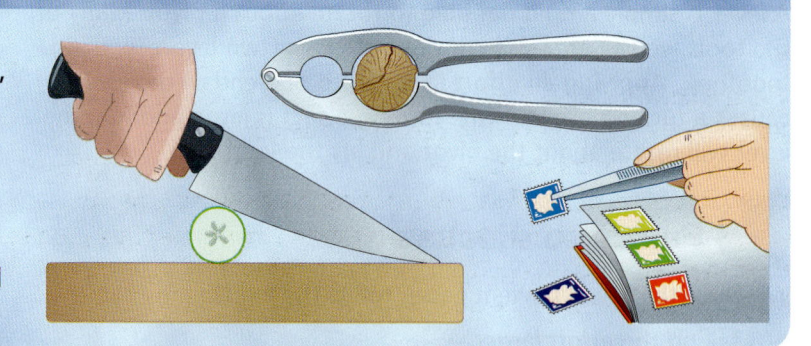

2 Human levers

Make a simplified model of the bones and muscles in a human arm. Use your model to demonstrate how the human arm acts as a lever.

a Write a brief report. Include a diagram, with pivot clearly labelled, showing what type of lever the human arm is and what each muscle does to move the arm.
b The biceps muscle is generally more developed than the triceps muscle. Suggest some reasons for this.
c Identify other levers within the human body. What muscles and joints are involved and what do they do?

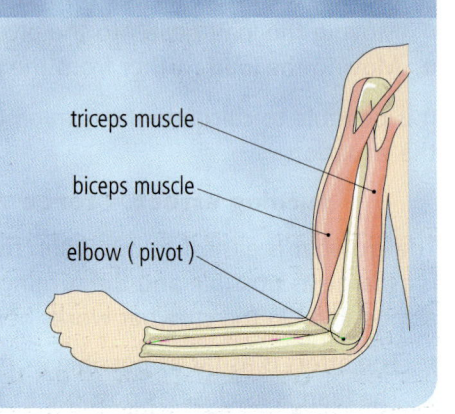

triceps muscle
biceps muscle
elbow (pivot)

PHYSICS — Pressure and moments

L4 How do things balance?

YOU WILL LEARN!
- that a force can make an object topple over
- that the turning effect of a force is called its moment
- how to plan and carry out an investigation into moments
- how to use the principle of moments to explain balance
- how to calculate the moments of forces about a single pivot

Because humans stand upright and walk on two legs we have to learn about balance at a very early age. We rapidly learn how it is possible to balance, and how it isn't.

1 Balancing

Try some of these balancing activities.
a Start with both feet together. Lean over as far as you can. What do you do instinctively to help you balance?
b Stand with your back to a wall, heels touching the wall. Try to pick up an object from the floor about 0.5 m in front of you.
c Stand with both feet together, with the side of one foot against the base of a wall.
d Stand facing a wall, about 3 foot-lengths from the wall. Put your hands behind your back. Lean forward until your nose touches the wall. (Be careful!)
e Which tasks are possible? Why are the others impossible?

If we lean too far, our weight moves too far to one side, we become 'top-heavy' and fall over. We instinctively try to stop this happening by either not leaning so far or by sticking out a 'counterbalance' weight that tends to tip us the other way. So how can we decide how far is 'too far' to lean for an object?

Did you know ?
Many animals use a long tail as a counterbalance weight to prevent them falling over when they are leaping from branch to branch or changing direction quickly. If possible, observe how a cat uses its tail for balance when jumping.

Stable and unstable

We can consider all the weight of an object acting straight down from the centre of mass. The centre of mass of an object is the place where you could imagine all the mass to be if it all collapsed down into a point, so the centre of mass of a sphere is at the centre of the sphere, the centre of mass of a ruler is half way along, the centre of mass of a pyramid is a small distance up from the base, directly beneath the point, and so on.

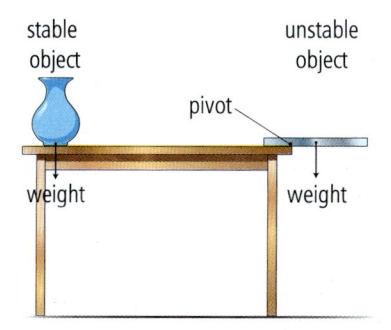

The ornament is stable because its weight is acting downwards through its base. The weight does not have any turning effect on the ornament, so the ornament does not tip over. The weight of the box acts downwards over the edge of the table. There is a turning effect with the edge of the table as the pivot. The box turns, tipping up and falling off the table.

PHYSICS   Pressure and moments

Points to discuss

The diagram opposite shows a candle holder in a stable and an unstable position.

1 What is the furthest that the candle holder could be tilted before it fell over?
2 What would happen if it were tilted less than this amount then released?
3 Suggest two ways the candle holder could be designed to make it as stable as possible.

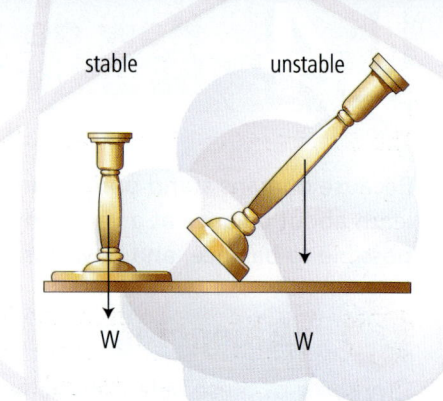

2 Investigating moments

The turning effect of a force is usually called its moment. So the moment of a force is found from

moment = force × distance from pivot

Suspend a metre rule from its centre point. Add a small weight, (plasticine or blu tack) to one end if necessary so the ruler hangs horizontally.

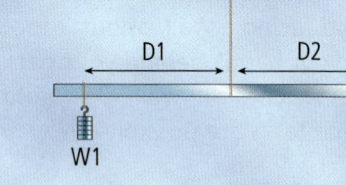

The weight W1 will try to make the ruler turn anticlockwise. The weight W2 will try to make the ruler turn clockwise.

a Experiment with different values of W1 and W2 different distances from the centre point of the ruler to find the combinations of W1, W2 and distances that will make the ruler balance.
b You might like to record your results in a table like this.

Weight W1	Distance D1	Anticlockwise moment	Weight W2	Distance D2	Clockwise moment

c For each set of values of W1, D1, W2 and D2, calculate the anticlockwise moment and the clockwise moment. Record them in your table.
d Use your results to draw a conclusion about the conditions necessary for the ruler to balance.

Points to discuss

1 The weight of the ruler acts downwards from its centre point. What effect does this have on the clockwise and anticlockwise moments in Activity 2?
2 Would it be possible to use weights to make the ruler balance if it was suspended from a point other than its centre point?
3 What effect would the weight of the ruler have in point 2?

PHYSICS   **Pressure and moments**

Using the principle of moments to solve problems

The principle of moments states that for any object that is balanced

total clockwise moment = total anticlockwise moment

Question 1

A mass of 400 g is hung from the 5 cm mark on a metre ruler, suspended from its centre point. What mass must be hung from the 80 cm mark to make the ruler balance?

Use the principle of moments to find the mass of the unknown weight W.

clockwise moment = anticlockwise moment
$$(80 - 50) \times W = (50 - 5) \times 400$$
$$W = \frac{45 \times 400}{30}$$
$$W = 600 \text{ g}$$

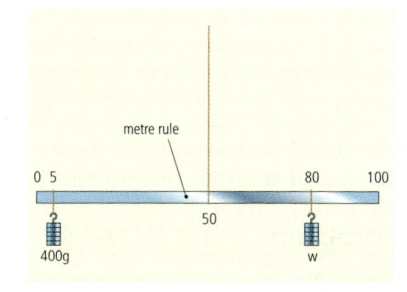

Question 2

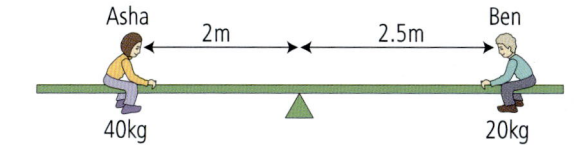

Kris wants to join the children on the see-saw. Kris has a mass of 30 kg.

Which side must he sit to make the see-saw balance? Why?

How far from the pivot must he sit?

Question 3

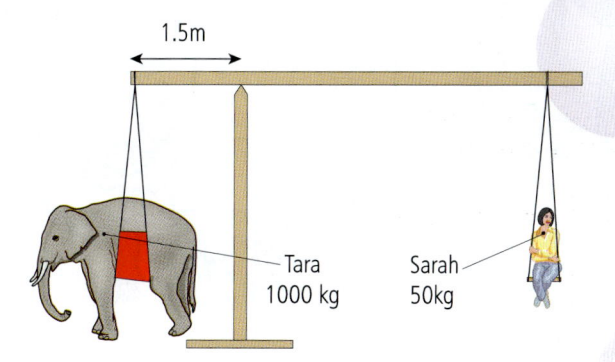

Suppose that Sarah has a mass of 50 kg. Tara, the baby elephant from the local zoo, has a mass of 1000 kg, and she is so large that the closest she can get to the pivot on a weighing machine is 1.5 m away. The arm of the weighing machine is 25 m long. Is it possible for Sarah and Tara to make the arm of the weighing machine balance?

Did you know

The Romans used to use a balance called a steelyard to weigh food. The food was hung from one end of a suspended metal arm. A fixed weight was then moved along the metal arm until the arm balanced horizontally.

PHYSICS   Pressure and moments

3 People have their moments too

Follow these instructions to make a model of a human back.

1. Use a long rod, such as a broom handle, with a hole at one end.
2. Pass a rod through the hole and fasten it firmly so the rod can pivot about its end. This pivot represents the lower end of the spine.
3. Tie string to the other end of the rod, about $\frac{1}{4}$ of the way from the end. Pulling on the string represents the back muscles tightening to straighten the spine.

a. Allow the rod to lean slightly from the vertical position. Pull on the string to bring the back vertical again. You probably pulled with the string at right angles to the rod. Why is this not a true representation of the muscles in your back?

b. Allow the rod to lean again. Pull it upright again, using an angle of 10° or less between string and rod? Why is this a better representation of the human back? How much force did you have to use?

c. Tie a weight to the top end of the rod. How does this affect the amount of force you have to use to pull the rod upright? (Keep the angle of the string at 10° or less.)

d. Doctors recommend that when lifting heavy weights we should bend our knees and keep our spine as straight as possible. How does this safe lifting technique help prevent back problems?

A safe lifting technique exerts a small moment on the back

PHYSICS — Pressure and moments

Summary

Pressure is a measure of how concentrated a force is. High pressures hurt.

Pressure can be calculated from the equation:

$$\text{pressure} = \frac{\text{force}}{\text{area}}$$

The units of pressure are N/m^2 or N/cm^2

The force exerting pressure on a surface is always measured at right angles to the surface.

Pressurised gases are gases that have been **compressed** (squashed) into a smaller volume than they would normally occupy.

All gases exert a pressure on the walls of the container they are in.

The **gas pressure** is caused by particles of the gas colliding with the container walls.

A liquid exerts a pressure on the walls of the container it is in.

The pressure in a liquid acts in all directions.

Pressure can be transmitted through a liquid because liquids are not compressible.

The pressure in a gas or a liquid increases as the depth increases.

The pressure at any point in a gas or a liquid depends on the height of the column of gas or liquid above that point.

A **lever** is a simple machine that uses a pivot.

The **moment** of any force is found from the equation:

moment = force × distance to pivot

All the weight of an object can be considered as acting downwards from its **centre of mass**.

An object is **unstable** if its weight causes a moment about its base.

The **principle of moments** states that for an object to balance

total clockwise moment = total anticlockwise moment

Key words

atmospheric pressure
centre of mass
compressed
effort
lever
moment
particle model
pivot
pressure
pressurised
principle of moments
turning effect

Summary Questions

1. Make your own glossary (list of meanings) for the Key words. Keep your definitions short.

2. Pressure is a measure of how concentrated a force is.
   a. Write the equation used to calculate pressure.
   b. The soles of a person's trainers have an area of 400 cm^2, and they normally exert a pressure of 0.125 N/cm^2. When they put on ice skates they exert a pressure of 1 N/cm^2. If the ice skate blades are 33 cm long, how wide are they, to the nearest cm?

3. A gas exerts a pressure on the walls of any container it is in.
   a. Use the particle model to explain why the gas exerts a pressure.
   b. Use the particle model to explain how the pressure exerted by a gas is affected by temperature.
   c. Use the particle model to explain why water boils at a lower temperature at the top of a tall mountain than at sea level.

PHYSICS — Pressure and moments

End of unit Questions

1 Sue pumps up a bicycle tyre. As she does so, she notices that the pump becomes hot.
  a Where, and how, was the energy stored before it was transferred in pumping up the tyre? *1 mark*
  b Explain how the gas molecules inside the tyre exert pressure on the walls of the tyre. *1 mark*
  c The air going into the tyre was warmed up by the pumping. What effect will this have on the motion of gas molecules in the air in the tyre? *1 mark*
  d When the air in the tyre becomes hotter, the pressure rises.
  Give **one** reason, in terms of the motion of gas molecules in air, why the pressure rises. *1 mark*
  e The pressure in the tyre increases as Sue forces more air into the tyre.
  Explain why a larger number of gas molecules increases the pressure in the tyre. *1 mark*

2 This question uses the principle of moments.
  a State the principle of moments.
  b A metre rule of mass 50 g is suspended from its centre point. A mass of 200 g is hung from the 30 cm point of the metre rule. What mass, M, must be hung from the 90 cm point to make the ruler balance?
  c The string is moved so that the metre rule is suspended from the 40 cm point. The 200 g mass is not moved. Draw a diagram to show the forces acting on the metre rule.
  d Where must the mass, M, be moved to, to make the metre rule balance again?

3 a Two syringes are connected together as shown in the diagram below.

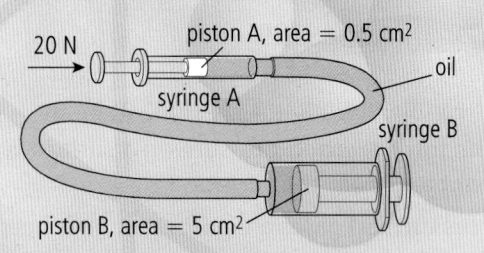

A force of 20 N is applied to the piston in syringe A.
  i Calculate the pressure that the piston in syringe A exerts on the oil. Give the units. *1 mark*
  ii Calculate the force needed to just prevent the piston in syringe B from moving out. Give the unit. *1 mark*

  b The diagram below shows the brake pedal used to operate the brakes in a car. The foot applies a force of 50 N.

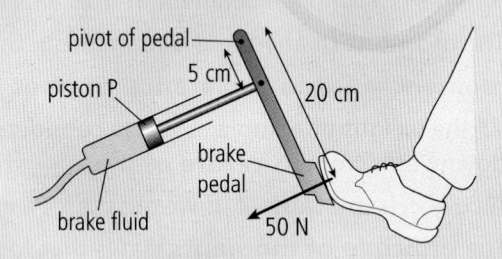

  i Calculate the force applied to the piston P. Give the unit. *1 mark*
  ii The brake fluid pushes another piston, Q, which is attached to the car's brakes. Piston Q has an area which is eight times larger than piston P. Calculate the force on the car's brakes. Give the unit. *1 mark*

Revision

How to revise

Towards the end of year 9 you will do **SATs** in Science, English and Mathematics. SATs cover all of the work you have done in years 7, 8 and 9. SATs are tests that check how much you know and understand about each subject. Your school may use the results of these tests to help decide what courses you will do in years 10 and 11. It is important that you do your best in your SATs! **Revising** means reviewing what you have done so that you remember and understand the work.

In order to revise effectively you will need all of the work you have done in Key Stage 3.

Plan your revision

1. You should begin your revision about three months before the actual tests. It is important that you plan your revision in advance. Find out the actual dates of the tests. Make a timetable of what you are going to revise and **stick to it**! If you have other activities planned for certain days then mark these on your timetable.

Revision timetable
March week 1

Day	Subjects to revise
Monday 2nd	English French
Tuesday 3rd	Maths Chemistry
Wednesday 4th	History Physics
Thursday 5th	Geography R.E.
Friday 6th	My Birthday !
Saturday 7th	German French Chemistry
Sunday 8th	Physics Maths Biology
Monday 9th	English Biology
Tuesday 10th	History Maths
Wednesday 11th	Geography field trip
Thursday 12th	Geography R.E.

2. Do not try to revise too much at once. Your brain gets tired and you will not be able to work properly. Two sessions of 30 minutes are more effective than one session of 90 minutes. Take a ten-minute break between each session.

3. Your brain needs food and water to work properly. Have a small snack in your break.

4. Revise a couple of different subjects in each day. This gives you a change and stops your revision from becoming too boring.

5. While you are asleep your brain carries on sorting out what you have learnt. So make sure you get plenty of sleep.

6. Don't plan to revise all of your work once in great detail. Draw up a plan to revise everything two or three times but in less detail. This will be more effective.

How to revise

If you just try to read all of the work you have done you will not remember very much of it. It is far more effective if you **use** the information you are trying to revise. Try to get some new paper, pens, pencils, coloured pens and highlighters to use in your revision. It's always more enjoyable to work with new things.

1. Make notes. When you make notes you condense your work into something much shorter. This involves a lot of thinking about what are the most important bits. Thinking about your work helps you to remember it.
   - Start by reading through your work and making lists of key points and key words under different headings. Make notes on an A3 sheet of paper. You can display these in your bedroom, study area or anywhere else you are allowed!
   - Write headings in a different colour from the rest of your work.
   - List other important points in another colour.
   - Make sure your notes are neat enough to read easily.
   - Once you have completed all of your notes for a subject you can rewrite them onto index cards or into a small notebook. You will find these useful to carry around and look at when you have a spare moment e.g. on the bus, between lessons, before you go to sleep, etc.

207

REVISION

- There are different ways to make notes which are illustrated below. Some of these were covered in topic 7A. Decide which is best for you.

FOOD TYPES

Protein
- used for growth and repair.
  making enzymes.
  skin, hair, muscles, contain protein.
- found in eggs, cheese, milk, fish, meat, chicken, beans, lentils.
- test for protein – biuret test – add dilute sodium hydroxide, then add dilute copper sulphate solution. Purple colour indicates protein.
- made of long chains of amino acids.
- digested by pepsin.

Carbohydrates
- used as a source of energy.
- found in . . . .

Food		Good sources	How we use it	Food test and result
carbo-hydrate	sugar	cakes, jam, sweets, fizzy drinks, fruit, biscuits	As a source of energy	Benedict's test. Mix food with Benedict's reagent and heat to over 90°C. Blue colour → orange/red
	starch	potatoes, flour, bread, rice, pasta, chapattis, poppadoms, cereal		
Protein				
Fat				

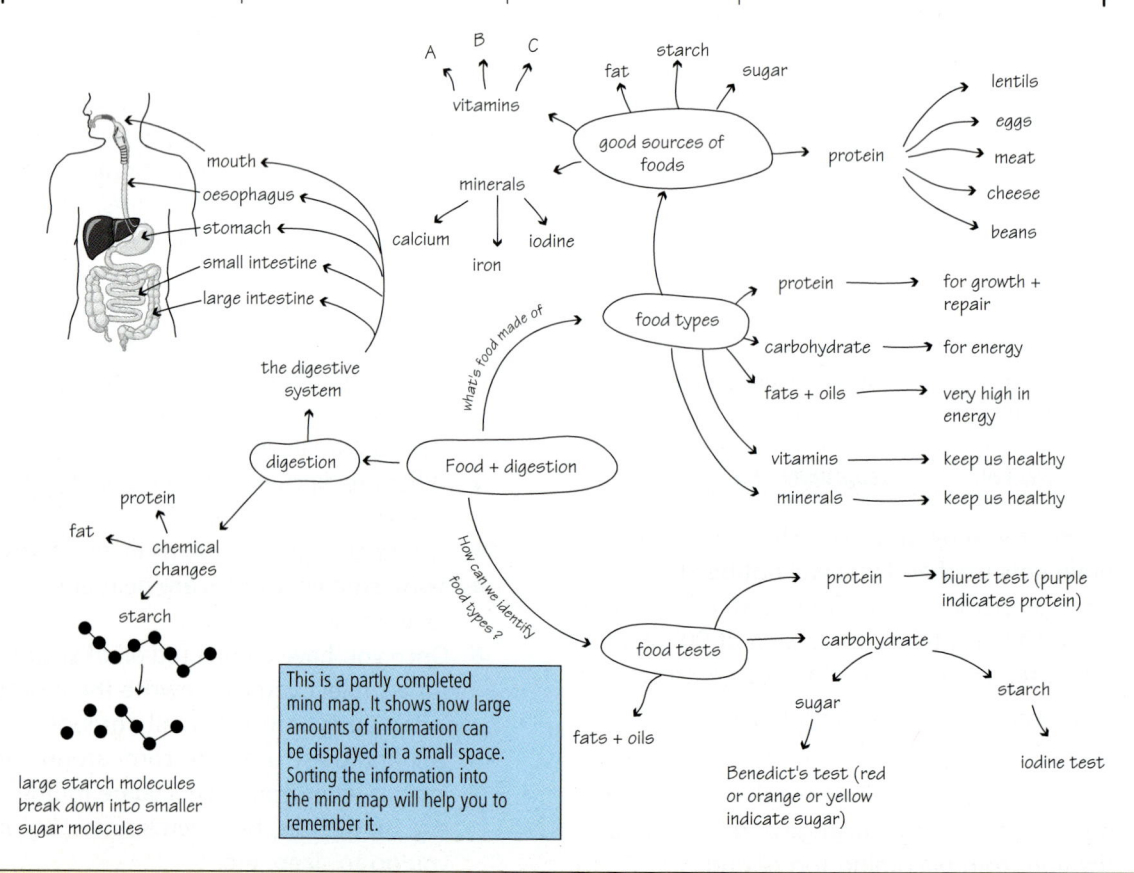

This is a partly completed mind map. It shows how large amounts of information can be displayed in a small space. Sorting the information into the mind map will help you to remember it.

REVISION

2. Use mnemonics. These are a way of helping you to learn basic facts, especially when they form a list. If they are funny or rude they are even easier to remember! In topic 7L you used the mnemonic *My Very Easy Method Just Speeds Up Naming Planets* to learn the names of the planets in order from the Sun.

3. You are not alone! It can be helpful and more fun to revise with someone else. Working in pairs or small groups can assist your revision and lets you test each other. Working with others can help you to fill in gaps in your knowledge and understanding. Don't let it become all fun and no work though!

4. Using the Internet is a good way of revising. If you are lucky you will have Internet access at home. If you don't you might be able to use facilities at school or in public libraries. There are some really good websites to help you revise.

5. Test yourself. If you have some key facts to remember then try look, cover, write, check. *Look* at the facts for 3 minutes and try to remember them. *Cover* up the facts. *Write* down what you are trying to learn (without cheating!). *Check* how many you got right. Try again after an hour.

6. Study past papers. Your science teacher should give you recent science SATs papers. Study these and make sure you are familiar with the layout of the paper, the types of questions asked and how you gain marks.

Remember that there will be questions about practical work and its results. For example, you could be given a graph or table of results and asked to interpret or explain the data. Other questions are designed to test your understanding of science. These questions are often set in unfamiliar contexts. They require you to apply the work you have done in lessons to new situations.

REVISION 7A Cells

In this topic you found out:
- that cells are the basic units of life
- that cells are organised into tissues from which organs are made
- about cell structure and the differences between plant and animal cells
- about the functions of some cells.

Key words
cell	multi-cellular
chloroplast	nucleus
cytoplasm	organ
fertilisation	tissue
gene	vacuole
membrane	wall

Summary of content

Living things are made of cells. Most organisms are multi-cellular – made of millions of cells.

All cells have a **membrane**, **cytoplasm** and a **nucleus**.

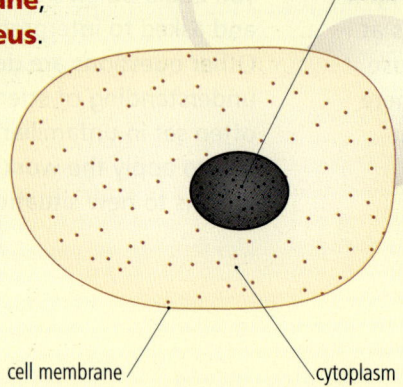

Plant cells also have a **cell wall**, a **vacuole** and often have green **chloroplasts**.

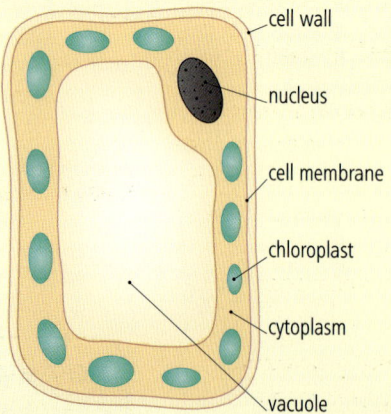

Although cells have these same basic parts they have different structures so that they can carry out specialised functions.

A group of cells of the same type is called a **tissue**. A group of tissues that work together is called an **organ**.

Organisms grow by cells dividing into two new cells that each then gets bigger before dividing again.

The nucleus of a cell contains **genes** that carry information about how to make new cells, tissues and organs. **Fertilisation** is when genes from a male and a female organism join together to make a new set of information for a new organism.

Review Questions
1. Draw diagrams of four specialised cells. Explain how each one is adapted for its function.
2. Draw a table summarising the differences between animal and plant cells.
3. Make a table to summarise some cells, tissues and organs that make up organ systems in humans.

REVISION

7B Reproduction

In this topic you found out
- more about reproduction in humans and how they protect and care for their offspring
- about how reproduction in other animals is similar to, and different from, humans
- about how your body changes during adolescence

Summary of content

Fertilisation is where a sperm nucleus fuses with an ovum nucleus. Some animals reproduce using **internal fertilisation**. Other animals reproduce using **external fertilisation**. Once fertilised, some animals' eggs develop internally while others have eggs that develop externally. In humans, fertilisation and development are both internal.

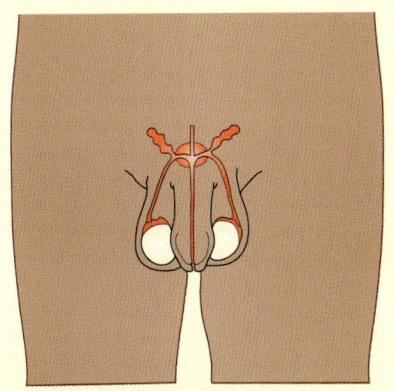

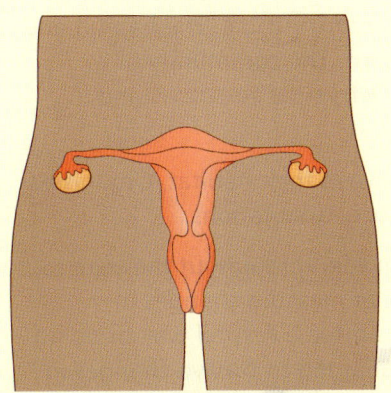

Key words
- adolescence
- amniotic sac
- cell division
- fertilisation
- fetus
- menstrual cycle
- ovary
- placenta
- puberty
- secondary sexual characteristics
- umbilical cord
- uterus

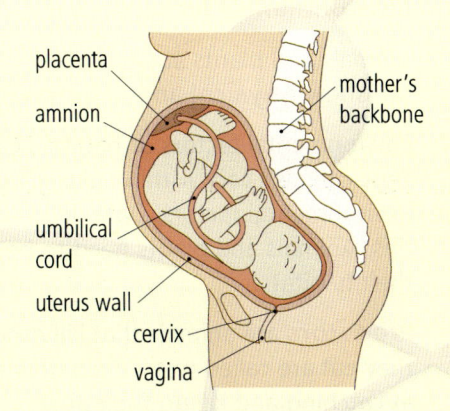

Male reproductive system

Female reproductive system

The reproductive organs of a human are designed to give the best chance of fertilisation and development. The **fetus** develops in the **uterus**. The fluid in the **amniotic sac** protects it. It gets nutrients and oxygen from its mother via the **placenta**. It removes carbon dioxide and other waste through the placenta. The **umbilical cord** connects the fetus to the placenta. Harmful substances from the mother can reach the fetus through the placenta.

Ova are released from the **ovary** once every month in a woman. Every month, the lining of the uterus thickens to get it ready for a fertilised ovum. If an ovum is not fertilised then the uterus lining breaks down. It comes out of the vagina as a **period**. These are stages of the **menstrual cycle**.

When the fetus is ready to be born, the muscles of the uterus wall push it out through the vagina. When babies are born they feed on milk, which contains nutrients and provides protection against disease.

Animals grow by **cell division** followed by cell growth. In humans, growth is rapid at first then slows down. There is a **growth spurt** around the time of **puberty**. **Adolescence** is when children change into adults. This includes puberty when **secondary sexual characteristics** develop. Hormones control puberty.

Ready to be born

Review Questions

1. Describe the route taken by a sperm from the testes to fertilising an ovum.
2. List the different ways in which the fetus is protected whilst inside its mother.
3. Explain how a fetus gets food and how it gets rid of waste carbon dioxide.

211

REVISION

7C Environment and feeding relationships

In this topic you found out

- how to identify differences between habitats and how they affect the animals and plants that live in them
- how animals and plants are adapted to live in a particular habitat
- how animals and plants are adapted to changes in their environment
- how animals are adapted to feed on particular foods
- how related food chains are part of food webs
- how energy is passed through food chains
- why it is important that there are different types of habitat

Key words
adaptation
community
consumer
ecosystem
environmental features
food chain
food web
habitat
physical features
predator
prey
producer

Summary of content

A **habitat** is any place where animals and plants live. The animals and plants that live there are called a **community**. The habitat and its community are called an **ecosystem**. The community of a particular habitat will depend on the **physical features** and **environmental factors** of the habitat.

Animals and plants are **adapted** to live in their habitat. Organisms can show **physical** and/or **behavioural** adaptations.

Environmental factors of habitats can vary throughout the year. They can also vary within a day. We can measure changes in environmental factors. Datalogging is often a helpful way of doing this. Animals and plants need to be adapted to survive changes in their habitats.

Predators are animals that kill other animals for food. The animals they eat are called **prey**. Predators are adapted to make them good at catching and killing their prey.

Prey animals are adapted to help them avoid being killed and eaten.

Plants often have adaptations that deter animals from eating them.

Animals and plants can be linked together in **food chains**. A food chain shows how energy flows from **producers** (plants) to **consumers**. All the food chains in a habitat can be linked together to form a **food web**.

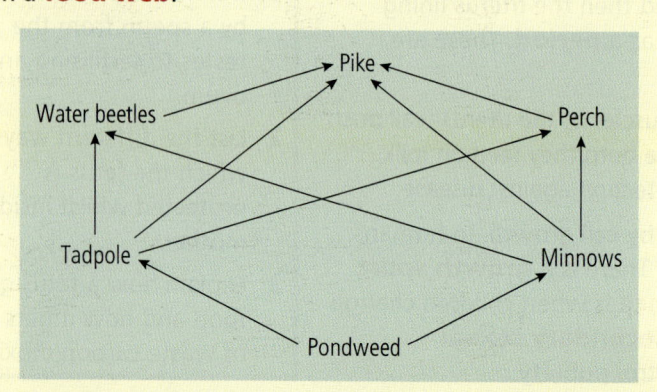

[Food web diagram showing: Pike, Water beetles, Perch, Tadpole, Minnows, Pondweed]

Review Questions

1. Draw four food chains from the food web on this page. Name a predator and a prey animal in each.
2. Give four examples of animals and plants that are adapted to live in different habitats. For each one explain how it is adapted. Include one example of behavioural adaptation.
3. Explain what is meant by a 'producer' and a 'consumer'.

REVISION

7D Variation and classification

In this topic you found out

- the similarities and differences between different species of organisms
- about variation within a species
- why variations occur
- how and why scientists classify species of animals and plants
- different methods, including spreadsheets, of showing patterns of variation

Key words

gene	species
inherited	taxonomic
invertebrate	variation
kingdom	vertebrate

Summary of content

A **species** is a group of organisms that can breed together to produce fertile offspring. Members of the same species have many features in common but there will be **variation** between the individuals.

Some variations are **inherited**. They are passed on from the parents in their genes. Other variations are due to the **environment**. Some variations can be due to a combination of inherited and environmental factors.

Scientists around the world use the same system of classifying organisms. They divide them into **taxonomic** groups. There are five **kingdoms**: plant, animal, bacteria, fungi and protists. These kingdoms can be sub-divided.

The animal kingdom can be divided into **vertebrates** and **invertebrates**.

Vertebrates can be divided into **fish, amphibians, reptiles, birds** and **mammals**.

Invertebrates can be divided into **coelenterates, flatworms, roundworms, segmented worms, molluscs, echinoderms** and **arthropods**.

Some animals are more difficult to classify than others.

Review Questions

1. Write out a description of the characteristics that identify each of the following vertebrates:
   fish, amphibian, reptile, bird, mammal
2. Make a table showing inherited and environmental characteristics in humans. (Some characteristics could be in both columns.)
3. Make an identification key to identify these made up organisms opposite.

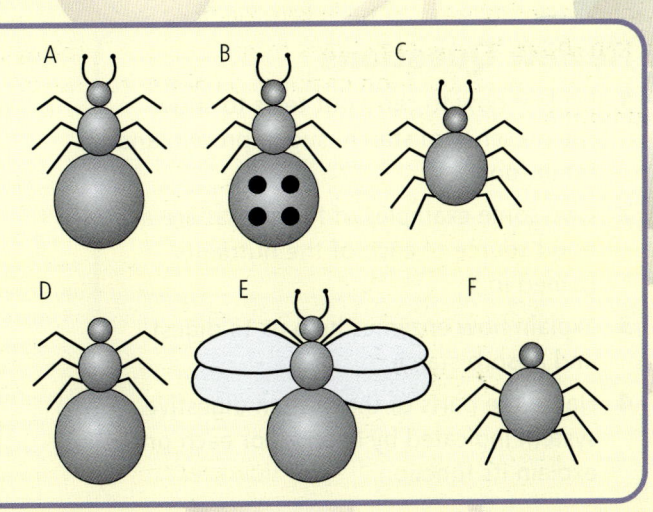

REVISION

8A Food and digestion

In this topic you found out

- the names of the different components of a balanced diet and why they are important to us
- how and why our body breaks down large molecules in digestion
- how nutrients are carried round our body in our blood
- how to use secondary sources to find information about food and to display the information in graphs
- why it can be difficult to interpret evidence about food and health
- how to carry out reliable investigations about how enzymes work

Key words
absorption, fibre, carbohydrate, mineral, digestion, nutrient, enzyme, protein, fat, vitamin

Summary of content

Food provides us with five types of **nutrient**. These are:

protein, which is essential for growth and repair of the body; **carbohydrate** and **fat**, which give us energy; and **vitamins** and **minerals**, which help keep the body working efficiently.

We also need **water** and **fibre**.

We can carry out tests to find out which nutrients are present in particular foods.

To stay healthy we need a **balanced diet** that contains the right amounts of these nutrients.

Some food molecules are broken down into smaller ones in the process called **digestion**. This happens in the gut. **Enzymes** speed up digestion of foods. Enzymes work best at optimum conditions of temperature and pH.

Digested food is absorbed in the small intestine. Nutrient molecules are carried to where they are needed in the blood.

Review Questions

1. Explain how to carry out tests to show the presence of starch, sugar, protein and fat in food.
2. Give some examples of foods that are a good source of each of the nutrients named in **1**.
3. Explain how enzymes help us to digest and absorb starch.
4. Name the parts of the human digestive system indicated by letters. For each one, explain its function.

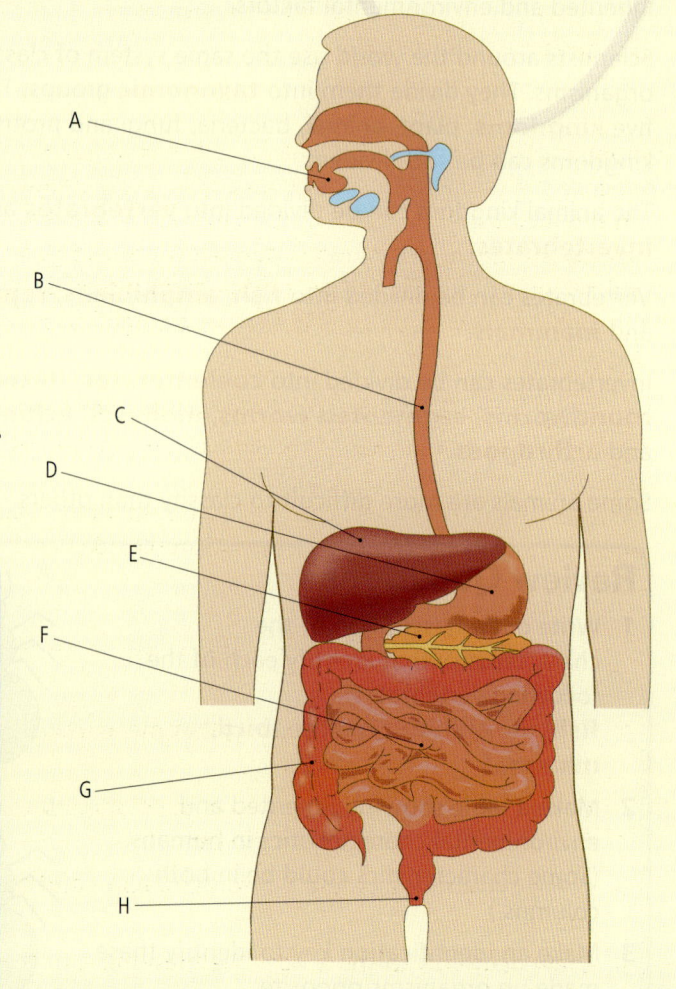

214

REVISION 8B Respiration

In this topic you found out

- about how cells get the glucose and oxygen they need for respiration
- how animal and plant cells release energy
- that respiration is similar in all animal and plant cells
- how historical ideas about circulation have changed with time
- how to use living organisms in investigations and to take into account factors that cannot be controlled

Summary of content

Your body uses **glucose** as a source of energy. Glucose is absorbed in the intestine and carried around the body in the blood. Energy is released from glucose in **respiration**.

Aerobic respiration is a chemical reaction between glucose and oxygen:

glucose + oxygen → carbon dioxide + water + energy

Anaerobic respiration does not need oxygen but gives much less energy:

glucose → lactic acid + energy

Blood is pumped around the body by the heart. When blood reaches the smallest vessels, called **capillaries**, oxygen passes from the blood to the cells. Carbon dioxide passes from the cells to the blood. The blood is pumped to the lungs where it picks up more oxygen and gets rid of carbon dioxide. Our ideas about how blood circulates have changed over the last 2500 years.

Our lungs are well adapted to allow exchange of gases. They have a thin wall, a large surface area and a good blood supply.
Exhaled air has a different composition from inhaled air. Inhaled air has more oxygen, less carbon dioxide, less moisture and is cooler.

Key words
- aerobic respiration
- alveolus
- anaerobic respiration
- bronchiole
- bronchus
- capillary
- diaphragm
- glucose
- thorax
- trachea

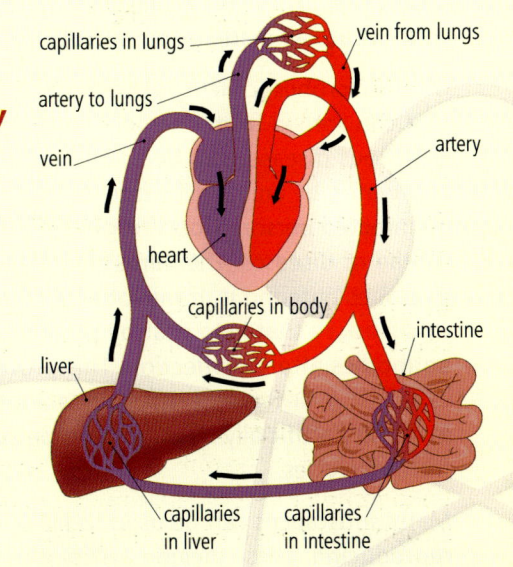

Simplified diagram of the human circulatory system

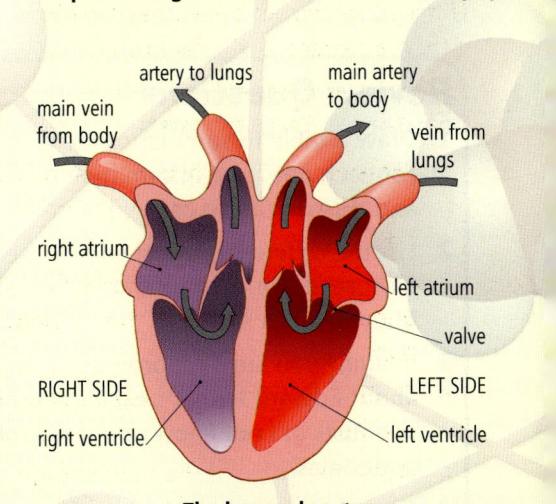

The human heart

Review Questions

1. Explain the features of the lung that make it well adapted for gaseous exchange.
2. Describe the route taken by a molecule of glucose from the intestine to a muscle in the leg.
3. Draw a diagram to show the route of air in and out of the lungs.
4. Draw diagrams to show how the movement of the ribs and diaphragm makes us breathe.

REVISION

8C Microbes and diseases

In this topic you found out

- that bacteria, fungi and viruses are all types of microbes
- how infectious diseases are spread
- how the body defends itself against infectious diseases
- how we use scientific knowledge to prevent and treat infectious diseases
- how microbes can be useful

Key words
- antibiotic
- antibody
- antigen
- antiseptic
- bacteria
- disinfectant
- fungus
- hygiene
- immunity
- infectious
- pathogen
- penicillin
- vaccination
- virus

Summary of content

There are many different types of microbes. They include **bacteria**, **fungi** and **viruses**.

Some of these microbes are very useful and are used to make foods, medicines and chemicals. Cheese, bread, wine, beer and yoghurt are all made using microbes.

Other microbes, called **pathogens**, can cause diseases. Diseases that can spread from one person to another are called **infectious**. Infectious diseases can be spread in the air, in contaminated food and water, by animals, by infected blood or by direct contact with an infected person. Good **hygiene** is important for preventing the spread of diseases. The human body has many barriers to stop microbes entering it. If microbes do enter the body it produces **antibodies** that help destroy pathogens. The body produces antibodies after an infection. This protects the body in future and is called **immunity**. **Vaccination** is a method of producing immunity artificially by injecting a person with harmless material from microbes.

Many substances can be used to kill microbes or to stop them from reproducing. These include **antiseptics**, **disinfectants** and **antibiotics**. **Penicillin** was the first antibiotic.

Review Questions

1. Draw a table to summarise the different types of microbes. For each one, give information about its structure, its uses and diseases it can cause.

2. List the different ways in which disease-causing microbes can be spread. For each method of spreading, explain how the body defends itself.

3. Imagine you are a reporter in 1756. Write a newspaper report about Edward Jenner's experiment. Remember that in 1756 scientists did not know about microbes, antigens or antibodies.

4. Give a modern day account of the way diseases can be prevented by vaccination.

REVISION

8D Ecological relationships

In this topic you found out

- how to classify plants
- how the resources found in a habitat affect the type and number of animals and plants found there
- how to draw pyramids of numbers to show the numbers of organisms in a habitat
- how to measure and present information about the conditions found in a habitat
- how to use sampling to find and count the animals and plants in a habitat

Key words
carnivore
conifers
consumer
ferns
flowering plants
food chains
food webs
herbivore
kite diagrams
mosses and liverworts
photosynthesis
pitfall traps
pooters
producer
pyramid of numbers
quadrat
sample
sweep nets
transect
tree beating

Summary of content

Green plants can be classified into four groups. These are **mosses and liverworts**, **ferns**, **conifers** and **flowering plants**.

Environmental factors can affect the size of the population in a habitat. To measure the size of a population it is usually best to **sample** a small area then estimate the total population from this. **Quadrats** are useful to help do a random sample.

Sweep nets, **pooters**, **pitfall traps** and **tree beating** are all methods of finding small invertebrates in a habitat. **Transects** are a method of observing and measuring gradual changes in a habitat. **Kite diagrams** are a good way of displaying what is found out by doing a transect.

Food webs are a way of representing what eats what in a habitat. Food webs are made up of a number of **food chains**. All food chains start with a **producer**. Producers can use light energy to convert carbon dioxide and water into food containing energy. Most producers are green plants which make food in the process called **photosynthesis**. **Primary consumers** are animals that eat plants. Primary consumers are **herbivores**. Animals that eat herbivores are called **secondary consumers**. Animals that eat other animals are called **carnivores**. **Pyramids of numbers** can be used to represent the size of the population at different levels in a food chain.

Review Questions

1. Summarise the characteristics that enable us to classify green plants into four main groups.
2. Make a list of environmental factors that could affect the distribution of animals and plants in a school's grounds.
3. Explain how you would use a quadrat to estimate the number of daisies on a football pitch.
4. List four ways of collecting small invertebrates. Explain how you would carry out each method.

REVISION
7E Acids and alkalis

In this topic you found out
- the uses and properties of acids
- how we use indicators to detect acidic and alkaline solutions
- about the pH scale
- about acids reacting with alkalis (neutralisation)

Summary of content

There are many useful **acids** and **alkalis**.

Some acids and alkalis are hazardous to handle. They are very corrosive.

You need to know these hazard symbols:

Corrosive
These substances attack and destroy living tissues, including eyes and skin.

Irritant
These substances are not corrosive but can cause reddening or blistering of the skin.

Harmful
These substances harm you if swallowed or breathed in or absorbed through your skin. They are not as dangerous as toxic substances (which can cause death).

Key words
acid
alkali
corrosive
equation
harmful
hazardous
hydrochloric acid
indicator
pH values
react
sodium hydroxide
solution

Weak acids are often found in foods.

You can make a corrosive acid or alkali safer by making it more dilute.

Indicators are dyes that are different colours in acid and alkali. Universal indicator is a mixture of dyes. It has a range of colours. The lower the pH value, the more strongly acidic a solution. A liquid with a pH of 7 is neutral (neither acidic nor alkaline). pH values above 7 indicate an alkali.

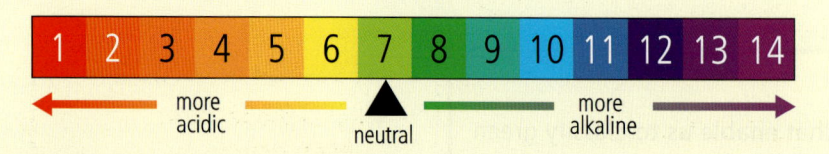

1 2 3 4 5 6 7 8 9 10 11 12 13 14
← more acidic   neutral   more alkaline →

When acids react with alkalis they neutralise each other. They form a salt and water.

ACID	+	ALKALI	→	A SALT	+	WATER
hydrochloric acid	+	sodium hydroxide	→	sodium chloride	+	water

There are many useful neutralisation reactions, including indigestion remedies to get rid of excess acid in your stomach.

Review Questions
1. Name a strong acid and a strong alkali.
2. How would you describe the solutions with the following pH values?
   i 1   **ii** 7   **iii** 9   **iv** 14
3. Describe how you could make a sample of sodium chloride in the lab.
4. What type of substance do all indigestion remedies contain?

REVISION
7F Chemical reactions

In this topic you found out
- the new substances made in chemical reactions
- reactions of acids that produce a gas
- about burning as a chemical reaction
- the tests for hydrogen, oxygen and carbon dioxide gases
- word equations to describe chemical reactions

Key words
calcium carbonate
carbon
carbon dioxide
hydrogen
methane
oxygen
product
reactant
word equation
zinc

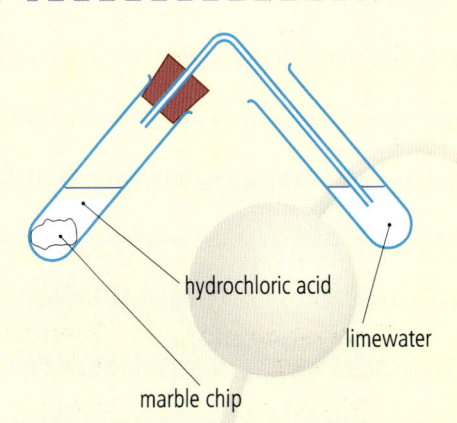

Summary of content
In a chemical reaction, we get new substances formed.
We can represent these using word equations, in which:

reactants → products

Examples include:

acid + a metal → a salt + hydrogen

Many (but not all) metals react with acid, giving off hydrogen gas. The hydrogen 'pops' when tested with a lighted splint.

acid + a carbonate → a salt + water + carbon dioxide

The carbon dioxide turns limewater milky.

metal + oxygen → metal oxide

When substances burn in air, they react with the oxygen present to form oxides.

fuel + oxygen → carbon dioxide + water

Fuels containing carbon and hydrogen burn in air to give the products shown above.

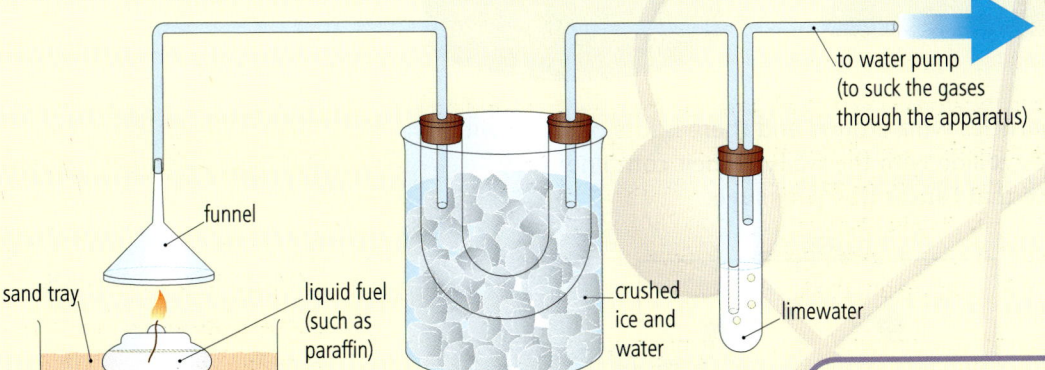

We can test the water formed by seeing if white anhydrous copper sulphate turns blue (or blue cobalt chloride paper turns pale pink). There are also other products formed when we burn fuels containing carbon and hydrogen if the supply of oxygen is limited. (See Unit 9H.)

Review Questions
1. What is the test for:
   i hydrogen
   ii carbon dioxide
   iii oxygen
   iv water?
2. Complete these word equations:
   i aluminium + oxygen → ?
   ii methane + oxygen → ? + ?

REVISION

7G Particles

In this topic you found out

- how the particle model can explain differences between solids, liquids and gases
- the way experimental evidence is explained by, and can affect, scientific theories and models

Key words

diffusion
evidence
gas pressure
model
particle
theory
vibration

Summary of content

We can explain the properties of solids, liquids and gases using **particle theory**. This describes a model that matches the observations we make of how materials behave.

In a **solid** the particles are lined up next to each other. They are fixed in position but do vibrate.

In a **liquid** the particles are still very close together, but can slip and slide over each other.

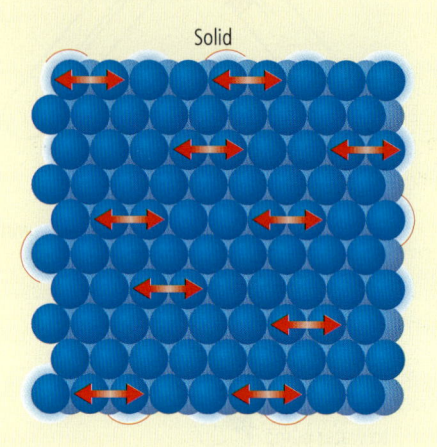

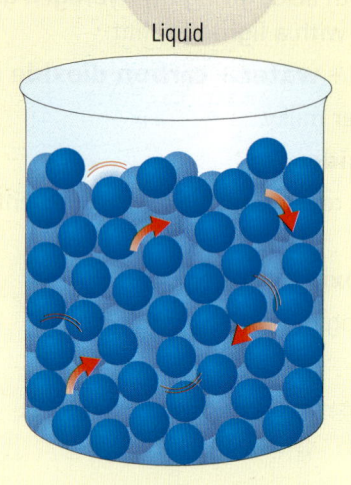

In a **gas** the particles whiz around and there is lots of space within the gas. As they collide with the walls of their container they produce a force that causes **gas pressure**.

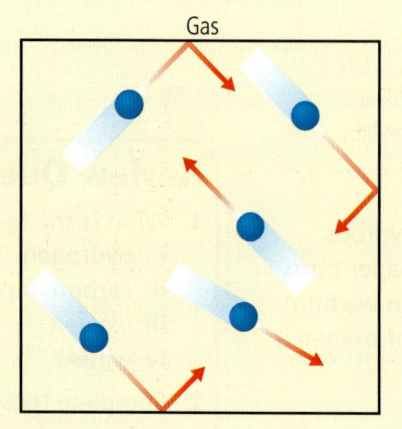

Diffusion is when substances mix without us stirring them up. This happens automatically in liquids and gases because their particles are free to move around.

Review Questions

1. Make a table that shows the properties of the 3 states of matter.
2. Explain each property in your table using particle theory.

220

REVISION
7H Solutions

In this topic you found out

- more techniques for separating mixtures
- how to distinguish between a pure substance and a mixture
- how to apply particle theory to explain techniques of separation
- about saturated solutions and solubility curves

Key words
chromatogram
chromatography
distillation
filtration
insoluble
saturated solution
solubility curve
soluble
solute
solution
solvent

Summary of content

When solids dissolve in a liquid their particles become intermingled. The solid is called the **solute**, the liquid is the **solvent** and the resulting mixture is a **solution**.

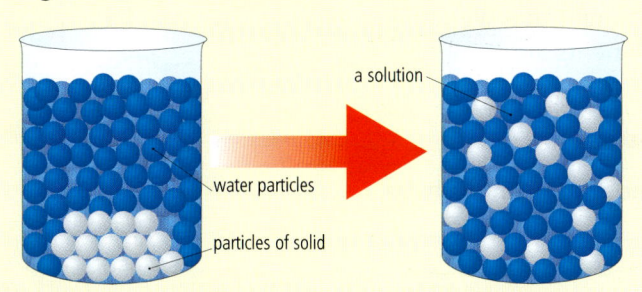

We can collect the solvent (liquid) from the solution by **distillation**.

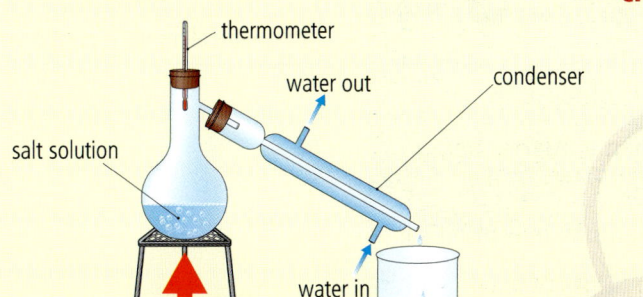

If a solvent contains two or more solutes, we can separate the solutes by **chromatography**.

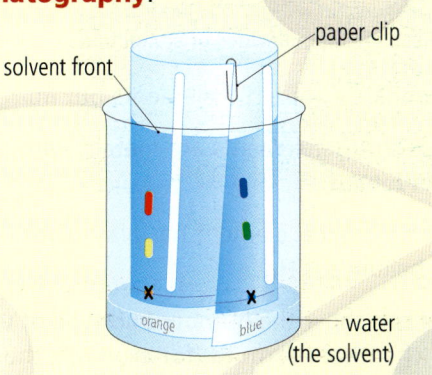

A solution that will not dissolve any more solid is a **saturated** solution.

The **solubility** of a substance varies with temperature.

This can be shown on a **solubility curve**. (See opposite.)

Review Questions

1. When you make a cup of black coffee:
   i. What is the solvent?
   ii. What is the solute?
   iii. Explain, using the particle theory, why coffee dissolves more quickly in hot water than in cold water.
2. How would you separate:
   i. water from a solution of copper sulphate in water
   ii. the dyes in a food colouring?

221

REVISION

8E Atoms and elements

In this topic you found out
- the huge range of materials that exist, and the relatively small number of elements they are made from
- about elements consisting of only one type of atom
- the properties of various elements
- how to use the particle model to explain what happens when elements combine

Key words
atom, molecule, compound, Periodic Table, element, symbol, formula

Summary of content

Elements are substances that cannot be broken down into any simpler substances. The smallest part of an element that we can still recognise as the element, is an **atom**. Elements are made up of only one type of atom.

When atoms bond together they form **molecules**.

If the atoms in a molecule are not all the same type, then we have a **compound**.

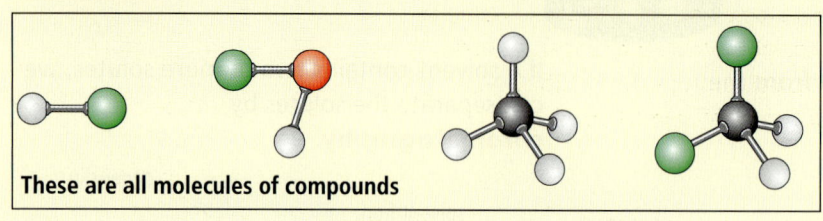

These are all molecules of compounds

These are all molecules of elements (hydrogen, oxygen, sulphur)

There are about 100 elements but millions of compounds.

Most of the elements are metals, with less than a quarter being non-metals.

Each chemical element has a **symbol** (for example, hydrogen's is H, helium's is He).

We can show the number and type of each atom in a molecule by its chemical **formula** (for example, the formula of carbon dioxide is CO_2).

The elements have been sorted out into a useful structure called the **Periodic Table**. This shows us patterns in the properties of elements.

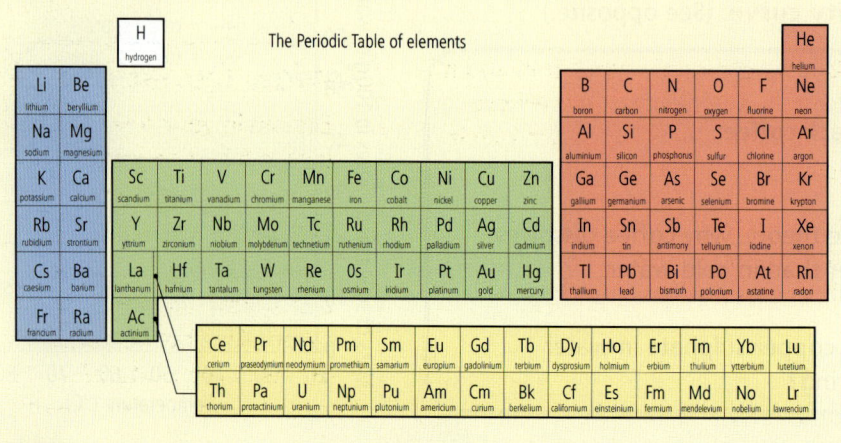

The Periodic Table of elements

Review Questions

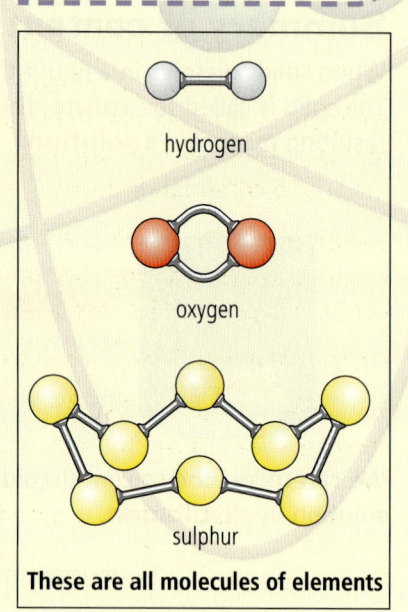

1. Write down the chemical formula of:
   i each element drawn on this page
   ii each compound drawn on this page (black atoms = C, white = H, green = Cl and red = O)

2. In carbon dioxide:
   i How many elements are there?
   ii How many atoms are there in each molecule?

REVISION

8F Compounds and mixtures

In this topic you found out
- how to distinguish between compounds and mixtures
- how to distinguish between chemical reactions in which new substances are formed and the formation of mixtures

Key words
composition, mixture, compound, proportion, element, pure, formula, ratio, impurity

Summary of content

Compounds contain more than one type of atom bonded together.

The ratio (or proportion) of each element is fixed for any particular compound. For example, the ratio of calcium : carbon : oxygen in any sample of calcium carbonate is always 1 : 1 : 3 and its formula is $CaCO_3$. So compounds have a **fixed composition**.

The properties of a compound bear no resemblance to those of the elements which make up the compound. The elements in a compound can only be separated by some kind of chemical reaction.

On the other hand, **mixtures** do not have any fixed composition.

The amount of each substance in a mixture can vary. Because no new substances have been formed, it is usually possible to separate out the different substances in a mixture. (Methods such as filtration, evaporation, distillation and chromatography can be used.)

Simple 'two-element' compounds have chemical names that end in **–ide** (for example, magnesium oxide, MgO). Compounds whose names end in **–ate** contain at least three elements of which one is oxygen (for example, copper sulphate, $CuSO_4$).

We can use melting points and boiling points to identify pure substances from values given in data books or databases. However, the melting point and boiling point of a mixture will vary depending on its composition.

Review Questions

1. Explain in your own words the changes taking place in the diagram above.
2. How could you tell when a chemical reaction had taken place between the atoms in the mixture?

REVISION

8G Rocks and weathering

In this topic you found out

- that the texture of rocks is one of the key characteristics of different rock types
- about the processes of weathering, erosion, transportation and sedimentation
- about processes, such as evaporation and dissolving, that are involved in the formation of rocks
- how the process of rock formation operates over different timescales

Key words
abrasion
deposit
erosion
evaporite
sediment
transport
weathering

Summary of content

Rocks are broken down at the surface by weathering.

Chemical weathering is when the rock is attacked by weakly acidic rainwater (or by oxygen).

Limestones are weathered more quickly by acid than granite rock.

Rocks are also broken down by **physical weathering**.

Water can collect in cracks in the rock. If this freezes the ice takes up more space than the water and the crack opens up bit by bit, until a piece eventually breaks away.

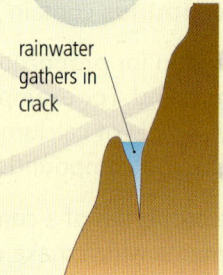

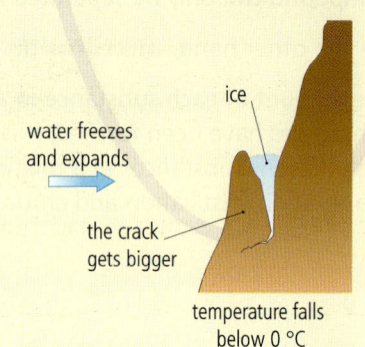

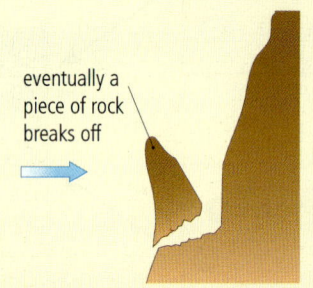

Changes in temperature also put rocks under great forces.

The minerals in the mixture that make up the rock will each expand and contract at different rates. Again, this cracks the rock and breaks bits off.

The weathered rock is then **transported** to another place, mainly by moving water. On its journey the rock fragment will get smaller, smoother and rounder the further it is carried along. It will also wear away rock that it passes over.

This is called **erosion**.

Eventually, the rock fragment is **deposited** as a **sediment** (sedimentation).

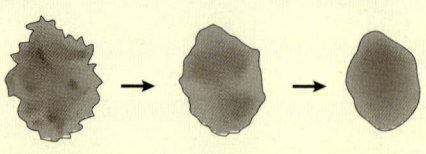

These sediments build up in layers. The sediments can be made from the remains of animals and plants as well as bits of rock.

Other layers are formed when dissolved compounds come out of solution as solids as the water evaporates. These are called evaporites.

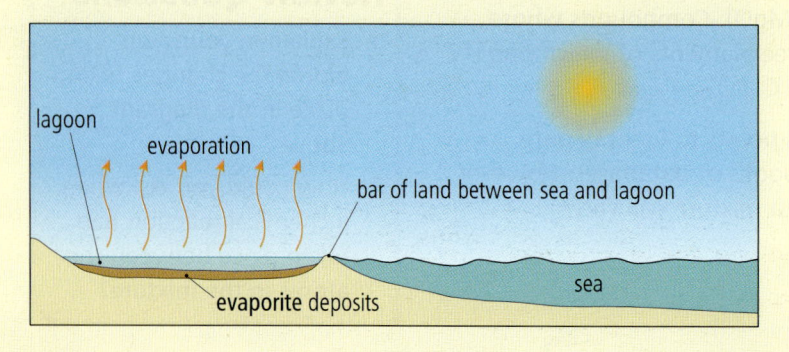

rainwater gathers in crack

water freezes and expands

ice

the crack gets bigger

temperature falls below 0 °C

eventually a piece of rock breaks off

Review Questions

1. Explain the difference between weathering and erosion.
2. How are rock fragments sorted according to size when they are deposited by a river?
3. List the 3 general types of material that can make up deposited sediments.

REVISION
8H The rock cycle

In this topic you found out
- the major rock-forming processes
- how rock-forming processes are linked by the rock cycle
- that rock texture is one of the key characteristics of the main different types of rock
- how to apply your previous work on processes, such as crystallisation, to the processes involved in the rock cycle
- processes operating over different time scales

Key words
basalt
cementation
compaction
gabbro
gneiss
granite
igneous
obsidian
pumice
schist
sedimentary
slate

Summary of content

Sedimentary rocks are formed when layers of sediment are buried under more recent deposits. Under the pressure (compaction) and with the help of mineral 'cements' (left behind when water evaporates from between the particles of sediment) rocks are formed.

Metamorphic rocks are formed when existing rock is put under increased pressure and/or temperature (without melting).

The existing rock has its structure (and possibly its minerals) changed. Bands of minerals are visible if the metamorphic rock is formed under pressure.

Igneous rocks are formed when molten rock solidifies.

Slow cooling, inside the Earth's crust, produces rock with large crystals, such as granite. Faster cooling, at or near the Earth's surface, produces rock with small crystals, such as basalt.

The processes of rock formation happen in a natural cycle that we can summarise in the **rock cycle**.

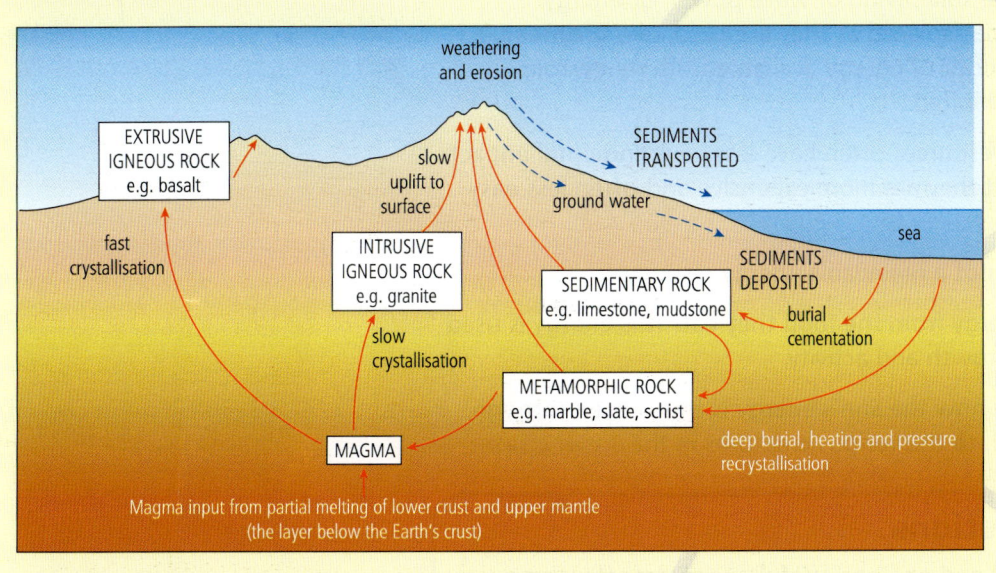

Review Questions
1. Make a bullet pointed list of the stages involved in the formation of sedimentary, metamorphic and igneous rock.
2. Draw a flow diagram to summarise the rock cycle.

REVISION

7I Energy resources

In this topic you found out

- how to use energy transfer diagrams to represent the changes taking place when fuels are used
- how to compare the advantages, limitations and environmental impact of different fuels
- the range of renewable energy resources available and what they can be used for
- the energy requirements of different people and the transfer links between the Sun, energy resources and people

Key words
diet
efficiency
energy
energy consumption
energy transfer
flammable
food chain
fossil fuel
fuel
joule
nuclear power
renewable energy

Summary of content

Fuels are substances that are burned to release their stored energy. When fuels are burned, the energy stored in the fuel is transferred to heat, movement and other forms of energy. Much of the energy is transferred to 'waste' forms of energy.

An **energy transfer diagram** shows the energy changes taking place.

Chemical energy stored in candle wax   changes to   **useful light energy + waste heat energy**

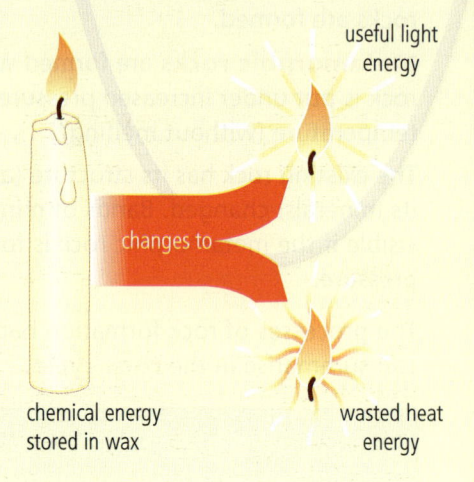

It is important to conserve fuels because **fossil fuels** will run out.

Renewable energy resources are energy resources that are always available, like solar, wind or wave power, or energy resources that can be replaced as they are used, like **biomass**. At present, the amount of energy available from renewable energy resources is limited.

Renewable energy resources often have less environmental impact than fossil fuels, but they are more expensive and often less easy to use.

Nuclear power is not a renewable energy resource.

People get their energy from the food they eat. This energy is used for life processes, growth and activity.

Food chains show how the Sun's energy is transferred through plants then, in food, to the various creatures in the **food chain**.

Review Questions

1. Give one useful and one non-useful energy transformation happening when oil is burned in an oil lamp.
2. What is the difference between renewable and non-renewable energy resources?
3. Where do people get their energy from? Describe two energy transformations that happen in people.

REVISION

7J Electrical circuits

In this topic you found out

- how to measure current and compare its size in different circuits
- about current flow in series and parallel circuits
- about developing models to explain current flow in circuits
- about the energy transfer in circuits and how to relate this to voltage
- why electricity can be hazardous, and how some electrical safety devices work

Key words
ammeter
circuit
component
conductor
current
current rating
energy transfer diagram
fuse
parallel
resistor
series
voltage

Summary of content

You need to know these circuit symbols.

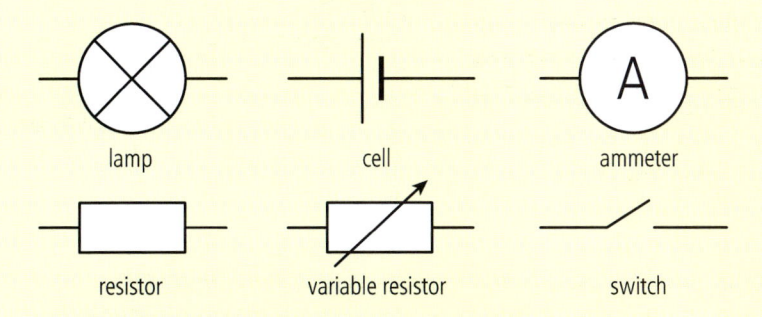

- lamp
- cell
- ammeter
- resistor
- variable resistor
- switch

Current in a circuit is measured using an **ammeter** connected in **series**.

The current in any given circuit can be increased either by increasing the **voltage** or by decreasing the **resistance**.

In a series circuit, the size of the current is the same at all points around the circuit. In a **parallel** circuit, the current splits up, some of it going along each available path.

Current and **voltage** can be imagined using a 'people in corridors' model, where the people represent the current, wide corridors represent low resistance, narrow corridors represent high resistance. The voltage of the cell or battery is represented by someone pushing the people along the corridor.

Current flow around a circuit transfers **energy** from the battery or power supply to the components in the circuit.

Increasing the voltage in any given circuit, increases the energy being transferred around that circuit.

Electricity can be dangerous because the energy it carries can cause serious or fatal burns. Electrical safety devices work by breaking the circuit, switching off the electric current.

Review Questions
1. State two factors that affect the size of the current in a circuit.
2. How is energy transferred around a circuit?
3. What is the difference between a series circuit and a parallel circuit?
4. How does a fuse work?

REVISION

7K Forces and their effects

In this topic you found out

- the difference between mass and weight
- the effect of balanced and unbalanced forces on an object
- how forces can be used to explain floating, air resistance and friction
- how to relate changes in the motion of an object to the forces acting on the object

Summary of content

The **mass** of an object tells us how much matter there is in the object.

The **weight** of an object tells us how hard it is being pulled downwards by **gravity**. Weight is a force, measured in **newtons**.

Unbalanced forces change the shape of an object, make it move, or change its movement.

Floating objects have 2 balanced forces acting on them, weight acting downwards and **upthrust** acting upwards.

Denser (heavier) liquids are easier to float in.

Elastic materials stretch until the force pulling them is exactly balanced by the forces inside them trying to pull them back to their original shape.

Friction is a force that acts to slow down the movement of surfaces sliding over each other. It is less between surfaces that are smooth or lubricated.

Friction is very important in car brakes and tyres to slow cars down and stop them skidding.

Graphs of distance against time can be drawn to show how quickly an object is moving.

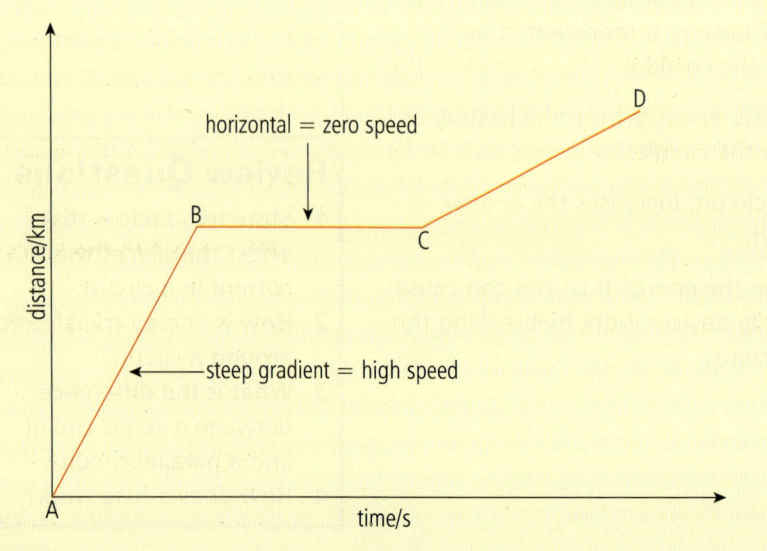

Key words
density
displacement
elastic
extension
force
friction
gravity
mass
newton meter
stopping distance
upthrust
weight

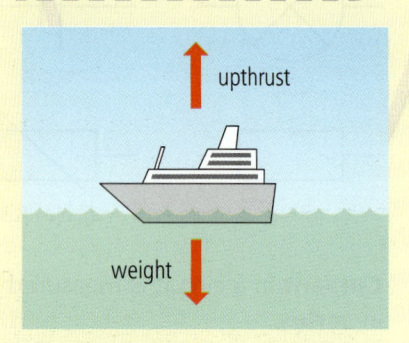

For floating objects weight and upthrust are balanced

Review Questions

1. What is the difference between mass and weight?
2. State three effects unbalanced forces can have on an object.
3. Explain how some objects are able to float.
4. Give two ways to decrease the friction between surfaces.

REVISION

7L The solar system and beyond

In this topic you found out

- why we sometimes see eclipses of the Moon and Sun
- what causes the seasons and why they are different in different places
- what different planets are like, and whether there is any life on other planets
- what is beyond the solar system

Key words
axis of rotation
date line
elliptical orbit
luminous
lunar eclipse
orbit
parallax
phases of the Moon
planet
solar eclipse
star
Universe

Summary of content

The Earth takes 24 hours to turn once on its own axis, causing day and night, and one year to **orbit** the Sun.

The Moon takes 28 days to orbit the Earth, causing the **phases** of the Moon.

The Sun is **luminous**; it gives off light. All other bodies in the solar system are visible because they reflect the Sun's light.

Lunar eclipses happen when the Earth's shadow falls on the Moon.

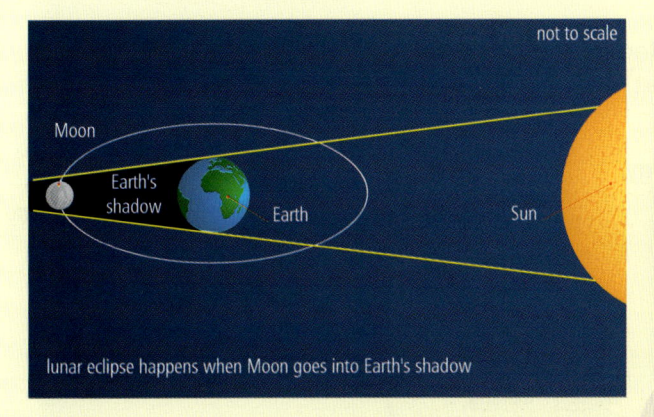

Solar eclipses happen when the Moon passes between the Earth and the Sun.

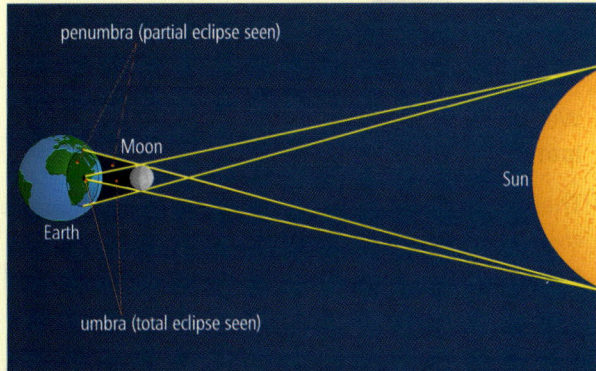

lunar eclipse happens when Moon goes into Earth's shadow

penumbra (partial eclipse seen)
umbra (total eclipse seen)

The **seasons** occur because the Earth's axis is tilted relative to its orbit around the Sun so, as the Earth moves around the Sun, the northern hemisphere is sometimes tilted towards the Sun (summer) and sometimes tilted away from the Sun (winter).

There are nine known **planets** in the solar system. Going outwards from the Sun they are Mercury, Venus, Earth, Mars, Jupiter, Saturn, Uranus, Neptune and Pluto.

The Earth is the only planet known to support life.

There are billions of other stars similar to our Sun in the **Universe**.

Review Questions

1. Why do we see phases of the Moon?
2. When does a solar eclipse happen?
3. The Earth's axis is tilted with respect to the Sun's radiation. In the UK, explain the effect this tilt has on:
   i day length throughout the year
   ii temperature throughout the year.

REVISION

8I Heating and cooling

In this topic you found out

- why temperature scales are needed and how to make one
- the difference between temperature and heat
- the ways in which heat can be transferred from one place to another
- how to use the particle model to explain heat transfer, expansion and change of state

Key words
change of state
conduction
conductor
convection
density
heat
insulation
melting point
particle model
radiation
temperature
temperature scale

Summary of content

Heat tells us how much heat energy an object has. The **temperature** of an object tells us how concentrated the heat energy in the object is.

The most common temperature scale used in science is the **Celsius** scale.

Thermal conductors transfer heat energy easily, **thermal insulators** don't.

Thermal insulators can be used to reduce unwanted transfers of heat energy.

There are three ways in which heat energy is transferred; **conduction**, **convection** and **thermal radiation**.

We can use the **particle model** to explain how materials behave when they gain or lose heat energy.

There are certain **fixed temperatures**, called the **melting point** and the **boiling point**, at which materials **change state**. These temperatures are different for different materials.

A material is always solid at a temperature lower than its melting point.

A material is always a gas above its boiling point.

Between its melting point and its boiling point a material can be either liquid or gas. **Evaporation** is the change of state where a material changes from a liquid to a gas at a temperature below its boiling point.

The higher the temperature, the more rapidly a liquid evaporates.

Review Questions
1. Name the three ways in which heat energy can be transferred.
2. Use the particle model to explain the difference between a thermal conductor and a thermal insulator.
3. What are the two fixed temperatures for pure water?
4. What is the difference between heat and temperature?

REVISION 8J: Magnets and electromagnets

In this topic you found out

- about making magnets and testing their strength
- what a magnetic field is and how to plot the magnetic field for a magnet
- about making an electromagnet and investigating the factors affecting its strength
- some of the places where magnets and electromagnets are used

Key words
bar magnet
compass
electromagnet
geomagnetic pole
magnetic field
magnetic force
magnetic material
magnetic north pole
magnetic pole
non-magnetic
repel
soft iron core

Summary of content

The only **magnetic materials** are **iron**, **steel**, **cobalt** and **nickel**. **Magnets** can be made from magnetic materials. Ceramic or rubber magnets contain large amounts of magnetic material.

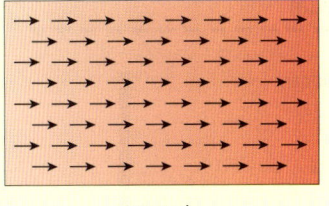

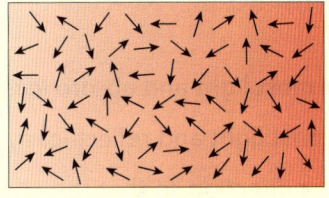

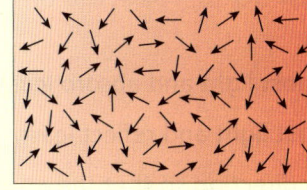

magnet

S → N
microscopic magnet

magnetic material

All magnets exert forces, called **magnetic forces**, on magnets and magnetic materials around them.

Magnetic forces can act through non-magnetic materials, but not through magnetic materials.

A **compass** is a magnet that is able to rotate freely.

The Earth has two **geomagnetic poles**; a 'magnetic south' near the North Pole and a 'magnetic north' near the South Pole.

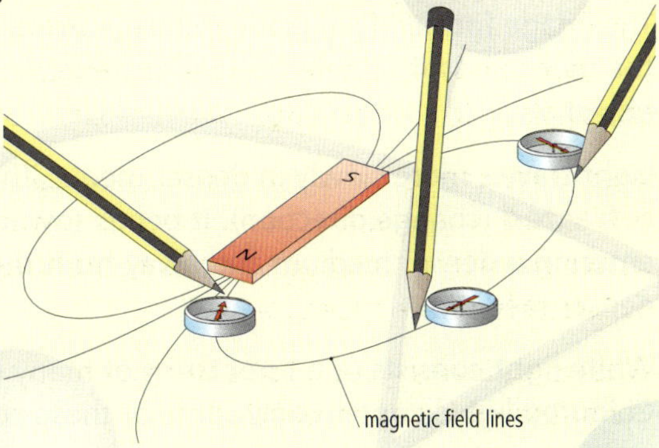

Magnets have two **poles**, a north pole (short for north-seeking pole) that is attracted to the magnetic pole near the Earth's North Pole, and a south pole (short for south-seeking pole) that is attracted to the magnetic pole near the Earth's South Pole.

All magnets have a **magnetic field**, showing how strong the magnetic force is in different places.

The closer together the lines are in the magnetic field, the stronger the magnetic force.

An **electromagnet** can be made from a coil of wire, with a current flowing through it.

The strength of an electromagnet is increased by putting a **core** of magnetic material inside the coil.

magnetic field lines

Review Questions

1. What is the difference between a magnet and a magnetic material?
2. What is the area of magnetic force around a magnet called?
3. Give two factors that affect the strength of an electromagnet.
4. How can a permanent magnet be used to navigate around the Earth's surface?

REVISION

8K Light

In this topic you found out

- how light travels and the speed at which it travels
- what happens to light when it hits different types of materials
- why we see images in mirrors
- why coloured lights and coloured filters can make objects 'change colour'

Summary of content

Light travels in straight lines at 300 000 km/s.

The path of light can be represented by **rays** (straight lines with arrows to show the way the light energy travels).

Light falling on an object can be **transmitted**, **reflected** or **absorbed**.

Light coloured, shiny objects reflect most light and absorb least.

Dark coloured, dull objects absorb most light and reflect least.

Light reflects from a plane mirror in a direction so that the **angle of reflection** equals the **angle of incidence**.

An **image** is formed where light rays appear to have come from.

The image formed by a plane mirror is virtual, upright and behind the mirror. It is the same size and distance from the mirror as the object.

Light travels more slowly in denser media. This can cause it to be **refracted** (change direction). It bends towards the normal on entering a denser medium and away from the normal on leaving a denser medium.

White light consists of a **spectrum** of many different colours. Coloured lights contain only some of these colours.

Coloured filters transmit only some colours of light, and absorb all other colours. For example, a yellow filter will transmit red and green light, and absorb blue light.

The colour of an object tells us what colour light it reflects. For example, a turquoise object will reflect blue and green light and absorb red light.

Key words
- absorption
- coloured filter
- incident ray
- plane mirror
- primary colour
- reflection
- refraction
- scattering
- spectrum
- speed of light
- transmission
- virtual

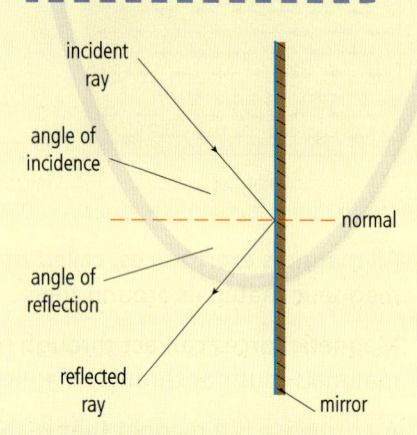

Reflection from a plane mirror

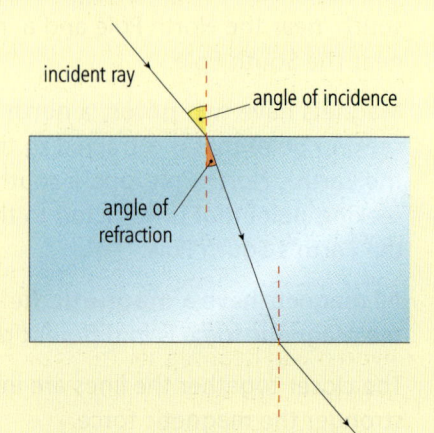

Refraction through a glass block

Review Questions

1. How could you make an object reflect more light?
2. What are the three primary colours of light?
3. What is the difference between reflection and refraction?
4. What colour would a red object appear when seen through a yellow filter?

REVISION

8L Sound and hearing

In this topic you found out

- how to change the pitch and loudness of sounds
- how sound travels through different materials
- how the human ear works and how human hearing differs from that of some other animals
- why sound can be dangerous and the effects loud sounds can cause

Summary of content

Sound is produced by **vibrating** objects.

When a sound wave travels through a material, the particles are alternately squashed together (**compression**) and spread apart (**rarefaction**).

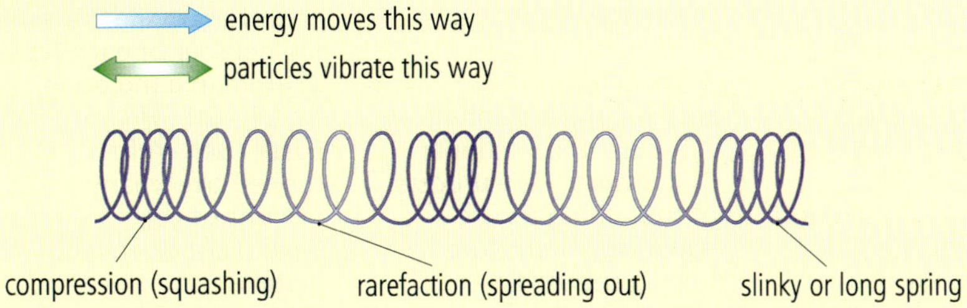

→ energy moves this way
↔ particles vibrate this way

compression (squashing)   rarefaction (spreading out)   slinky or long spring

Sound waves are **longitudinal**. The sound energy travels in the same direction as the particles vibrate in.

The loudness of a sound is its **amplitude**. Large vibrations cause a loud (high amplitude) sound.

The **pitch** (**frequency**) of the note from a string or drum skin can be increased by increasing the tension (stretching it more) or by decreasing the length or area.

The pitch (frequency) of the note from a wind instrument can be increased by decreasing the length of the vibrating air column.

An oscilloscope can be used to compare the amplitude and frequency of different sound waves.

Sound waves must have a **medium** to travel through. They cannot travel through a vacuum.

Sound travels further and faster through solids and liquids than through gases.

Adult humans can generally hear sounds in the range 20 Hz to 20 000 Hz. Children can hear higher frequency sounds. The ability to hear high frequencies decreases with age.

Many animals can hear **ultrasound**, frequencies too high for humans to hear.

Very loud sounds can permanently damage the ear, causing hearing loss.

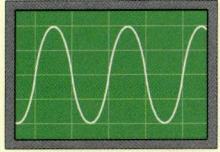

large amplitude 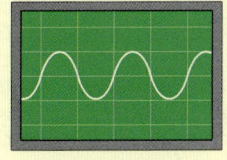   small amplitude 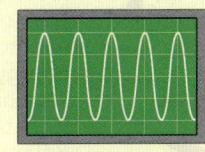   high frequency 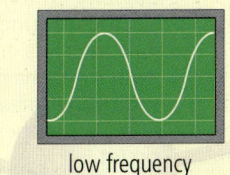   low frequency

Key words
compression
decibels
frequency
longitudinal
loudness
medium
noise pollution
pitch
rarefaction
speed of sound
ultrasound
vibration

Review Questions

1. Explain how increasing each of these would affect a sound you heard:
   i amplitude,
   ii frequency.
2. State two ways to lower the pitch of a note made by a stringed instrument.
3. Use the particle model to explain why sound can't travel through a vacuum.
4. What is the difference between sound and ultrasound?

Glossary

Acceleration – is the rate of change of speed, so the higher the acceleration the more quickly the speed is changing.

Adaptation – Feature of an organism's structure or behaviour that enables it to survive in a particular habitat.

Aerobic respiration – A type of respiration where oxygen is used:
glucose + oxygen → carbon dioxide + water

Amniotic sac – A bag of fluid surrounded by a thin membrane. The fetus develops in this inside the uterus. It protects the fetus if the mother is knocked or bumped.

Anaerobic respiration – A type of respiration where oxygen is not used.
In animals – glucose → lactic acid
In plants – glucose → ethanol + carbon dioxide

Antibody – A substance made by the white blood cells that helps to destroy microbes. Each antibody works against a specific microbe.

Atom – The smallest particle that can still be identified as an element.

Bacteria – A type of microbe, consisting of simple single cells.

Balanced equation – A way of describing a chemical reaction that shows the formulae of reactants and products so that the number of each type of atom is the same on either side of the equation.
e.g. $2 Mg + O_2 \rightarrow 2 MgO$

Balanced forces – Forces are balanced when the forces in one direction are equal in size to the forces in the opposite direction. An object acted on by balanced forces does not change speed or direction.

Carbohydrate – Nutrients such as sugar and starch. They are made of carbon, oxygen and hydrogen and are the main source of energy in the diet.

Cementation – The process whereby dissolved solids come out of solution to 'stick' rock fragments together, helping to form sedimentary rock.

Chlorophyll – A green pigment, found in the chloroplasts of plant cells, which absorbs light energy for photosynthesis.

Chloroplast – An organelle found in plant cells where photosynthesis takes place.

Chromatography – The process whereby small amounts of dissolved substances are separated by running a solvent along a material such as absorbent paper.

Clone – An individual organism that has been produced from only one parent and is genetically identical to that parent.

Compaction – The process whereby pressure builds up on sediment as layers are deposited on top, resulting in the particles fusing together, helping the formation of sedimentary rock.

Compound – A substance made up of 2 or more different types of atom.

Conservation of mass – The mass of reactants before a reaction equals the mass of products formed after the reaction.

Convection – The transfer of heat energy through a material by particles themselves moving. Hot parts of the liquid or gas become less dense and move upwards, cooler parts become more dense and move downwards.

Current – The flow of electricity round a circuit that transfers energy from the power supply/batteries to the other components in the circuit.

Cytoplasm – Where all of the main chemical reactions in the cell take place.

Diffusion – The automatic mixing and movement of one substance through another, without the need to stir up the substances.

Digestion – The process by which large, insoluble molecules are made smaller and soluble by 'digestive juices' such as enzymes.

Displacement reaction – The reaction in which a more reactive metal takes the place of a less reactive metal in its compound.
For example:
zinc + copper sulphate → zinc sulphate + copper

Distillation – The process of separating a pure liquid from a mixture by boiling the mixture containing the liquid, then condensing the gas and collecting the pure liquid.

DNA – Deoxyribonucleic acid, the chemical in chromosomes which contains genetic information.

Efficiency – The efficiency of an energy resource is a measure of how much of the stored energy is changed into useful types of energy when the energy resource is used.

Electromagnet – A magnet made by passing an electric current through a coil of wire, usually wound on a soft iron core.

Element – A substance made up of only one type of atom. Elements cannot be broken down chemically into simpler substances.

Energy transfer – The movement of energy from one place to another.

Energy transformation – The change of energy from one form to a different form.

Enzyme – Protein molecules which help chemical reactions in living organisms to take place.

Erosion – The wearing away of rocks as they come into contact when moving over each other.

Fertilisation – The joining together of male and female sex cells, e.g. egg and sperm.

Fetus – An unborn baby which has developed the main organs and limbs which will be present after it is born.

Formula – The abbreviation that tells us the number of each type of atom in a molecule.
e.g. H_2, CH_4, H_2O

Fossil fuel – A fuel formed over many millions of years from dead plant or animal material.

Frequency – The number of complete sound waves in one second. A sound wave with a high frequency is a high pitched sound.

Friction – The force that acts between two moving forces. It acts in the opposite direction to the movement, so slows down the movement.

Fuse – A safety device designed to melt if too high a current flows through it. This turns off the current and prevents overheating or damage to other components.

Gamete – A sex cell such as egg cells, sperm, pollen and ovules.

Gas pressure – The force per unit area exerted as gas particles collide with the walls of their container or other objects.

Gene – Part of a chromosome, found in the nucleus of a cell, which controls a characteristic in an organism.

234

GLOSSARY

Geomagnetic pole – One of the poles of the Earth's magnetic field. One end of the imaginary bar magnet through the centre of the Earth.

Gravity – The attractive force that pulls masses together. On Earth all things are pulled towards the centre of the Earth by the Earth's gravity.

Igneous – Rock types formed by the solidification of molten rock.

Immunity – Your body's ability to destroy a particular pathogen before it is able to make you ill.

Luminous – Any object that gives off light, rather than simply reflecting light shining on it.

Lunar eclipse – When the Moon passes into the shadow cast by Earth.

Membrane – Controls what goes in and out of the cell.

Menstrual cycle – The monthly cycle where the uterus is prepared for a fertilised egg, an egg is released and, if it is not fertilised, the uterus lining breaks down and a period occurs.

Metamorphic – Rocks whose structure and/or mineral content has been changed by the action of heat and/or pressure.

Molecule – A group of 2 or more atoms bonded together.

Moment – The turning effect of a force. It is calculated from the equation:
Moment = force × distance from pivot

Neutralisation – A chemical reaction in which an acid reacts with a base to form a salt and water (plus carbon dioxide if the base is a carbonate).

Nucleus – Carries genetic material/genes/chromosomes/DNA and controls activities of the cell.

Ovary – The organ in a female which releases an ovum every month and which also produces female hormones.

Periodic Table – A table of the chemical elements listed so that similar elements line up in vertical columns (called groups).

Placenta – An organ which develops in the uterus where oxygen and nutrients pass from the mother's blood to the fetus and carbon dioxide and other waste material pass from the fetus's blood to the mother's.

Photosynthesis – The chemical process in which plants make food. Photosynthesis can be summed up in the equation:

carbon dioxide + water $\xrightarrow[\text{chlorophyll}]{\text{light energy}}$ glucose + oxygen

pH value – A number on the pH scale that indicates how acidic or alkaline a solution is. A pH value of 7 is neutral. Values below 7 are acidic (the lower the number the more acidic a solution is) whereas pH values above 7 are alkaline (the higher the value the more alkaline a solution is).

Power rating – A measure of how rapidly a device transforms electrical energy into other types of energy.

Primary colour – A colour of light that cannot be made by mixing other colours. The primary colours of light are red, green and blue.

Principle of moments – The principle that states that for a balanced object the total clockwise moment acting on the object is equal to the total anticlockwise moment.

Producer – A plant that can make food from simple substances, e.g. carbon dioxide and water, using energy from sunlight. Producers are always found at the start of a food chain.

Product – A substance that is formed in a chemical reaction.

Pyramid of numbers – A diagram that shows the numbers of organisms at each level in a food chain.

Qualitative data – Information gathered by observations from experiments.

Quantitative data – Information gathered by taking measurements during experiments.

Rarefaction – A region of a sound wave where the vibrating particles are stretched further apart than normal.

Reactant – A substance that we start with before a chemical reaction takes place.

Reactivity Series – A list of the metals in order of their reactivity.

Refraction – The change in direction that happens when a ray of light travels from a medium of one density to a medium of a different density. Refraction is caused by light travelling more slowly in the denser medium.

Reliable – The word that describes data that we can expect to be reproduced if collected again under the same conditions.

Renewable energy – Energy coming from sources where the energy is continually available (like solar power) or where the energy used can be replaced (like wood).

Saturated solution – A solution in which no more solute will dissolve at a given temperature.

Sediment – Rock fragments or bits of organic matter that are deposited.

Sedimentary – Rock types formed from the compaction and cementation of sediment.

Selective breeding – Means of producing individual organisms with desired characteristics by breeding from parents that possess those characteristics.

Solar eclipse – When the Moon passes between the Sun and the Earth, casting a shadow over part of the Earth's surface.

Temperature – A measure of the concentration of thermal energy within a material. An object where the thermal energy is concentrated has a high temperature. If the thermal energy is very spread out the object will be cold.

Terminal velocity – The fastest speed that a moving object can reach. When an object is travelling at terminal velocity its forward forces are exactly balanced by the forces resisting its motion.

Tissue – A group of cells of the same type which work together to carry out a particular function.

Uterus – The organ in a female where a fetus grows and develops until it is ready to be born.

Vaccination – Giving a person antigens so that they produce antibodies against a disease.

Variation – Differences between members of the same species.

Virus – A type of microbe that has to 'take over' a cell in order to reproduce.

Voltage – A measure of the force with which a battery or power supply 'pushes' electrical current round a circuit. Voltage is measured in volts.

Weathering – The breakdown of rocks in nature.

Weight – The force that acts downwards on any object, due to the force of gravity pulling it towards the centre of the Earth.

Word equation – A way of describing a chemical reaction that names what we start with and what we finish with after the reaction.
For example:

magnesium + oxygen
↓
magnesium oxide

Index

All page numbers in **bold** type show places where information is contained in a table or an illustration.

A

absorption, food 214
absorption, light 232
acceleration 179–81, **179**
  in free fall 187, **187**, 188
acidic soil 109, 110, **110**
acid rain 112, 113–17
acids 218
  reactions 78–88, 219
    and metal reactivity 98–9
    titrations 86–7, **87**
adaptations 8, 48, **48**, 212
addictive substances 28, 33, 37
adolescence 211
aerobic respiration 23, 215
aerosols 196, **196**
air 94, 195
  and plants 42, **42**, 43
  see also atmosphere
air pollution 118–20, **118**
  see also acid rain;
    greenhouse effect
air pressure 195, **195**, 198
air resistance 179, 182–4, **182**
  and free fall 186, **187**
  and heat 185, **185**
  and speed 184, **184**
  and terminal velocity 188, **188**
alcoholic drinks 33, **33**, 36
  ethanol in 126
alkaline soil 109, 110, **110**
alkalis 84, 86, 96, 218
  in titrations 86–7, **87**
aluminium **83**, 103, **103**
  reactivity 98–9, **99**
aluminium oxide 99
amino acids 49
ammeters 147, **147**, 227, **227**
amniotic sac 211, **211**
amplitude 233, **233**
anaerobic respiration 215
angle of incidence 232, **232**
angle of reflection 232, **232**
animal cells 210, **210**
animals 52, 213
  asexual reproduction 18, **18**
  breeds of 11–13, **11**, **12**
  cloning 16–17, **16**
  in food webs 212, **212**, 217
annual plants 59
antibiotics 216
antibodies 216
antiseptics 216
appliances 151–3, **151**
Archimedes 199
area and pressure **192**, 193
Aristotle 42
arteries, coronary 34, **34**
artificial fertilisers 63, 64
artificial satellites 170–2, **170**, **171**, **172**
asexual reproduction 17–18, **17**, **18**
asthma 27
atmosphere, gases in 52, **52**
  plants affect 42, **42**
  see also air

atmospheric pressure 195, **195**, 198
atoms 222

B

bacteria 213, 216
balance 201–4
balanced equations 80, 83
balanced forces 182, 188, **188**
bar magnets 231, **231**
basalt 225, **225**
bases 84
batteries 150, **150**
bell jar model 26, **26**
bioaccumulation 69, **69**
biochemistry 132, **132**
biofuel power stations 156
biological control 70
biomass 43, 49, 52, 62
  as an energy resource 226
birds 66–7, **67**
blood 34, 215
blood cells 35
blood vessels 28, 215, **215**
  coronary arteries 34, **34**
boiling points 75, 230, **230**
bones 34–5, **35**
braking systems 197, **197**
breathing 25–7, **26**
breeds, animal 11–13, **11**, **12**
brittle materials **76**
bronchioles 27
bronchitis 28
budding by hydra 18, **18**
building materials 112, **112**
burettes 86–7, **86**, **87**
burning see combustion

C

caesium 97, **97**
caffeine, investigating 38, **38**
calcium 30, **62**, **83**, 97
calcium carbonate 115–16
  reaction with acid 136, **136**
  as marble 219
candles 139, 226, **226**
capillaries 215, **215**
carbohydrate 214
  see also cellulose; sugar
carbon 62, 77, **77**, 127
carbonates **83**
  and acid rain 115–16
  reactions 82–3, 136, **136**, 219
carbon dioxide
  in the atmosphere 52, **52**
  and global warming 121, **121**, 122
  in blood 215
  carbonates give 82, 219
  combustion gives 126, 139, 219, **219**
  from fossil fuels 52, **52**, 53
  and plants 43, 45, **45**
  in glasshouses 70

photosynthesis 46, 52
  in rain 113
  and respiration 23, 52
carbon monoxide 28, 127
carcinogenic substances 28
cardiac muscle 34
carnivores 217
cars 181, 183, **185**
  efficiency 157, **157**
  fuel 126, 127, 185
  pollution from 119, 127, **127**
  and acid rain 113
cartilage 35, **35**
catalytic converters 123, **127**
Cavendish, Henry 163
cell division 211
cells, electrical 149–50, **149**
  and reactivity 130, **130**
  and voltage 148
cells, organisms' 210, **210**
  nucleus of 6, 16, **16**, 210
cellulose 49
Celsius scale 230
cementation 225, **225**
centre of mass 163, **163**, 201
CFCs (chlorofluorocarbons) 121
chalky soil 108, 109
change of state 230, **230**
  melting 136
  sublimation 77
charge on ions 81, **81**
chemical energy 129, 130, **144**
  in candles 126, **226**
  cells store 150
  and voltage 148
chemical industry 132, **132**
chemical properties 104
chemical reactions 134–41, 219
  energy from 129–30
  burning fuels 126–8
  metals 78–89, 91–106
chemical weathering 112, **112**, 224
chlorides 78, **79**
chlorophyll 44, 46, **62**
chloroplasts 48, **48**, 210
cholesterol 34, **34**
chromatography 221, **221**
chromosomes 6, **6**
circuits 147, **147**, 227
  models of 149, **149**
circular motion 168–9, **168**, **169**
circulatory system 39, 215, **215**
  see also blood; blood
    vessels; heart
classification 213
clay soil 108, 109
climate change 121–2, **121**
clones 16–18, **16**, **17**, **18**
cobalt chloride test **126**, 219
colour 232
coloured filters, light 232
combining power 80, 81, **83**, **83**
  metals 100
combustion 139–40, 219
  fuels 126–8, 139
  carbon dioxide from 113
  and electricity generation 156

and global warming 121, 122
communities 212
compaction 225
compasses 231
competition and plants 66–7
components **227**
composition 223
compost 63
compounds 222, **222**, 223, **223**
compressed gases 195
compression 233, **233**
conduction 230
conductors **74**, 75, 230
  non-metals **76**, 77, **77**
conifers 217
conservation of energy 158
conservation of mass 135, 136
consumers 212, 217
convection 230
Copernicus 167
copper **93**, 101–2, **102**
  with water 95–6, **95**
copper(II), combining power **83**
copper oxide 84, **84**
copper sulphate 82, **87**
  preparing 84–5, **84**, **85**
  tests with **126**, 219
cores, electromagnet 231
coronary arteries 34, **34**
corrosion 99, **99**
  rusting 93–4, **93**, **94**
  tarnish 92–4, **92**, **93**
corrosive substances **218**
crop plants 65, 70, **70**
  and fertilisers 62–5, **63**
  and herbicides 66, **66**
  and pests 68–9, **68**, 70
  varieties of 9–10, **9**, 14, **14**
crude oil 132, **132**
crystallisation 225, **225**
current 149, 151, 227
cuttings 17, **17**
cytoplasm 210

D

Davy, Sir Humphry 97
DDT 68–9
deceleration 179, **179**
deforestation 52, 53, **53**
density **74**, 75
  and floating 228
  and light refraction 232
dependent variable 99
deposition 224, **225**
diamond 77, **77**
diaphragm 25, 26, **26**
diet 30–2, **30**, 214
diffusion 220
digestion 132, 214
digestive system 39, **214**
diseases and microbes 216
disinfectants 216
displacement reactions 101–3
  energy from 129, 130
distance and speed 176, **176**

236

INDEX E–H

distance-time graphs 187, 228
distillation 221, **221**
DNA 6
dogs, breeds of 11–12, **11**, **12**
drugs 36–8, **36**, **37**, **38**
  see also alcoholic drinks; smoking
dry cells 150, **150**
ductile materials **74**
dull materials **76**
dynamos 154–5, **155**

E

Earth 229, 231
  mass of 163, **163**
  movement of 168–9, 177, **177**
  see also atmosphere
eclipses 229, **229**
ecological relationships 217
ecosystems 212
Edison, Thomas 155
efficiency 157, **157**
effort 199–200, **199**, **200**
eggs 6–8, **8**, 211
  in cloning 16, **16**
elastic materials 228
elastic potential energy **144**
electrical conductivity **74**, 75
  non-metals **76**, 77, **77**
electrical energy 130, **144**, 146
  and appliances 151–2
  and cells 150
  and efficiency 157
  and electric generators 154
  and voltage 148
electric generators 154–5, **155**
electricity 143–60
  as an energy source 146, **146**
  and energy transfer 147–50
  generating 122, 154–6
  paying for 151–3, **152**
electromagnets 231
electromotive force 148
electrons 147
  free electrons 75, 77, **77**
elements 222, **222**, 223, **223**
embryos in cloning 16, **16**
endothermic reactions 130, **130**
energy 143–6, **144**, 226
  in chemical reactions 129–30
    burning fuels 126–8
  in circuits 227
  conservation of 158
  and electricity 147–52
  in food chains 217, 226
  from glucose 23, 49, 215
  heat see heat
  light see light
  and sound waves 233, **233**
  and voltage 148
  wasted energy 144, **145**, 157–8
energy flow diagrams 145, **145**, 158, **158**
energy resources 226
  see also fuels
energy transfer 144, 145, 226
  and electricity 147–50
  energy transfer diagrams 226, **226**
  energy transformations 144–5, **145**

  by appliances 151–2
  and wasted energy 157
environment 52–3
  and energy resources **156**, 157, 226
  and farming 67, 68–9
  and variation 5, 10, 213
  see also pollution
environmental chemistry 107–24
environmental factors in habitats 212
environmental variation 5, 213
enzymes 214
epidermis, plant 48, **48**
equations 80
  acid-alkali reactions 86, 218
  acid-carbonate reactions 82–3, 219
  acid-metal oxide reactions 84
  acid-metal reactions 78, 219
  burning 219
  metal-oxygen reactions 219
  oxygen-hydrogen reaction 135
  photosynthesis 46, 52, 132
  respiration 52, 132
erosion 224, **225**
ethanol, burning 126–7, **126**
ethics 17, 38
eutrophication 120, **120**
evaporation 230
evaporites 224, **224**
evidence 220
exercise 22–4, **24**, 34
exothermic reactions 126, 129, 131
expiration 26, **26**

F

Faraday, Michael 154
farming 13, 67
  crops see crop plants
  and soil 111, **111**
fat, body 23
fats and oils 49, 214
feeding relationships 212, **212**
female reproductive system 211, **211**
ferns 217
fertilisation 7, 210, 211
fertilisers 51, 62–5, **63**
  and soil type 109
  testing 64, **64**
fetuses 33, 211, **211**
fibre in diet 214
filters, light 232
fitness 22–4, **22**, **24**, 34
floating 228, **228**
flowering plants 6, 14, **14**, 217
food 49, 57–61, **57**, **58**
  and digestion 132, 214, **214**
  energy from 226
  and microbes 216
  and photosynthesis 43–9
food chains 212, 217, 226
  and pesticides 68–9, **69**
food webs 212, **212**, 217
  and pesticides 68–9, **68**
forces 162, 191, **191**, 228
  and acceleration 179, 180–1
  in free fall 186–8, **187**

  and terminal velocity 188, **188**
gravitational 164–5, **165**
  and planets 168, 169
  and satellites 170–1, **170**
levers 199–200, **199**, **200**
in liquids 197, **197**
magnetic forces 231
and moments 202–4, **202**, **203**
and motion 179–88, **182**
  circular motion 169, **169**
  and pressure 192, **192**, 193, **193**
  and speed 179–81
forests 52, 53, **53**
  and acid rain 116, **116**
formulae 80, 83, 222, 223
  acids and salts **78**, **79**, 83
fossil fuels 52, **52**, **53**, **156**
  and acid rain 113–14, **113**, 117
  as energy stores 145, 226
  and global warming 121, 122
  see also fuels
francium 97
free electrons 75, 77, **77**
free fall 186–7, **186**, **187**
  in space 166, **166**
frequency 233, **233**
friction 179, **179**, 182, **182**, 228
  compensating for 180, **180**
  and free fall 186
  heat from 185, **185**
fuels 52, **52**, **53**, **156**
  and acid rain 113–14, **113**, 117
  burning 219, **219**, 226
    energy from 126–8, 144, **144**
  as energy stores 145, 226
  and global warming 121, 122
fungi 213, 216

G

Galileo 167
gametes 6–8, **7**, **8**
gases 220, **220**, 230, **230**
  atmospheric 42, **42**, 52, **52**
  greenhouse gases 121, **121**, 122
  pressure in 195–6, **196**, 220
  in reactions 136, **136**
gas pressure 220
gas turbine power stations **156**
genes 6–7, **7**, 210
  and selective breeding 12
  and variation 10, 213
genetic information 6, 10
  and clones 16, **16**, 17
geomagnetic poles 231
geostationary orbits 171–2, **171**
geothermal power stations **156**
glasshouses, crops in 70, **70**
Global Positioning System 172, **172**
global warming 121–2, **121**
glucose 23, 52, 215
  in plants 46, 49, 50, 52
gold 75, **75**, 93, **93**
  low reactivity 104, **104**
GPS (Global Positioning System) 172, **172**

grafting 18, **18**
granite 225, **225**
graphite 77, **77**, 150
graphs
  distance-time **187**, 228
  reaction products 138
  speed-time 187–8, **187**, **188**
gravitational potential energy **144**
gravity 161–6, 180, 228
  and fluid pressure 198, **198**
  and free fall 186, **186**
  in space 166, **166**
  and satellites 170–1, **170**
  planets 168, 169
Greenhouse Effect 121, **121**
greenhouse gases 121, **121**, 122
Group 1 metals 75, **76**, 104
  reactions with water 96–7, **97**
growth 211
  plants 41, **41**, 70
  and acid rain 116, **116**

H

habitats 67, **67**, 212
hardness 75
harmful substances **218**
hazard symbols 218, **218**
health 21–40, **21**
hearing 233
heart 34, **34**, 215, **215**
  and smoking 28
heat/heat energy **144**, 230
  from chemical energy 226, **226**
  displacement reactions 129
  exothermic reactions 126, 131
  and friction 185, **185**
Helmholtz, Hermann 158
herbicides 66, **66**
herbivores 217
Hopkins, Sir Frederick Gowland 31
horses, breeding of 12, **12**
human body
  circulatory system 215, **215**
  food **49**, 57–61, **57**, **58**, 226
  and digestion 132, 214, **214**
  health 21–40, **21**
  levers in 200, **200**
  and microbes 216
  moments 204, **204**
  reproduction 6–8, **8**, 211, **211**
humus 64, 108
hydra 18, **18**
hydraulic jacks 198, **198**
hydrocarbons 126, 127, 139
hydrochloric acid **78**, **79**
  reactions 79–81, 84, 218
    with carbonates 136, **136**, 219
  in titrations 87, **87**
hydro-electric power **156**
hydrogen 78, **78**, 80, 219
  as fuel 127
  in plants 45, 62
  and water 134–5, **134**
hydroxides 83, 96
hygiene 216

237

INDEX I–P

I

identical twins 10
igneous rocks 225, **225**
images 232
immunity 216
incident rays 232
incomplete combustion 127
independent variable 99
indicators 87, 218
infectious diseases 216
inheritance 5–20, 213
inherited variation 5, 213
insecticides 68–9, **69**
inspiration 25, **26**
insulators 230
intercostal muscles 25, 26, **26**
invertebrates 213
iodine 30, 44, **44**
ionic lattices 81, **81**
iron 30, **62**, 75, **75**, 231
   reactions 96, 131
      rusting 93–4, **93**, **94**
iron(III) oxide 94, 131
   thermit reaction 103, **103**
irritant substances 218

J

joints 35, **35**

K

Kevlar 132–3, **133**
kinetic energy **144**
kingdoms 213
kite diagrams 217
Knop, Wilhelm 62
Kwolek, Stephanie 132–3, **132**

L

lactic acid 215
lakes, pollution of 120, **120**
   and acid rain 116–17, **117**
lattices 81, **81**
Lavoisier, Antoine 139–40
leaching 63, 108
leaves 48, **48**, 49, 59
   testing 44, **44**, 45, **45**
Leclanché, Georges 150
legumes 65
levers 199–200, **199**, **200**
ligaments 35, **35**
light **144**, 232
   from chemical energy 226, **226**
   in food webs 217, 226
   and plants 45, **45**, 46, 47
   in glasshouses 70
light bulbs, investigating 158
light gates 177–8, **177**
limestone 136, **136**, 224
   in neutralisation 111
   acidified lakes 117, **117**
limewater test **126**, 219, **219**
Lindzen, Richard S. 122
liquids 220, **220**, 230, **230**
   pressure in 197–8, **197**
lithium 75, **75**, 92, **92**
   reaction with water 96
loamy soil 108, 109
longitudinal waves 233

loudness 233
luminous objects 229
lunar eclipses 229, **229**
lungs 25–7, **25**, **26**, 215, **215**

M

magnesium **62**, 83
   reactions 103, **103**, 129, 137
      with acid 78, **78**, 79–81
      with water 95–6, **95**, **96**
magnesium chloride 79–80
magnesium oxide 137–8, **137**, **138**
magnesium sulphate 78, 129, 135
magnetic fields 154, 231, **231**
magnetic forces 231
magnetic materials 74, 231, **231**
magnets 231, **231**
male reproductive system 211, **211**
malleable materials **74**
manure 63, **63**, 64
mass 162, 163, 228
   and acceleration 180–1, **180**
   of the Earth 163, **163**
   in reactions 135–6, **136**
matches 127–8, **127**
materials 91, **91**, 115
   making new 132–3
media, wave 233
meiosis 6
melting 136
melting points 230, **230**
   of metals **74**, 75
   of non-metals **76**
membranes, cell **210**
menstrual cycle 211
metal oxides 92, 99
   in reactions 84–5, 86, 219
      displacement 103, **103**
metals 73–90, 104
   and acid rain 115
   combining power 83, **83**
   corrosion see corrosion
   properties 74–5, **74**, **75**, **76**
   in reactions 100, 219
      with acids 78–81, 98–9, 219
      displacement 101–3, **101**, **102**
      with water 95–7, **95**, **96**
metamorphic rocks 225, **225**
meteors 185, **185**
methane 113, 126
microbes 216
   see also bacteria; fungi
minerals 30, **30**, 32, 214
   in plants 50, 51, 62, **62**
   and fertilisers 62–3, 65
   in rocks 224
mirrors, reflection at 232, **232**
mixtures 223, **223**
models 220
   breathing 26, **26**
   electricity 149, **149**, 227
   particles see particles
molecules 222, **222**
moments 202–4, **202**, **203**, **204**
Moon 169, **169**, 229
   gravity on 164–5, **164**

N

natural fertilisers 63–4
negative acceleration 179, **179**
neutralisation 84–7, 218
   acidic soil 110, 111
   acidified lakes 117, **117**
Newton, Sir Isaac 162, 170, **170**
nicotine 28
nitrates 78, **79**, 83
   and plants 50
   see also nitrogen
nitric acid 78, **79**, 113, **114**
nitrogen **52**, 198
   and acid rain 113, 114, **114**
   in plants 50, **62**
   see also nitrates
non-metals 76–7, **76**, **77**
nuclear power 156, 226
nucleus, cell 6, 16, **16**, 210
   at fertilisation 211
nutrients 30, 214
nylon 133, **133**

O

offspring 6–8
oils
   and fats, in diet 49, 214
   as fuel see fossil fuel
orbits 168–9, 229
   satellites 170–2, **170**, **171**
organs 210
ovaries 211
ovules 6
oxides, metal see metal oxides
oxidising agents 128
oxygen **52**, **52**
   in blood 215
   in burning 126, 139–40
   and eutrophication 120
   metal reactions with 100, **219**
      magnesium 137
      potassium **100**
      rusting 94, 131
   and plants 46, **46**, 62
      photosynthesis 45, 46, 47, 52
   and respiration 23, 52
   and water 134–5, **134**
ozone layer depletion 121

P

parallel circuits 227
particles 220, **220**
   and air pressure 195, **195**
   and air resistance 182, **182**
   and heat 230
   in reactions 80, **80**
passive smoking 29
pathogens 216
peaty soil 108, 109
penicillin 216

Perey, Marguerite 97
Periodic Table 75, 222, **222**
periods 211
persistence of pesticides 69
pesticides 68–9, **69**
pests 68–9, **68**, 70
pH 218, **218**
   and acid rain 113, 116
   and neutralisation 85
   and soil 109–11, **110**
phases of the Moon 229
phloem vessels 49, 51
phlogiston 139–40
phosphorus, plants need **62**
   as phosphate 50
photosynthesis 41–9, **54**, **61**
   and the atmosphere 52
   equation for 46, 52, 132
   in food webs 217
physical changes 136
physical factors 212
physical properties 104
   metals 74–5, **74**, **75**, **76**
   non-metals 76–7, **76**, **77**
physical weathering 224, **224**
pitch 233
pitfall traps 217
pivots 199–200, **199**, **200**
placenta 211, **211**
plane mirrors 232, **232**
planets 167, 168–9, 229
   see also Earth
plant cells 210, **210**
plants 52–3, 213
   and acid rain 115–16, **116**
   and competition 66–7
   crops see crop plants
   in food webs 212, **212**, 217
   forest see forests
   growth 41, **41**, 70
   and acid rain 116, **116**
   and pests 68–9, **68**
   and photosynthesis see photosynthesis
   reproduction 6, 14, **14**
      vegetative 17–18, **17**, **18**
   respiration 47
   and soil pH 110, **110**
   storage organs 59, **59**
polar orbits 171–2, **171**
poles 231
pollen 6, 14
pollination 14
pollution 107, **107**, 118–20
   and acid rain 113–14, 117
   and cars 113, 119, 127, **127**
   and global warming 121–2
   from power stations **52**, **113**, 122, 156
polymers 132
pooters 217
population, size 217
potassium 83, 92, **92**
   plants need 50, **62**
   reactions 96, **100**
potassium hydroxide 86, 87, **87**
potential energy **144**
power ratings 152–3, **153**
power stations 155–7, **155**, **156**
   pollution from **52**, 113, 122, **156**
precipitation reactions 135
predators 212
pregnancy 33, 211, **211**
pressure 191–8, 220

238

INDEX P–Z

pressure cookers 196, **196**
pressurised gases 195, 196, **196**
prey 212
Priestley, Joseph 42, 139, **140**
producers 212, 217
products 219
propagation 17–18, **17**, **18**
propane 126
properties 104
    see also physical properties
proportions in compounds 223
protein 49, 214
protists 213
puberty 211
pure substances 223
pyramids of numbers 217

Q

quadrats 67, 217
qualitative observations 99
quantitative data 99

R

radiation 144, 230
random samples 67
rarefaction 233, **233**
ratios in compounds 223
reactants 219
reactivity 91–106, 130
Reactivity Series 100, **100**, 104
rechargeable batteries 150
recovery time, measuring 23
reflection 232, **232**
refraction 232, **232**
renewable energy resources 226
reproduction 6–8, **7**, **8**, 211
    asexual 17–18, **17**, **18**
    flowering plants 6, 14, **14**
resistance, electrical 227
resistance to insecticide 69
resistance to motion see air resistance; water resistance
resistors **227**
respiration 23, 132, 215
    and the atmosphere 52
    by plants 47, 59
respiratory system 25–7, **25**
rib cage 25, 26, **26**
rivers, pollution of 120, **120**
    and acid rain 116–17, **117**
rock cycle 225, **225**
rockets 165–6, **165**, **166**
    space shuttle fuel 135
    see also space craft
rocks 224–5, **224**, **225**
    as building materials 112, **112**
    effects of acid rain 115
    as soil fragments 108
roots 50–1, **50**, 59
rubidium 97, **97**
rusting 93–4, **93**, **94**

S

salts 78–88, 219
    formulae **78**, **79**, 83
    structure 81, **81**
    uses of 87, **87**

sampling 67, 217
sandy soil 108, 109
Sankey diagrams 158, **158**
satellites 168–9
    artificial 170–2, **170**, **171**, **172**
saturated solutions 221
Scheele, Carl Wilhelm 139
schist 225
seasons 229
secondary sexual characteristics 211
sediment 108, 224, 225, **225**
sedimentary rocks 225, **225**
sedimentation test 109
seeds 60
selective breeding 12–14
separation techniques 221, 223
series circuits 227
sexual reproduction 6–8, **7**, **8**, 211
    plants 6, 14, **14**
S-factors in fitness 22–3, **22**
shiny materials 74, 75, 92
silty soil 108, 109
silver nitrate 101–2, **102**
skeleton 34–5, **35**
slate 225
smog 118, **118**
smoking 28–9, **28**, **29**, 36
    and drugs 37, **37**
soda lime 45, **45**
sodium 83, 96
sodium chloride 81, **81**, 218
sodium hydroxide 84, 218
sodium oxide 84
sodium sulphate 83, **83**
soil 108–11, **108**, **110**
    and acid rain 115–16
solar eclipses 229, **229**
solar power **156**, 226
solar system 167, **167**, 168, 229
    meteors 185, **185**
    see also Earth; Moon; planets; Sun
solids 220, **220**, 230, **230**
solubility 221
solubility curves 221, **221**
solutes 221
solutions 218, 221, **221**
solvents 221
sonorous materials **74**
sound **144**, 233
space 166, 167–72
    see also solar system
space craft 185
    see also rockets
space travel 165–6, **165**, **166**
specialised cells 8
species 213
spectrum of white light 232
speed 175–90
    and fitness 22, 23, **24**
    and forces 179–81
        air resistance 184, **184**
        circular motion 169, **169**
    of light 232
    measuring 177–8, **177**, **178**
    of sound 233
speed guns 178, **178**
speed-time graphs 187–8, **187**, **188**
sperm 6–8, **8**, 211
stable objects **20**, 201–2, **201**
stamens 14, **14**

stamina 22, 23, **24**
starch 44–5, 58–60
    in leaves 44, **44**, **45**, 49
    in potatoes 60, **60**
stars 229
steam, reactions with 96, **96**
stems 51, **51**
stigmas 14, **14**
storage organs 59, **59**
storing energy 145–6, **146**
    and power stations 155
streamlined shapes 183, **183**, **185**
strength 22, 23, **24**
sublimation 77
sugar 60, **60**, 61
    see also glucose
sulphates 78, **79**, 83
sulphur, pollution from 113, 117
sulphur dioxide 118, **118**, 119
    and acid rain 113–14, **113**, **114**
    and plant growth 116
sulphuric acid **79**, 82
    and acid rain 113, **114**
    copper sulphate from 84, **84**
    magnesium sulphate from 78, **78**
Sun 167, 226
suppleness 22, **24**
surveying habitats 67, **67**
sweep nets 217
symbols 218, **218**, 222, **227**

T

tar 28
tarnish 92–4, **92**, **93**
taxonomic groups 213
temperature 70, 230, **230**
temperature scales 230
terminal velocity 186, 188
theories 220
thermal conductors **74**, 75, **76**, 230
    non-metals **76**, 77
thermal pollution 120
thermal radiation 230
thermit reaction 103, **103**
thorax 25, **25**, 26, **26**
thrombosis 34
tidal flow power stations **156**
time and speed 176, **176**
tissues 210
titration 86–7, **87**
touch test 109
transects 217
transmission of light 232
transport, rock 224, **225**
tree beating 217
turning effect 199, 201–2
twins, identical 10

U

ultrasound 233
umbilical cord 211, **211**
unbalanced forces 228
units
    of electricity 152–3, **152**
    for speed 176–7, **176**
Universe 229
unstable objects **20**, 201–2, **201**

upthrust 228, **228**
uterus 211, **211**

V

vaccination 216
vacuoles **210**
vagina 211, **211**
van Helmont, Jan Baptista 42, 43
variables, controlling 47, 99
variation 5, 9–10, 213
variegated leaves 44, **44**
varieties 9–10, **9**, 14, **14**
    comparing 15
vascular bundles 51, **51**
vegetative reproduction 17–18, **17**, **18**
vertebrates 213
vibration 220, 233, **233**
virtual images 232
viruses 216
vitamins 30–2, **31**, 214
Volta, Count Alessandro 149
voltage 147–9, 227
    measuring 148, **148**
    and reactivity 130
voltmeters 148, **148**

W

walls, cells **210**
wasted energy 144, **145**, 226, **226**
    reducing 157–8
water 134–5, **134**, 219
    in the atmosphere 121, **121**
    burning gives 219, **219**
    in diet 214
    in glasshouses 70
    metals reacting with 95–7, **95**, **97**
    in plants 45, 50, 51
        photosynthesis 45, 46, 50, 52
    and respiration 23, 52
    in rusting 94
water pollution 120, **120**
water resistance 182–3, **183**, 184, **184**
wave power 226
weathering 112, 224, **224**
    in the rock cycle 225
    and soil formation 108
weedkillers 66, **66**
weeds 66, 67, 70
weight 162, 164, **164**, 228
    and floating 228, **228**
    and free fall 186, **186**, 187
    and terminal velocity 188, **188**
wildlife 116, 122, **122**
wind power **156**, 226

X

xylem vessels 51

Z

zinc **83**, 96, 129, 150

239

Acknowledgements

AA Photolibrary: **99**; Ace Photolibrary: Gari Williams **112tc**; Action Plus: Mike Hewitt **22tr**, Glyn Kirk **22ml**, **178b**, Neil Tingle **22tl**, Michel Pissotte (DPPI) **186**; Adams Picture Library: **108**; AIP Emilio Segre Visual Archives: **97r**, Aquarius Picture Library: **16**; Associated Press: Katsumi Kasahara **114**; Biophoto Associates: **31br**, **77tr**; Bodleian Library: **167b**; Boots plc: **49tl**; Bridgeman Art Library: **140r** (Joseph Priestley (1733–1804), 1801 (oil on canvas) by Rembrandt Peale (1778–1860), New York Historical Society, New York, USA); British Museum: **93b**; British Rail: **103r**; Cafedirect: photo courtesy of Cafedirect **49bl**; CERN: 18.06; Cooke Corporation: **178m**; Corbis: Paul A Souders **22mcl**, Gary Brash **93tl**, Gillian Darley, Edifice **112bl**, Corbis (NT): **37l**; Corel (NT): **22mr, mcr, b, 49mcl, 52, 66t, 75t, b, 77b, 104r, 110mt, 112tr, br, 113, 116**; Daihatsu UK: **185mr**; Digital Vision (NT): **120t**; Empics Sports Photo Agency: Adam Davy **133b**, Tony Marshall **178T**, Ross Kinnaird **179t**; Food Fertiliser Technology Centre: **111**; Frank Lane Picture Agency: Richard Brooks **67**, R Bird **148**, D Hosking **179b**; Garden Picture Library: **110br**, J S Sira **109**, Brian Carter **110t**, Brigitte Thomas **mb**; Geoscience Features Picture Library: **92bl, br**; Getty Image Bank: Jeremy Walker **167t**; Getty Images Stone: Martin Barraud **10**, Peter Dokus **22cr**, Ben Edwards **87l**; Getty Images Taxi: Barry Yee **87cl**; Grabber **131**; Holt Studios International: Nigel Cattlin **64, 68, 70, 87r**, Gordon Roberts **132t**; Hulton Getty: **118**; Hutchison: **156r**; ICI: **63l, r**; International Potato Centre: **49tcl**; JVC: **146bl**; Mamod Ltd: **145**; Martyn Chillmaid: **9, 14, 30, 38, 48t, 49mr, 75m, 77tl, 79l, r, 92tl, tr, 93tc, 120b, 146t, 150t, 151, 156bl, 196l, r, 197, 204l, r**; NASA **132b, 166t, b, 169, 170, 185b**; National Museums of Scotland: **112tl**; Natural Visions: Heather Angel **44, 64**; New Media: **97l**; Olivio USA: **49tcr**; Oxford Scientific Films: **50**, Mantis Wildlife Films **17**, Mike Birkhead **43l**, Ted Levin **43br**, Carolina Bio Supply **48b**, Science Pctures Ltd **60**, Archie Allnutt **122**, Peugeot: **185tr**; Porsche: **185tl**; Pressens Bild Stockholm: Sven-Erik Sjoberg **53t**; Robert Harding Picture Library: Dr Denis Kunkel, Phototake **8l**; Science & Society Picture Library: **140l, 149, 150br**; Science Photolibrary: **35, 157, 172**, Biophoto Associates: **6, 31tr**, Pascal Goetgheluck **8r, 104l**, David Parker **15**, Matt Meadows, Peter Arnold Incorporated **29t, b**, Chuck Brown **51, 87cr**, Charles D Winters **103l**, Ron Church **198b**; Scottish Hydroelectric: **152**; Shout Pictures: **133t**; St Bartholomew's Hospital: **31l, 34**; Still Pictures: Mark Edwards **117, 127t**, Harmut Schwarzbach **127b**; Stockbyte (NT): **43tr, 49tr**, Tate & Lyle: **49mcr**; Topham Picturepoint: Photo News Service Ltd **37r**; Trevor Baylis: **146br**; TRIP: A Lambert **100**, UKAEA: **156tl**; Varta: **150bl**; Volkswagen Press: **185ml**.

Picture research by johnbailey@axonimages.com

Every effort has been made to trace all the copyright holders, but if any have been overlooked the publisher will be pleased to make the necessary arrangements at the first opportunity.